CARIBBEAN STORY
Book Two: The Inheritors

William Claypole PhD (UWI)
John Robottom BA

Assignments provided by Coleridge Barnett
Principal, Wolmers Boys' School, Kingston, Jamaica

Editorial adviser Dr Bridget Brereton
Department of History, UWI, St Augustine, Trinidad

Longman Caribbean

Longman Group UK Limited
Longman House, Burnt Mill, Harlow,
Essex CM20 2JE, England
and Associated Companies throughout the world.

Carlong Publishers Caribbean Limited
P.O. Box 489
43 Second Street
Newport West
Kingston 10
Jamaica

Longman Trinidad Limited
Boundary Road
San Juan
Trinidad

© Longman Group Ltd 1981
This edition © Longman Group UK Ltd 1989

First edition 1981
Second edition 1989
Seventh impression 1993

Printed in Malaysia by PA

ISBN 0 582 03985.1

Claypole, William
    Caribbean story. — (New ed)
    Bk. 2, The inheritors
    1. Caribbean region, history
    I. Title II. Robottom, John
    909'.09821

ISBN 0–582–03985–1

Acknowledgements

The authors are grateful to the many people who
advised on the manuscript. In particular they would
like to thank Dr Sahadeo Basdeo, Dr Bridget
Brereton, Anne Hickling-Hudson, Professor Keith
Laurence, and Constance Morgan.

The Publishers are grateful to the following for their
permission to reproduce photographs.

The Aviation Picture Library for fig. 23.1; Anne Bolt
for figs. 6.4, 11.3, 14.3, 15.1, 15.4, 16.1, 18.3 and
23.2; Camera Press for figs. 20.4, 21.5, 21.6, 21.7 and
21.8; Caribbean Development Bank for fig. 23.3;
Central Office of Information/Crown Copyright for
fig. 16.2; Mary Evans Picture Library for figs. 3.1
and 6.3; Foreign and Commonwealth Office Library
for figs. 6.1, 7.1, 7.3, 12.1, 12.2, 12.4 and 17.4;
Hulton-Deutsch Collection for figs. 1.1, 1.2, 2.1, 2.2,
2.3, 6.2, 9.1, 9.2, 9.4, 10.6, 11.1, 12.5, 13.3, 13.6,
14.1, 18.2, 18.4, 19.2, 19.3, 19.4, 20.5, 21.1, 21.2,
21.4, 22.1, 22.2 and 22.3; Institute of Jamaica for
figs. 1.4, 9.3, 10.7, 13.1 and 17.2; Mansell Collection
for figs. 3.2, 4.1 and 4.2; Peter Newark's Western
Americana for figs. 7.2, 19.1, 20.1; Nigeria Magazine
for fig. 8.1; Popperfoto for figs. 10.1, 10.3, 11.2,
12.3, 14.2, 15.2, 17.3, 20.2, 20.3 and 21.3; Royal
Commonwealth Society Library for figs. 4.3, and
13.2; Trinidad Guardian for fig. 17.1; U.S.P.G. for
fig. 1.5; West India Committee for figs. 1.3, 10.2 and
10.5.

Fig. 10.4 was taken from "The Island of Montserrat"
by J. R. Alexander and fig. 8.2 was taken from a
biography of H. S. Williams by J. R. Hooker
published by Rex Collings.

We regret that we have been unable to trace the
copyright holders of the following and would welcome
any information enabling us to do so:

13.4, 13.5, 15.3 and 18.1

The cover photograph of C. Chang's mural painting
'Inherent Nobility of Man' was kindly supplied by
Mrs Mary Norton.

Introduction

To the student

This book has been written to help with your studies for the CXC examination. To encourage you to study in the way which the examiners expect there are assignments at the end of each chapter. Some will help you to be sure of understanding the main points and the most important ideas in the chapter. Some raise issues which you might like to discuss and others give ideas for further investigation.

The assignments have been chosen so that you can become familiar with the types of question, and the way that they are written, in Paper 2 of the examination. You will see that some questions set a topic for an essay and others start with a piece of stimulus material – which means a picture or quotation which you are asked to explain and give the background to. You will need to practise writing answers so that they deal with the question you are asked and so that you do not just copy information in the book.

Thirty per cent of the marks for the final result are given for school-based assessment which can be done as nine assignments (three per term for three terms), or one term's assignments may be replaced by a longer project. Many of the assignments in this book could be used for school-based assessment, although your teacher may give you different ones.

At the end of the book you will find the guidelines for the examination papers and the course work you will need for the CXC.

CONTENTS

THE FIRST YEARS OF FREEDOM

Work and land

Full freedom for ex-slaves in the British colonies in the Caribbean began when apprenticeship ended on 1 August 1838. The first aim of the ex-slaves was to escape from forced and unpaid labour. Many moved away from the plantation as soon as apprenticeship ended. Many others preferred to stay in their old homes among friends and relatives. They expected to become wage-earners on the estate and earn enough cash to buy the simple items of furniture and tools which they had not owned as slaves.

These plans were usually shattered within a few years. Masters began to cut wages and sometimes raised rents at the same time. They often evicted free people who were not needed or whom they disliked. As a result free people throughout the colonies felt the urge to leave the estates even when they had been the family home for very many years.

Earning a living

Skilled craftsmen had the best chance of moving. Masons, carpenters, barrel-makers, wheelwrights and cart-builders could find work from one estate to another. The semi-skilled domestic workers such as seamstresses, laundresses and cooks were not so fortunate. Now they had to pay wages, many planters could not afford so many domestic servants. They could either join the field gangs or take their chance in the towns. But most towns were small and workers from the estates could not compete with the craftsmen and domestics who had lived in the towns as slaves and apprentices. Most of the newcomers spent years of unemployment in desperate poverty.

Some apprentices who had saved their wages bought small stocks of goods to become pedlars, petty retailers and shopkeepers. On the large plantations, masters opened their own supply stores to sell cloth, pins, needles, saltfish and other items. But on the small properties the labourers relied on pedlars and small roadside shops. In the larger colonies a number of freemen became higglers and hucksters, buying provisions from the labourers' plots and selling them in port towns and market places.

Many freemen moved to Trinidad and British Guiana where the chance of earning a living was greater. Most travelled from the Windwards where wages were lower, or the Leewards where land was scarce. In Trinidad one group of freemen asked the governor for money to hire a ship to take them back to Africa. He passed on the request to the Colonial Office in London which turned it down.

Acquiring property

Free people only felt completely independent of the plantation if they could acquire their own land. The simplest method of getting property was to buy unoccupied land. This was of two kinds. There was land belonging to plantations which was not farmed by the owner and there was land belonging to no one person which was known as Crown land. Such Crown land was most commonly found in Trinidad, British Guiana and the interior of Jamaica.

Planters objected that having the right to buy Crown land encouraged labourers to move away from plantations. To make this more difficult they suggested that people should be able to become owners only if they bought and planted a large number of hectares. Few purchasers could afford the costs of clearing, planting and paying taxes on large farms. At first, the Colonial Office refused to accept the planters' proposal. Then, in 1846, Britain did agree that Crown lands should be sold only in large parcels which were most commonly fixed at 16 hectares or more. She did this partly to compensate the planters for the Sugar Duties Equalisation Act of 1846 which brought down the price of sugar and faced many planters with ruin.

Planters in Trinidad feared that the new farmers would be able to manage 16 hectares so they convinced the governor that the figure should be raised to 130 hectares. But it was still difficult to stop people gaining farms by squatting on unused Crown land in the remote interiors of the large colonies. In the past, the law had allowed a squatter to become the owner if he occupied land for twelve months and made some improvements. This was no longer legal, but constant patrols of militia would have been needed to stop squatting in districts a long way from the coast in Trinidad, British Guiana or Jamaica.

It was often just as difficult to prevent squatting on unused plantation lands. In Trinidad and British Guiana, plantation boundaries had not always been surveyed and planters did not know the exact extent of all they owned. Some planters or their agents even encouraged families to buy or squat on unused plantation lands to keep them close to the cane fields where they could work in the crop times.

Free villages

Missionary help

A few fortunate Africans bought land outright with savings from the sale of provision crops during slavery or overtime wages paid during apprenticeship. People who purchased property outright were more fortunate than squatters. They gained written proof of ownership and the land they bought was usually already cleared and close to markets. But outright purchase was the exception, not the rule. Most people simply lacked the money to buy land and the tools needed to till it.

In some cases, sympathetic nonconformist missionaries stepped in to help the ex-slaves acquire land. In 1835, a Baptist missionary, James Phillips, bought 10 hectares in the mountains behind Jamaica's Spanishtown. He subdivided the land into small lots for sale on easy terms to his congregation. The new community was named Sligoville after the Marquis of Sligo, then governor of Jamaica. Sligoville was the only settlement to be started during apprenticeship. But as apprenticeship drew to its end, the

Fig. 1.1 *Newcastle, a free village, in the Jamaican Blue Mountains.*

Baptist missionary, William Knibb, foresaw that planters would try to force extra work from their free labourers by increasing rents on homes on the estate. Knibb took steps to help his congregation meet this threat. In July 1838, he told them:

> I have had an offer of a loan of £10,000 from a friend in England; and if it be necessary, that sum shall be appropriated towards the purchase of lands on which you may locate yourselves if your present employer force you to quit the properties on which you now live.

The planters acted as Knibb had foreseen and by 1839 he was busily organising a number of 'free villages' for labourers who did not want to risk rising rents on their homes and garden plots on the plantations. Knibb, and most of the missionaries who followed his example, never planned the free villages as a complete alternative to working on the estates. It was generally reckoned that the people in the villages would still work for wages on the plantations for three to four days a week. The reason was quite practical. The missionaries and their congregations did not have the money to buy large enough lots for fully independent small farming. In most villages, land was broken down into plots no larger than one hectare. However, one hectare was sufficient to give the labourers enough independence to negotiate for better working conditions and wages on the estates. They were

Fig. 1.2 *A view of British Honduras now Belize, in the early nineteenth century.*

an important step in the process by which ex-slaves became a true free people.

Much of the money used to buy land was borrowed from missionary societies in England or from individuals who were sympathetic to the freemen. The emancipationist, Joseph Sturge, lent £400 to the Reverend John Clark to buy land for his congregation in St Anns, Jamaica. This made it possible to settle a hundred families and build a church and day school. In rapid succession, similar villages were established in Jamaica at Clarksonville, Wilberforce, Buxton, Bethany, Salem, Harmony and Mount Cary. By 1842 over 8,000 Africans were settled in those free villages which had been sponsored in their early stages by missionaries and their supporters.

Planters' sales

In Jamaica, it had been the missionaries who had seen the importance of making African land ownership possible. In the eastern Caribbean it was much less common for missionaries to help their congregations in this way. The few free villages they did organise came later than in Jamaica. It was not until 1842 that the Moravians sponsored a village in Antigua although all slaves had been freed there in 1834. On that island it was the governor, Sir William Colebrooke, who first suggested free villages as a means of encouraging the ex-slaves to remain agricultural labourers. In 1837 he suggested to the Antigua assembly that settlements should be created which 'if judiciously encouraged and carefully watched over, would inevitably become nurseries of labour for the whole island.' At first the assembly was reluctant to carry out the scheme so Colebrooke threatened to open the island's Crown lands to the labourers. However, by 1840, the planters changed their minds when they found that ex-slaves, at least in Antigua, had saved enough during slavery to be able to pay attractive prices for poor land. As a result the planters found they could easily sell waste lands for up to £120 per half hectare. The plots were generally not large enough to make a living from. Just as Colebrooke had intended, they were a means of keeping labour near the plantation. By the end of 1842 there were twenty-seven independent villages in Antigua.

Other estate owners in the eastern Caribbean followed the Antiguan example. When planters in Montserrat, Nevis and St Kitts found labourers eager to leave for better-paid jobs in Trinidad and British Guiana, they sold provision grounds and house lots to encourage them to stay. In Trinidad and British Guiana, some planters subdivided their front lands and offered to let labourers buy the plots by working for reduced wages until they were paid for.

Exploitation of purchasers

The missionaries and governors who sponsored the new independent villages believed it would bring benefits to both the African population and the landowners. The governor of Jamaica wrote to the Secretary of State for the Colonies in 1840 explaining this: 'Were the labourer comfortably settled in a home from which he could not be removed, or not at least without sufficient notice, there would, I am almost sure, be a better chance of obtaining willing labour from him.'

He went on to say that 'I shall do all I can to promote it from a conviction that it will increase the happiness and content of the negro population, and from a belief that it will also tend to the benefit of the landlords.'

The governor knew, however, that the movement from the estates to free villages often involved the exploitation of the African people.

Unless a missionary or government official kept a watchful eye, land purchase could be an opportunity for dishonest land speculators. A perfect example was reported to the governor in 1839. A certain Mr Drummond purchased 283 hectares of land in Clarendon for £500. This he divided into lots of 7 to 11 hectares for sale to smaller land speculators at four times the amount he had paid. The small speculators redivided the lots in turn and mortgaged them in parcels of 1 to 2 hectares to ex-apprentices at up to eight times the original purchase price. In 1840 the custos of St Elizabeth parish wrote to the governor complaining of land speculators. He explained that:

> designing individuals . . . have purchased at a low rate large tracts of land, and resold the same in small lots to the peasantry at a shamefully exorbitant profit, the lands being at the same time very poor and unproductive, and so situated as to prevent the labourers from being able to procure sufficient employment and support their families, thus exposing them to indigence and poverty instead of comfort, happiness and affluence.

Guyanese co-operatives

In British Guiana groups of ex-slaves pooled their savings to form co-operatives which bought entire plantations. The first co-operative village was built in 1839 when freemen paid $10,000 for North Brook Plantation on the east coast of Demerara. The legal owners were a committee of six, but eighty-four members each bought one share in the property including a house lot and farmlands. Each member gave either a period of work or a sum of money to maintain the drainage and irrigation ditches which were essential in coastal Guyana. Co-operatives usually bought up cheap abandoned cotton plantations but occasionally became owners of sugar estates. Among the larger purchases between 1834 and 1844 were the 202 hectare Plantation Friendship for $80,000, Plantation New Orange Nassau (later known as Buxton Village) for $50,000 and the 162 hectare Plantation Beterverwagting for $22,000. By 1850 there were more than twenty-five Guyanese co-operatives with land valued at over a million dollars.

In 1852 the colony's planters persuaded the governor to pass a measure which checked the growth of co-operatives. Known as Ordinance number 1, it prohibited the purchase of land by a group of more than twenty people. In 1856, Ordinance number 33 limited common ownership to ten or fewer people and said there had to be a cash payment for the upkeep of drainage. It was no longer legal for co-operative members to take turns to supply the labour needed. The ordinances stopped the growth of large co-operatives and broke the common bond between members which had come about from sharing in the drainage work. Several of the early co-operatives failed after Ordinance number 33 and were sold as separate plots to the original members. On their own, the owners found it difficult to borrow money for improvements or to keep the drainage systems in good repair. Trenches backed up, dykes wore away and bridges collapsed.

The planters had succeeded in their aims. Many co-operative members were forced to leave their flooded fields and return to working on plantations for wages. Some chose to find less fertile land to squat on in the interior. But the lessons were remembered. Present-day local government in Guyana is based on the democratic procedures worked out to manage these early co-operatives.

Small farming
Farms of their own

Every attempt to force labourers back to the cane fields made them more determined to leave the plantation. In the first twenty years or so after the end of apprenticeship a remarkable number succeeded. Even so, people in the larger colonies were more fortunate than those living where land was scarce.

In 1861, twenty-three years after apprenticeship, a Baptist missionary, William Underhill, reported that 120,000 Jamaicans earned a living away from the plantation. This was about a third of the island's total population. Sixty-five thousand of them owned small farms totalling over 143,264 hectares. Two hundred independent villages had been built. At the same time in Trinidad there were 11,000 small farmers, as well as many other freemen who had set up as small shopkeepers or wandering tradesmen. It was reckoned that fewer than 5,000 Africans worked regularly on plantations, where much of the labour was done by the indentured Indians (see Chapters 3 and 4).

By 1850, twelve years after apprenticeship, 42,000 Guyanese out of a total of 82,000 had managed to become completely or partly independent of the estates. The desire for freedom in Guyana had been strengthened by the action of the planters. To make up for their losses after the Sugar Duties Act, they had reduced wages from 48 to 32 cents a day in 1846 and cut them again by a quarter in 1848. To make it harder for labourers to make a living from growing food, the colony had reduced duties on imported food and many planters stopped freemen from fishing in irrigation trenches, collecting grass for their stock and gathering fruits from the plantations' hedgerows. All these measures made Africans more determined than

ever to find land away from the plantations.

In Antigua, St Kitts and Barbados scarcity of land made it less easy to withdraw altogether from plantation work. But, wherever possible, labourers moved away to build their homes and plant small garden plots. By 1858 15,600 Antiguans lived in 'independent' villages and could at least bargain with planters for better wages and living conditions. In Barbados the planters were stronger than in any other colony because so few of them were absentees. Here only 3,500 Africans had managed to buy property by 1860 out of a population of 150,000. Others, however, had used the threat of emigration to force planters to agree to a 'located-labour' system which allowed them garden plots on the plantations.

In the Windwards, Nevis and Montserrat, a mixed situation was found. Labourers could take over small plots of land in the hills but most still did seasonal work on the estates or moved to Trinidad during crop time. In some cases, the labourers went into sharecropping the sugar fields with the plantation owner. The

Fig. 1.3 *A view of Old North Sound, Antigua, in the nineteenth century.*

result of these movements was that many islanders became owners of tiny plots of land. In 1848, there were 8,200 small farmers in St Vincent who between them cultivated 4,884 hectares, an average of about three-fifths of a hectare each. Grenada, St Lucia and Tobago each had about 2,500 small freeholders.

Metayage

In St Lucia and Tobago planters found another way of keeping the labour they needed. They put pressure on the small farmers to become sharecroppers or *metayers* on their estates. Under the metayage system a property owner supplied the sharecropper with land, tools and the use of carts. He paid no rent for this but he had to grow cane and then work for a season in the factory. The earnings from the crop were then shared, half to the owner and half to the sharecropper.

Some metayers also owned a smallholding off the estate. However, its small size and the long hours they had to work as sharecroppers meant that they could not grow enough to make a profit from selling produce.

Selling crops

The small farmers grew produce for their own use but they also sold in local markets and, as we shall see, in the 1860s began to export their crops. With the cash they earned they bought tools, little luxury items and trade apprentice-ships for their children. After three hundred years of plantation slavery, many people looked on any agricultural work as a form of bondage. They saw their new farms as a way of placing their children in other occupations.

The simplest form of trade was carrying fruit and vegetables to the local Saturday market and selling them for cash. Often the small farmers' produce became part of a complicated higgling trade. In Jamaica, farmers in the mountainous eastern parishes sold their fruit and vegetables to coastal traders who carried them to the south-west where many wage-earners still worked on sugar plantations. Small farmers in Montserrat

supplied nearly all the fresh produce eaten in Antigua and St Kitts.

Crops for export

For export, Jamaican farmers grew ginger, pimento and coffee which were sold to local brokers who supplied European merchants. The small farmers in the Leewards grew arrowroot as a staple export crop. In 1857 St Vincent alone sold 613,380 kilograms. Small freeholders in Grenada exported coffee, cotton, cocoa, copra, honey and beeswax. As the squatters cleared Crown lands in Trinidad they sold the timber for charcoal burning and exported some for boat building. Later they planted and exported coffee and cocoa.

The Guyanese had difficulty in finding a suit-able export crop as their fields were generally too wet for coffee and cocoa. They were off the main West Indian trade routes, which made it difficult to attract the traders who purchased most of the smallholders' crops in the Antilles. It was not easy to make a living from growing and higgling fruit and vegetables as the popu-lation was small and there were plenty of provision grounds. Guyanese smallholders managed to get away from subsistence farming only when they began to grow rice for export later in the century.

New forms of society
In Jamaica

The new farmers, small traders and craftsmen were laying the foundations for new patterns of social and economic life in the Caribbean. In the middle of the nineteenth century this could be seen most clearly in Jamaica, because of the size of the island's interior which had been mostly uncultivated in the days of slavery. Twenty or so years after emancipation there were two quite different forms of settlement. Near the coast, the plantations still remained and planters continued to produce sugar by the old methods with the encouragement of the British govern-ment. Inland, towns and villages grew up despite the lack of good roads, schools and health facilities. Shopkeepers, provisioners, tailors, shoemakers and blacksmiths settled there to supply goods and services to the surrounding farmers.

The only sound roads were those which ran along the coastline linking plantations to the ports and government towns. Yet a system of tracks and pathways developed to link the interior towns and villages with each other and with the coast. Along these came higglers and wholesalers to buy their fresh fruit and vegetables, cocoa, coffee, pimento, arrowroot and ginger. Goods for sale were taken down to the coastal towns to be prepared and shipped by another new group of merchants. These men worked a two-way trade. They sold the farmers' produce to Europe and imported manufactured goods and provisions which they wholesaled to the new village shopkeepers. So there was soon a system of trade separate from that between the plantations and the large English merchant firms.

The new merchants gave the coastal towns a new importance. In the days of slavery they had held little more than government buildings, depots for plantation trade as well as a few inns and shops to serve sailors on shore leave and thirsty planters from the country. Now they held a new class of merchants and craftsmen who formed themselves into a group ready to challenge the plantocracy's control of the colony. The new free townspeople became the spokesmen for the small cultivators in the interior, their best customers. The first Jamaican political parties began to form. The Country Party represented the interests of the plantocracy and was opposed by the Town Party which worked for the concerns of the local merchants, the small farmers and the professional coloured classes. In the assembly, the Town Party began to demand that funds be set aside for better roads and facilities for the interior towns and villages.

Drawing away from the Europeans

In Trinidad, the clash of interests between the political spokesmen for plantation owners and the farmers of new crops was not as sharp as in Jamaica because there were fewer ex-slaves on the island. Yet, similar political divisions began to appear as cocoa farmers cleared lands in the foothills of the northern range. Some of them were Venezualan immigrants of mixed Spanish, American and African descent. Their spokesmen began to call for new roads to service these areas. They said that more funds were to be spent on helping independent farming and less on assisting Indian immigration which was of benefit only to the plantations, especially the large ones on the west coast.

By the 1850s, it was possible to see in British Guiana some early signs of a society divided, like Jamaica's, between the coastal towns and plantations on the one hand and the interior settlements on the other. In the more crowded colonies, it was difficult for this development to take place. Yet, the Africans had other ways of standing up to European dominance. In many places, this took the form of creating their own separate forms of religious organisation.

Missionaries and planters

Many nonconformist missionaries in the colonies demanded forms of obedience from their church members which smacked of the days of slavery. In Antigua the Moravians appointed African 'helpers' who had the duty of reporting any backsliding by church members. Offenders were often expelled from the church at monthly disciplinary hearings. To control their members the European Baptist missionaries used a 'ticket and leader' system. A trusted member of the congregation was appointed to issue tickets to new converts when he thought they were properly instructed and willing to live by the church's teaching. The leader could also withdraw tickets from members he thought were misbehaving.

Such missionaries did not use their control of their congregations for religious purposes only. They also insisted that labourers must accept the planters' and overseers' discipline on the estates and sometimes this displayed a racist belief that Europeans were superior and blacks inferior. It also meant that the missionaries sided with the planters in matters such as conditions of work, pay and penalties for work that overseers said was done badly. An English opponent of slavery toured a Moravian mission in Antigua after emancipation and described how some planters relied on missionary support.

> The people are more in fear of the church discipline than of legal punishment; and some planters employ the authority of the minister, rather than that of the magistrate, in enforcing due discipline and subordination on their estates.

The backing given to planters caused many people to support break-aways from the English missionary societies. The lead was taken by Jamaican Methodists led by Edward Jordan and the Reverend Thomas Pinnock. In 1836, during apprenticeship, they broke with the British Methodist Association and set up the Jamaican Wesleyan Association. The new body appointed native ministers, set up their own local committees and opened training schools. The Jamaican Baptists followed suit in 1843 by withdrawing from the British Baptist Missionary Society. The moves were repeated throughout the colonies so that there were very often two rival churches, the one having mostly white ministers and accepting control from London, the other having local ministers and managing its own affairs.

The English missionary societies gradually lost their sole control over Christianity in the Caribbean. They could never find enough missionaries willing to follow the church members to new villages in the interior. They sent less money to the Caribbean as they found new fields for missionary work in Africa and the Far East, usually among people who had not yet begun to demand independence. As the English societies' position weakened, new churches that had grown in North America moved into the Caribbean. One of the first examples were the Disciples of Christ who opened their first church in Jamaica in 1858.

Afro-Christian beliefs

Africans had first accepted Christianity in the last fifty years of slavery. Then they had usually merged their traditional religion with its belief in a spirit world with Christianity. But, under slavery, it had been difficult to bring the African part of their beliefs into the open. All the Europeans often saw was the way that African singing, dancing and drumming were used in worship. When the new Caribbean churches were founded from the 1840s they were much more open about the African elements in their Christian faith.

This was most clearly seen in revivalism. It can be traced to the 'Great Revival' in Jamaica in 1860–61 when thousands declared that they had been born again and accepted Christ as Saviour. From that starting point, revivalist sects flourished in Jamaica and other colonies. Their practices took many African forms such as possession by spirits and going into trances. Often there was a great belief in the power of the leader or prophet to heal, by touch, by water or with herbal medicines.

Afro-Christian healing often stemmed directly from the widespread faith in Myalmen. In the years after emancipation Obeah was made illegal but this did not stop people's belief in its power to do harm. They turned to Myalmen to release them from the shadows and other charms of the Obeahman. The Myalmen did this with traditional dances and rituals and also called on the Christian God or Christ to take part in the struggle against evil. Gradually the Myalist struggle against Obeah and the struggle of Christians against the devil merged together.

The new churches and revivalist sects also suited the cultural needs of the black Caribbean people. They did not put up barriers against customs such as a couple living together without

Fig. 1.4 *Jamaicans waiting to be baptised in the sea by their pastors.*

an official marriage. Being illegitimate was not seen as a reason for not being baptised. Church ministers, deacons and 'prophets' accepted the importance of extended families, and owning property in common.

Along with the new forms of Christianity, some free people began to practise African religions openly. In Trinidad the Shango religion flourished. It had its roots in the beliefs of Yoruba people of West Africa. In Jamaica, Kumina was a religion from Central Africa which involved the worship of ancestors' spirits through dancing, drumming and spirit possession.

European opinion

The success of the new religious movements in satisfying the needs of the freemen to express their own culture and manage their own affairs was marked in the comments of missionaries. In 1849, Peter Duncan wrote a *Narrative of the Wesleyan Missions to Jamaica*. He described for his English readers the '. . . melancholy spectacle of the degradation of an ungrateful people, and the sin of such as apostatise from God.' Peter Duncan was not alone in failing to see that with emancipation the ex-slaves had won the freedom to decide themselves on their personal lives and beliefs. Other English writers were just as blind to what was happening in the Caribbean. The novelist, Anthony Trollope, toured the colonies in 1859 and wrote of the freeman:

> He has made no approach to the civilisation of his white fellows, whom he imitates as a monkey does a man . . . he is idle, unambitious as to worldly position, sensual and content with little sustained effort.

Ten years earlier Thomas Carlyle had written the *Occasional Discourse on the Nigger Question*. In it he said that emancipation had been a mistake; but it was not too late to correct it. The labourers could still be rounded up by force and returned to the plantations where they belonged.

All these writers shared annoyance that the ex-slaves had not behaved after emancipation in the way that it had been planned they should. Many emancipationists had believed that, once free, the Africans would be eager to imitate the lives of

workers in England. For most this would have meant a lifetime of plantation labour and for a few the chance of rising to higher positions after hard work and study. But this was not what the freemen had wanted. They had sought a truer freedom and the opportunity to own property and run their own lives.

The planters had made no effort to treat African labourers as being equal to free workers in England. An American journalist, William Sewell, described their attitude well in 1860:

> They do not seem to reflect for a moment that the interest of the proprietor is to elevate, not degrade his labour. They have misjudged the Negro throughout, and have put too much faith in his supposed inferiority.

The British government also failed to keep faith with its early schemes to build a truly free society in the Caribbean. It had quickly backed down before planters' demands that it should be made difficult for the ex-slaves to move about the colonies as they pleased or to acquire Crown lands. Perhaps the clearest example of its failure is in the story of education in the twenty years after emancipation.

Education
School grants

In 1835, two years after emancipation, the British government made the Negro Education Grant of £25,000 to help in the schooling of West Indians. This was only £5,000 less than the first grant made to English education in 1833 and was supposed to be used in the same way. In England the money was given to church societies which had opened schools for the poor. In the West Indies the money was divided among the missionary societies which had already started schools.

Much of the money was wasted. The missionary societies quarrelled about their shares. Some rushed ahead to open new schools to take a claim on the grant and then closed them when they received less money than expected. Often Anglican clergy, like some of those in Jamaica, refused the grants when they learned they were to be shared with the nonconformists. The Roman Catholic Church in St Lucia, Dominica and Trinidad also refused the grants.

The missionaries usually thought only of teaching reading and writing and sometimes mathematics to a simple level. Many English emancipationists saw education as a way of building a new free society by helping the ex-slaves to read and understand the law. But the British government believed the main aim of the new schools should be to train freemen in obedience to their masters. Sir George Grey wrote to the governor of Trinidad in 1838 to say that the schools were to teach 'love of employment'.

The grant was increased to £30,000 in 1836 and was paid for each of the next ten years. But it was not as well used as the Lady Mico Trust money. Lady Mico had left £1,000 in 1670 to pay ransoms for Christian seamen captured by Barbary pirates from North Africa. Soon after her death the pirates were defeated and the money was invested. In 1834, Thomas Buxton got the agreement of the English law-courts to use the money to promote 'education among the black and coloured population of British Guiana and the West Indies.' On the whole the money was used wisely. Religious quarrels were avoided by opening non-denominational schools in Trinidad, St Lucia, British Guiana and the Bahamas.

The future needs of schools were anticipated by opening teacher training colleges in Jamaica and British Guiana.

The failure of the educational schemes

Despite their valuable work, the Mico schools and colleges could not provide even a fraction of the education needed. In 1846 the British government stopped making its grants and handed over the responsibility for schools to the planter-dominated local governments. This was the same as saying that Britain no longer felt any responsibility to see that the children of African labourers were educated, for the planters had long been bitterly opposed to schools for them. The Superintendent of Police in Antigua had said in 1836:

> . . . the system of education has been overdone, and the rising generation will grow up without the ability or the inclination to engage at any further period, in the different branches of Field Labour or cultivation of the soil.

Immediately the grants ended the local assemblies cut back on all education programmes. In

Fig. 1.5 *Codrington primary school, Barbados. The school was run by a missionary society.*

Guyana in 1857, there was a school-age population of about 43,000, but only ninety-five church schools with a total attendance of 3,511. In 1861 the Jamaican assembly cut the island's education budget to just £8,700 which was shared among the major religious denominations. The following year the clergy were criticised for using the money to shingle their churches and the budget was cut still further.

Even when missionary societies received funds for schools from collections in England, they were not always successful. Many schools in the coastal districts closed in the 1840s. This was partly because the labourers were moving to the interior but also because the schools offered only subjects which pleased planters and missionaries. The chief subjects taught were religious knowledge and home-making skills. The freemen wanted something else for their children; the education which would allow them to turn their back on agricultural work and become teachers, clerks, book-keepers, doctors and lawyers. Very few had the chance.

Assignments

1 *Read this extract from the opening paragraph of Chapter 1 again. 'The first aim of the ex-slaves was to escape from forced and unpaid labour. Many moved away from the plantation as soon as apprenticeship ended. Many others preferred to stay in their old homes among friends and relatives.'*
Imagine that you are one of the 'ex-slaves' in the British Caribbean after 1838.
a) *List the advantages of 'moving away from the plantation' as soon as possible.*
b) *List the advantages of remaining in 'their old homes'.*
c) *In which British Caribbean territories were the ex-slaves most likely to 'move away from the plantations'?*
d) *In which British Caribbean territories were the ex-slaves most likely 'to stay in their old homes'?*

2 **a)** *Explain why most planters tried to prevent ex-slaves from acquiring their own land. What methods did they use?*
b) *Explain why some planters were willing to sell land to ex-slaves.*

3 *Describe the variety of ways by which an ex-slave could earn a living as a freeman. What do you think were the greatest problems that free blacks faced at this time?*

4 *Describe the part played by the missionary societies in the establishment of free villages. What problems were likely to arise between free villagers and missionaries?*

5 *Do you know of any villages, roads or markets that can be traced to a nineteenth-century freeman enterprise? Prepare a short research paper on how one or more of the developments came into being. Where possible use sketches, pictures or diagrams.*

2 THE CHANGING SUGAR PLANTATION

Rivals for markets

New competitors

As soon as apprenticeship ended, free people tried to leave the plantation to become small farmers, traders or craft workers. Some could not change their work but moved to another territory where field and factory wages were higher. These movements led to a drop of a third in the total amount of sugar produced in the British colonies. The biggest falls were in the territories which had produced most under slavery, British Guiana and Jamaica.

Despite the movements and the fall in production, plantation work remained the chief way of earning a living for most ex-slaves.

About half a million still worked on plantations and they were the real victims of the many difficulties faced by the sugar industry in the nineteenth century.

The problems had begun in the eighteenth century when British plantations had struggled against rivals who could produce more cheaply and on a larger scale. Their first important competitor had been the French colony of St Domingue but most of the plantations were changed into smallholdings when Haiti became independent. New rivals soon appeared on the scene. The most serious were in the Americas, as the United States, the Spanish islands and Portuguese Brazil all increased the size of their slave plantations. Then in the 1820s a new chal-

Fig. 2.1 *Crushing and boiling sugar in India, in 1822.*

Fig. 2.2 *A sugar mill in Brazil in 1845. The workers are slaves.*

lenge came from sugar produced in European colonies in Asia. It was shipped to Europe from the Dutch East Indies, the Spanish Philippines and British India, Malaya and Mauritius.

These new sugar producers seemed to have every advantage over the Caribbean estates. Their rivals in the Americas still had a steady stream of new slaves, while West Indian planters had to pay wages. In Asia there was little slavery but wages could be kept low because of the large numbers looking for work. Competitors in the Americas and in Asia were working new land while most British West Indian plantations had exhausted their soil from up to two hundred years of cane cropping. There was fresh soil in Trinidad and British Guiana but here there were too few workers.

Free trade

Against all these disadvantages the West Indian planters had just one defence, the Navigation Acts. These protected them by letting their raw sugar into Britain at much lower rates of duty than their rivals. However, a growing number of people in Britain believed that this system of protection was a hindrance to their industry and trade. They wanted 'free trade' which meant abolishing customs duties on goods brought to Britain from all parts of the world.

Behind the call for free trade lay the great industrial and business changes in Britain which are often called the 'industrial revolution'. Between 1800 and 1850 the amount of coal mined in Britain multiplied more than four times. By 1850 the country had 9,654 kilometres of railway and 6,436 kilometres of canals. These linked industrial towns whose houses and factories sprawled over more and more of the countryside. In 1801, Manchester had a population of 75,000; by 1873 it had grown to three-quarters of a million. In the same period Liverpool and Birmingham grew from 77,000 and 71,000 to over half a million each.

A favourite boast of the factory owners was

13

Fig. 2.3 *A cotton factory near the city centre of Manchester, England, in 1832.*

that they were making Britain 'the workshop of the world', importing raw materials, turning them into manufactured goods and selling them all over the globe. In 1750 Britain had imported less than 1,360 kilograms of cotton, by 1800 the annual figure had risen to 2,722 kilograms and in the next fifty years shot up to 360,612 kilograms. The raw cotton was made into millions of kilometres of cloth, mostly for export.

Such huge quantities of factory-made goods made nonsense of the Navigation Acts. Cotton factory owners, for instance, could not get more than a fraction of the raw cotton they needed from British colonies. They also had to import from the United States and pay the high duties. Many manufacturers of textiles and iron goods suffered because their foreign customers wanted to pay for British goods with raw materials but these too incurred customs duties when they came into Britain. Naturally, manufacturers called for an end to all import duties so they could get their raw materials cheaply from anywhere in the world.

A strong case was made for free trade in sugar which had become an important part of British diet. Each person consumed an average of about nine kilograms a year.

The main drink of factory workers, especially in the cold damp British winters, was sweetened tea. Cuts in the price of sugar from non-British producers would help to lower the cost of living. But that was only half the argument for free trade. Sugar refining was an important British industry, especially in port towns such as London, Liverpool, Bristol and Glasgow. Refiners found that the West Indian planters and those in other British colonies, could no longer supply all the raw sugar they needed. So they turned to other sources, especially from Brazil and Cuba. But the Navigation Laws said that a higher duty had to be added to raw sugar from Cuba and Brazil and this made the sugar dearer than that from the British Empire. In turn that meant that British refiners could not sell refined sugar as cheaply as their rivals in France, Germany and Holland.

Sugar duties equalised

Sugar Duties Equalisation Act

In 1846, the British Prime Minister, Lord John Russell, announced his plans to equalise sugar duties. By this he meant that all sugar should come into Britain at the same rate as West Indian sugar. The door was now open for a flood of sugar from the large slave-worked plantations. The West Indian interest protested vigorously, but it no longer had any real power in British politics. In the Caribbean some planters talked of leaving the British Empire and joining the United States. Russell would not give way. The only change he would accept to the Sugar Duties Equalisation Act of 1846 was to cut the duties on foreign-produced sugar gradually year by year, until full equalisation came in 1854. To help the planters cope with the competition from lower cost producers, Russell abolished restrictions on indentured immigration (see Chapter 4). He also promised British government backing for a private loan to Trinidad, British Guiana and Jamaica to develop schemes to recruit labourers.

The chart below shows how the Equalisation Act brought benefits to the British people. From 1846 the amount of sugar used by each person rose sharply. But you can see from the table that it was not British Caribbean sugar. Even before the sugar duties were fully equalised, foreign sugar was going to the refineries in Britain in far greater quantities than Caribbean sugar.

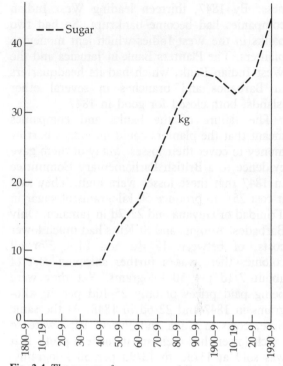

Fig. 2.4 *The amount of sugar consumed in a year by each person in Britain 1800–1939.*

First effects of the Equalisation Act

The news that foreign sugar was to be cheaper had two immediate effects in Britain. First, the price paid for sugar fell from 33/- to 25/10d per 50 kilograms. Second, Englishmen were no longer willing to lend money to companies and banks which specialised in West Indian busi-

Imports of sugar to Britain (yearly average in tonnes)						
	Last 4 years of slavery	Apprenticeship	First 4 years of freedom	Last years of high protection	First 4 years of falling protection	Second 4 years of falling protection	First 4 years of free trade
From	1831–4	1835–8	1839–42	1843–6	1847–50	1851–4	1855–8
British Caribbean	191,671	185,738	121,003	125,745	142,530	150,070	151,917
Other parts of British Empire	33,687	41,076	73,161	99,189	119,684	124,164	115,172
Foreign colonies	20,156	17,047	35,016	48,860	91,003	106,303	138,259
Total of non-Caribbean sugar	53,843	58,123	108,177	148,049	210,687	230,467	253,421

ness. By 1847, thirteen leading West Indian companies had become bankrupt. So had two banks in the West Indies which lent money to planters. The Planters Bank in Jamaica and the West Indian Bank, which had its headquarters in Barbados and branches in several other islands, both closed for good in 1847.

The failure of the banks and companies meant that the planters could no longer borrow money to cover their losses. Many of them gave evidence to a British Parliamentary Committee in 1847 that these losses were high. They said it cost 25/- to produce 50 kilograms of sugar in Trinidad or Guyana and 22/7d in Jamaica. Only Barbados, Antigua and St Kitts had much lower costs, of between 15/4½d and 21/-. For all colonies there was a further shipping cost of about 7/1d per 50 kilograms. Yet they were being paid prices of only 25/10d per 50 kilograms in 1847 and 22/6d in 1848. At the same time, costs in Cuba and Puerto Rico were so much lower that their sugar made a profit if it was sold at 11/3d to 13/9d per 50 kilograms. Perhaps some of these figures were exaggerated but 474 sugar and coffee plantations went out of business in Jamaica between 1846 and 1852. By 1858 sugar production in Grenada had fallen by half compared with the last years of slavery, while Montserrat, St Vincent and Tobago had all suffered production losses of about a third.

Effects on labour

After the Equalisation Act planters tried to reduce costs by cutting wages. Between 1838 and 1846 able-bodied workers in Trinidad and Guyana had earned about 2/- a day; in Jamaica the average rate was 1/8d. Wages in the smaller colonies averaged only 8d or 9d although workers were often given a cottage and perhaps a garden plot. From 1846 these rates were cut by as much as a half but the labourers did not take this quietly. In the Windwards many simply laid down their tools and retired to work their provision grounds. In St Kitts they were accused of setting fire to the cane fields. There were strikes in Trinidad and British Guiana.

In reply to the protests, planters made small efforts to compensate for the loss of earnings. More workers were offered housing or garden plots and sometimes also free medical care. But in most cases the labourers made no gains before their resistance was crushed. On the smaller islands there was no other way to make a living. As early as 1849 the governor of the Leewards reported on 'the peaceful submission of the labouring classes . . . to the reduction in wages.' In the larger colonies, the labourers lost the wage struggle because the planters could exploit the new immigrants they were now allowed to recruit from India.

Immigrant regulations laid down that indentured labourers must receive 1/1d (or 25 cents) for a task which would take a day. Such a daily rate must have seemed a promise of riches to poor Indian peasants whose money wages at home had been between 1½d and 2¼d a day. Yet by keeping the tasks long so they took seven hours, or nine in crop time, planters usually needed to pay for only four tasks a week. In 1900 the average weekly earnings for indentured men in Trinidad was only a dollar (or about 4/4d). Clearly, immigration did much to keep wage rates low for both East Indians and African labourers.

Mechanisation

New machinery

After the Equalisation Act, sugar could be the main export crop only if costs were cut by using machinery in the fields and factories. For the first time in three hundred years, ploughs, harrows, weeding machines and wheelbarrows began to replace human backs and hoes. In 1846 the lieutenant-governor of the Leewards reported that a man and a boy working with a plough and three horses could prepare half a hectare for planting as quickly as eight labourers using hoes; an entire weeding gang of sixteen could be replaced by a man, a boy, one horse and a weeding machine.

Even such simple machinery could not always be used. Horses pulling ploughs and weeding machines had great difficulty working the steep fields in Montserrat, St Lucia and Dominica. In other colonies, such as Nevis, loose stones in the light soils caught in the teeth of weeding machines or sheared off the cast iron points of ploughs. In Guyana, machines often stuck in the muddy fields while draft animals trampled down the sides of the vital drainage ditches. Where machines could not be used, planters could turn only to new hoes 'made entirely of steel, much thinner and . . . lighter than the common hoe.' Labourers could make more strokes per minute, but this was a pathetic attempt to make a seventeenth-century tool compete with nineteenth-century machinery.

Planters who could afford the new machines did save on wages. But machines could not replace the steady labour supply required during crop time. Then human arms and cutlasses were still needed to cut and top the canes. Harvesting machines were not invented for another century. The problem of finding enough labourers was greatest in colonies where freemen had their own holdings. Most of their crops needed to be harvested at the same time of the year as the cane. Once again it was the steady flow of indentured East Indian labour which solved the problem for the most successful planters, those in Trinidad and British Guiana.

Steam power

The greatest improvements came about when steam engines, made in the industrial cities of Britain, were bought to drive factory machinery. Steam power drove the rollers crushing cane better than wind, water or animals. This one change could result in 25 per cent more juice being expressed from the canes. If a planter could afford vacuum pans the sugar could be boiled at a lower temperature, which lessened the chance of destroying the sugar crystals by over-heating. Plantations with large enough steam engines could also install centrifugal driers to separate molasses from the sugar crystals. This saved the costs of the long curing process and stopped wasteful leakage on the voyage to Europe.

In Trinidad and Guyana there was enough unexhausted land to make it worthwhile to spend the money on machinery. Planters there could often borrow money for factory improve-ments on the understanding that they would open new cane fields. As early as 1852, there were 282 steam engines on 183 sugar properties in Guyana. Most were used to drive mills and driers but a few were connected to pumps to improve field drainage. In the smaller colonies, planters found it harder to arrange loans for machinery. Even a small steam engine cost over £1,200; and the price of vacuum pans was between £400 and £1,000. It was reckoned that a property needed a yearly output of 375 tonnes before it was profitable to buy a steam engine large enough to operate a drier. Not one single property in the Leewards produced that much sugar. Here the planters could only afford small steam engines for their mills and try to improve the quality of their canes by ratooning less often, using more fertiliser and planting thinner rows.

Central factories

The coming of field machinery and steam engines meant that there were many advantages from joining several estates together. The owners would have more funds to buy the machinery and could close the smaller factories using copper boilers. They could then replace them by a central factory using vacuum pans, heavy rollers and steam-driven driers. The first step towards amalgamation usually came when a planter fell into debt to a merchant company. By agreeing to cancel the debt, the company was able to buy the estate at a low price. It then joined several such plantations and ran them as one estate under a limited liability company. Often this company was itself controlled by a large British company which owned plantations and other businesses in many parts of the world. This meant that they could raise the money for improvements to their property and were not so likely to be ruined by a poor crop in one area.

In 1857 the merchant company Cavan and Lubbock began to buy sugar properties in the British West Indies and Puerto Rico. Within ten years they had installed $500,000 worth of the latest machinery. In 1866 the Company joined with Burnley Hume and Company to become the Colonial Sugar Company. By 1878 it owned one quarter of all the sugar properties in Trinidad and Guyana. It was the Colonial Sugar Company which opened the first central factory in the English-speaking West Indies at Ste Madeleine in Trinidad in 1872. Others followed at Napurima and on the northern plain. From this time on, the estates fell increasingly under the control of limited companies, and amalgamations went on steadily.

Rises in production

Wage cutting, machinery and amalgamations all played their part in helping some colonies, especially Trinidad and British Guiana, to cope with the effects of the Sugar Duties Equalisation Act. In British Guiana for instance the production figures went like this:

Year	Tonnes produced
1830	(before emancipation) 60,000
1851	(after Sugar Duties Act) 38,000
1861	63,000
1871	92,000

But a major reason for the growth of production was the low paid work and poor conditions of large numbers of immigrant labourers. Their story is told in the next two chapters.

Assignments

1 a) *Explain how each of the following provided competition at different times to the British West Indian Sugar Industry: i) the French colony of St Domingue; ii) the United States; iii) Brazil; iv) European colonies in Asia.*
   b) *How did the Navigation Acts protect the British West Indian sugar industry up to 1848?*

2 *Use the chart on page 15 to answer the following:*
   a) *In which period between 1831 and 1858 were imports of sugar to Britain from the British Caribbean highest?*
   b) *Give reasons for this.*
   c) *Name two 'other parts of the British Empire' and two 'foreign colonies' from whom Britain imported sugar.*
   d) *Which of the sources of imports of sugar to Britain showed the greatest increase?*
   e) *Give reasons for this.*

3 *Account for the survival of the sugar industry in some parts of the British Caribbean and not in others.*

4 *How do you think the ex-slaves would be affected by the changes on the sugar plantation between 1834 and 1858?*

3 MIGRATION

Free Africans on the move

The planters' labour problem

When apprenticeship ended, the three largest territories were faced with a shortage of plantation labour. For Trinidad and British Guiana it had existed since they were taken over by Britain in 1801 and 1815. There was much unused land which attracted planters to move there from other islands. But there were not enough labourers to work it, and after 1807 the British government tried to stop any sales of slaves from the more crowded islands to planters in Guyana and Trinidad. However, Jamaican planters faced a labour problem because their island was large enough for workers to leave the estates to settle in free villages in the interior.

Black migration in the Caribbean

From September 1838, labourers across the Caribbean were free to move in search of better working conditions or land of their own. British Guiana and Trinidad saw this as an opportunity to solve their labour problems. They appointed recruiting agents and paid bounties on each immigrant that a ship's captain brought into the territory. Other colonies objected. In Barbados, the Windwards, the Leewards and the Bahamas the assemblies passed acts forbidding recruiting agents to work in their colonies. The churches were brought in to help by preaching sermons on the horrors of the 'Guyanese slave trade'.

None of this stopped migration especially to Trinidad. In the first ten years after apprenticeship more than ten thousand blacks arrived there from the small islands, especially Barbados. This steady movement into Trinidad continued right through the nineteenth century. In 1897 there were about 14,000 Barbadians living on the island. Yet the migration did not solve the planters' problems. Like the ex-slaves

of Trinidad itself they preferred to work ground of their own, to squat or to settle in the towns. When railway and road building were important in the 1870s and 1880s they often took up this work. Some became seasonal workers on the plantations but even then planters found that people who had taken the great step of migrating to a new territory were not the sort to give up their independence. Planters often complained that they were disobedient and 'insolent'.

Some planters believed they might do better by recruiting in the United States. In her northern cities there were many blacks who had become free by escaping from the plantations in the American south. Perhaps they would welcome the chance to work in the warmer Caribbean. Only just over a thousand did and most of them came as craftsmen who would not work on the estates.

Liberated Africans

There was one more possibility. Since Britain had abolished the slave trade in 1807 her warships had patrolled the seas looking for foreign boats carrying slaves. Most of the captures they made were of Brazilian and Cuban ships. When the slaves had been released they were usually taken to two British colonies, St Helena in the Atlantic or Sierra Leone in Africa. Both these colonies were in danger of being overcrowded so the British government was willing to encourage the liberated Africans to emigrate to the Caribbean.

The first arrivals were often English-speaking Christians who had lived in Sierra Leone for some time. One group were descended from Maroons who had been deported from Jamaica in 1796, first to Canada and then to Sierra Leone. But few Africans were willing to make the journey back to West Indian plantations. This was also true of the people of the Kru coast, near to Sierra Leone. Recruiting agents persuaded a few hundred Krus to go to British Guiana and Trinidad. No more followed. News about bad conditions and the obstacles to becoming independent farmers travelled quickly back to Africa.

After 1841 most liberated Africans were brought to the Caribbean either as soon as they were taken from a slave ship or after a short time on St Helena. These Africans were unused to European ways and had not been seasoned to plantation labour. They usually left the plantations as soon as they could and settled as squatters or smallholders in the interiors. In Trinidad they remained quite separate groups through the nineteenth century, living in their own villages or on the fringes of towns and often speaking their own languages.

The liberated Africans obviously did not meet the planters' needs and no more were brought from the late 1860s. But in the thirty years 1838–68 a total of 36,130 had been landed.

Indentured labour

Black immigration failed to solve the labour problem of planters in British Guiana or Trinidad. Many believed they might have better fortune by turning to indentured labourers. They were returning to the system which had been tried in the sugar colonies before slavery, but with one important difference. The bond-servants of the seventeenth century had been poor Europeans. The indentured labourers of the nineteenth century came from the many parts of the world where European traders and soldiers had become powerful. In other ways the system was the same. Poor, landless people would be recruited to work on the plantations with promises of a free passage and a small plot of land after they had worked for a few years.

Chinese from Malaya

In Trinidad and British Guiana the search for indentured labourers began almost as soon as the territories had been taken over by Britain. In 1802 the first governor of Trinidad got permission to import Chinese labourers from Malaya. Many Chinese were already moving from their homeland to other places like Malaya in south-east Asia where European plantations and trading posts were growing fast. It was not difficult to persuade some to move on from Malaya and take up indentures in Trinidad with the promise of small plots of land after five years. One hundred and ninety-two made the trip half way round the world and landed at Trinidad in 1806. Sixty-one returned at their own request in 1807. Seven years later only thirty of the original immigrants lived in Trinidad and not one of them worked on a plantation.

Madeirans

In the 1830s planters in Trinidad and Guyana turned to Madeira, the Portuguese colony in the Atlantic where sugar was a main crop. Through Mr Seale, an English merchant on the island, they arranged for the first 125 Madeiran cane-workers to come to Trinidad in 1834. A year later 559 landed in Guyana. They were the first of many thousands to come to the Caribbean. Most headed for Guyana because the wages were higher. A few hundred came to Trinidad or found their way to the Windwards and Leewards, but practically none to Jamaica. The numbers of Madeirans declined after 1846, partly because the Portuguese government objected to so many of their subjects leaving. But it was also because the plantation owners were disappointed in the immigrants. After their indenture was over very few settled as free workers on the plantations. They either returned to Madeira, or became market gardeners, cocoa growers, or entered the retail trade. By 1856 Portuguese Madeirans controlled nearly all the retailing businesses in Guyana and St Vincent.

Indians

In 1836 a Guyanese plantation owner, John Gladstone, decided to try his luck with indentured East Indian labourers. He had read that planters on the island of Mauritius in the Indian Ocean were using indentured labour taken from

India. He contacted Gillanders and Company, the firm which supplied Mauritius with the labourers. They assured him that there would be no problem in persuading Indians to sign on for the much longer journey to an unknown land, the 'Natives being perfectly ignorant of the place they agree to go to, and the length of journey they are undertaking'.

In May 1838, 396 landed in Guyana. Their fate was terrible. Anti-slavery campaigners soon found evidence of flogging and other forms of harsh punishment. Ninety-eight of the Indians on Gladstone's estates died before their time of indenture was over.

Controls on indentures

When apprenticeship ended in September 1838, the anti-slavery movement wanted to be sure that indenture schemes did not become a new form of slavery. The Colonial Office in London issued regulations which had been written by James Stephen, a senior official who was also a leading emancipationist and son of the James Stephen who had been a leading emancipationist MP. The regulations were aimed at all schemes to bring in non-European indentured labourers whether they were Africans from the small islands or people such as the Chinese or Indians. They stated that contracts could not be signed before the labourer arrived in a Caribbean colony. In the colony they could only be for one year. It was illegal to pay ships' captains a bounty to bring in African labourers.

Some planters managed to ignore the regulations, especially those to do with paying bounties. But the regulations did make it harder to recruit indentured labourers. Planters were not willing to pay for an immigrant's passage if they had not got the power to make him work on the plantation for at least three or four years. They protested to the government in London and asked that they should be allowed to bring in East Indians. The minister in charge of the Colonial Office replied that it was more sensible to grow sugar in India where labour was cheap. He told the Caribbean planters, 'the plantation will be found for the labourer and not the labourer for the plantation.'

Bountied European immigrants

The regulations did not forbid schemes to attract immigrants from Europe. The assembly in Jamaica was eager to encourage Europeans to settle in the interior so that there would be less room for the ex-slaves who were leaving the plantations. The reasons for the scheme were openly explained in English newspapers:

> I would by my plan, endeavour to supersede the necessity of any black labourers in the mountains, and by having 50 to 60,000 whites there, bring down say, 100,000 blacks to the lowlands. This would benefit the planters without injury to the negroes: to the former it would give a greater quantity of labourers . . . to the latter it would make the necessity of work greater; consequently less fear of their relapsing into barbarism.

Some planters recruited their own settlers but the assembly also appointed agents to recruit in Europe. New immigrants were paid a bounty, usually of £12, if they stayed for at least six months. They were promised land if they remained for five years. Some were brought to three townships set aside for immigrants by the assembly.

Trinidad and British Guiana attempted similar schemes, although they looked for labourers on the main plantations more than the interior. But planters in all the colonies found that it was difficult to recruit Europeans. During the nineteenth century more than seven million people left Europe for North America, but the West Indies offered much poorer opportunities. The best land was already taken up and stories of the unhealthy climate were widespread. The few who did come advised others not to follow. They reported that they were not provided with housing or medical care and that they lacked the farming skills to clear the interior lands. Many died within the first months; others wandered off to the port towns and drank themselves to death. A few went home and a few headed west to the mainland.

By 1843 the colonies had abandoned nearly all schemes for European immigration. The Jamaican scheme had attracted only 2,865 British and 1,038 Germans. Only a few hundreds had gone to each of the Leewards, the Windwards,

Fig. 3.1 *Between decks, on a ship carrying emigrants from Europe to the Americas, in 1851.*

Trinidad and Guyana. Planters were objecting to paying bounties to Europeans who were unsuitable for estate labour. The editor of Jamaica's *Falmouth Post* wrote that it was a waste of public money to try to substitute 'a European for an African peasantry in the tropics'.

Government immigration schemes

Britain changes policy

Almost every scheme to recruit labour to the large territories had been tried and all had failed to solve the problem. In 1843, the British government began a complete turn-about in its policy. It allowed Trinidad, Guyana and Jamaica to borrow money to pay for the passage of new indentured labour. In the same year it lifted the ban on recruiting in India. In 1846 the British Parliament passed the Sugar Duties Equalisation Act which removed the protection that West Indian planters had in the English market. To compensate planters, the government took away all other restrictions on immigration.

Three years later in 1849 a complete scheme for encouraging immigration was drawn up. The British government agreed to guarantee a private loan to West Indian planters to pay for the scheme. But the planters were not trusted to care for their labourers or treat them fairly. So the

British government made itself responsible for recruitment, shipping and supervision of living conditions on the estates. The work of organising immigration was given to officials in the West Indies and the homelands of the immigrants.

Recruiting the Chinese

The British government's regulations stated that the length of the indenture, wages and arrangements for a return passage were to be clearly explained to each immigrant. Recruiters were not to bribe, threaten or use force. These rules were not obeyed in China where the British government had little power.

Between 1859 and 1866 about 15,000 Chinese came to Guyana, 2,600 to Trinidad and 4,800 to Jamaica. Most of them came from barracoons at

Fig. 3.2 *Canton in south China. The buildings along the side of the harbour are the warehouses of British traders.*

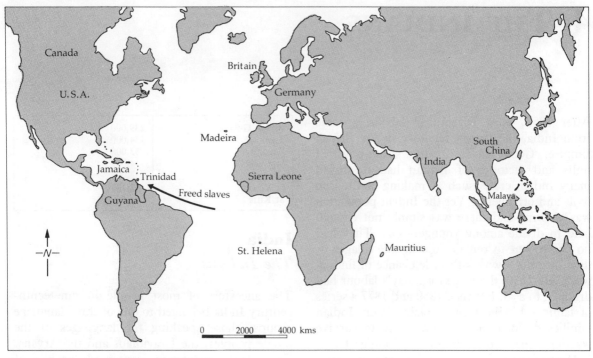

Map 1 *Sources of immigration to the Caribbean.*

Hong Kong, a small British colony on the south coast of China. They had found themselves in the barracoons after being taken prisoner in the civil war that was being fought across the whole of south China. Their captors handed them over to local indenture brokers who released them for a fee to British immigration agents.

Planters complained that the Chinese did not make good estate workers as few re-indentured themselves. They preferred to return to China or open small retail shops in the Caribbean. They were more expensive than East Indian labourers, who usually cost a planter about £15 as against £25 for a Chinese. In 1866 the costs rose greatly when the Chinese government insisted that indentures had to allow for a full return passage after five years. The planters wanted to pay this only after two five-year indenture periods had been served. The increased cost was enough to bring Chinese immigration to an end. Later Chinese immigrants to the Americas avoided the British-owned Caribbean. By 1890 150,000 Chinese had signed up to work in Cuban and United States cane fields. More came to work on the railways in the western United States and the Hawaiian sugar fields, where pay was better. Naturally the greater number of Chinese emigrants did not come to the western world; hundreds of thousands found work in the plantations, ports and warehouses of south-east Asia.

Assignments

1 *Using the map above answer the following questions:*
   a) *Why did immigrants come from Europe to the British Caribbean in the nineteenth century? Why was the number of European immigrants not much larger?*
   b) *Explain why immigrants from Africa came to the British Caribbean after emancipation.*
   c) *Which areas produced the largest number of immigrants to the British Caribbean? Why?*
2 **a)** *Give reasons why Trinidad and Guyana attracted immigrants from other British West Indian territories.*
   b) *What effects did this migration have: i) on the countries from which they migrated? ii) on the countries to which they migrated?*
3 *Why did the British government stop slavery but encourage the indentured system?*

4 THE INDIANS

After 1857, most indentured labourers came from India, the largest territory in the British Empire. Goods made in the steam-powered mills and factories of Britain had destroyed many Indian crafts such as making cloth, iron tools and ornaments. Yet the Indian population was growing and there was simply not enough land to divide among younger sons. They had no choice but to remain idle in the villages or drift into the towns with little chance of finding work. By 1850, the wage for a day's labour had dropped to a $\frac{1}{2}$d. Between 1850 and 1877 a series of famines hit the Ganges plain. Many Indian families decided that the only way to survive was for some of their members to emigrate.

Most of the emigrants went to other countries of the British Empire. Large settlements of Indians grew up in some of the colonies of East Africa (such as the modern Kenya and Tanzania). Other people settled in the modern South Africa. Most of these migrated from the western half of India. For those in the eastern half, the best chance to emigrate came when they were offered a shilling a day and steady work in Trinidad and Guyana.

The planters saw the Indians as ideal labourers. They were hard-working, used to low wages and poor diets and skilled in tropical agriculture. They re-indentured themselves more often than the Chinese or Madeirans. They were also easy to recruit, British control of India meant there were ready-made recruiting and collection centres in the country. The constant flow of British ships to India meant there were no difficulties over transport. The British government was satisfied, too. Because they ruled India it was easy to have recruitment supervised closely.

Between 1844 and 1917, 416,000 Indians were indentured to work in the British West Indies. They were divided among the colonies in this way:

British Guiana	239,000
Trinidad	134,000
Jamaica	33,000
St Lucia	4,000
Grenada	3,000
St Vincent	2,700
St Kitts	300

India

The Indians

The ancestors of most people in nineteenth-century India belonged to one of three language groups: those speaking the languages of the jungle peoples, the Dravidians and the Aryans. Each language group contained people of several different racial backgrounds. The first inhabitants were jungle tribesmen. Today their ancient dialects are spoken in only a few remote villages in the central highlands. The jungle peoples were forced to flee there by groups of nomads who moved in from the west more than 5,000 years ago. These newcomers spoke the Dravidian languages; they were dark-skinned and slightly built. Their first settlements were along the broad river plains of the Indus and Ganges but in the following centuries they spread through the whole peninsula.

The Dravidians were driven from the north by taller and fairer-skinned people who first arrived about 1500 B.C. These were the Aryan-speaking peoples. Their invasion accounts for the language divisions of modern India. In the south Dravidian dialects are spoken; in the north and along the western coast people tend to speak Hindi or other related languages which stem from the various Aryan dialects.

Western societies owe much to the early Indian civilisations. They devised the system of Arabic numbers, especially the use of '0' which allows for easy counting in multiples of ten. Their ancient written language, Sanskrit, has

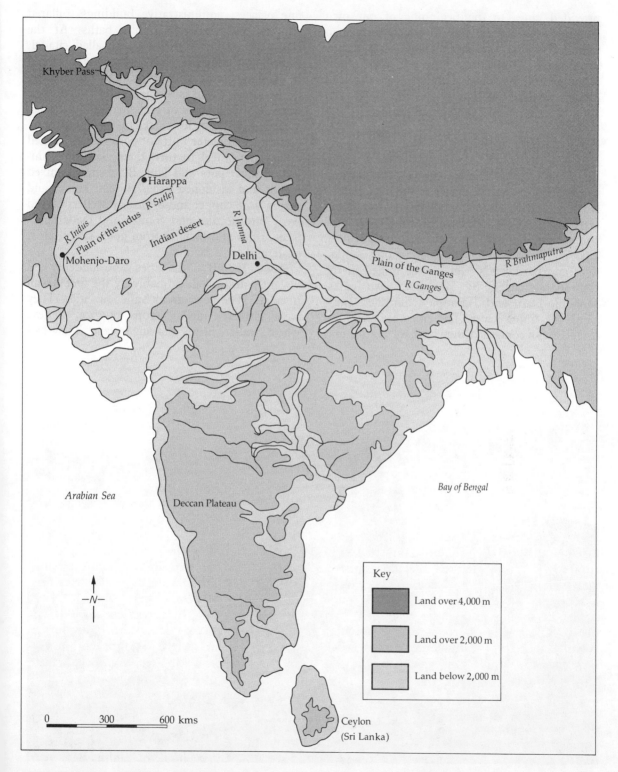

Map 2 *The Indian subcontinent: relief features.*

provided clues to the beginning of our own languages and to the way in which early man migrated across the face of the earth. They formulated Hinduism, one of the oldest religions still practised. Hinduism gave rise to other sects like the Jainists and the Sikhs, and another major world religion, Buddhism.

The wealth of India

For thousands of years the people of Africa and western Europe spoke in awe of India's fabulous wealth. The fertile plains along the Indus and Ganges Rivers were ideal for growing food crops and cotton, and herding sheep, goats and cattle. The southern forests provided exotic spices, dyes and hardwoods. Gems were mined in the central highlands. By 5000 B.C. two cities, Mohenjo-Daro and Harappa, controlled trade along the Indus River. The cities built of kiln-dried bricks contained thousands of houses and

fine palaces, administrative buildings, pillared temples and elaborate public baths. At the centre of each city was a high-walled citadel. Enormous granaries and warehouses stored trade goods and tributes which surrounding farmers paid as taxes to their rulers. The cities were also the homes of craftsmen and artisans. Wheelwrights made carts to be pulled by domesticated water buffalo; potters had learned to use the wheel to turn their clay into thin-walled jugs, pots and jars. Blacksmiths mixed metals and fashioned axes, chisels, knives and razors from copper and bronze. Jewellers carved ivory into needles and combs, and made necklaces, rings and bangles from gold, silver, jade, agate and lapis lazuli.

About 1500 B.C. the cities were suddenly and violently destroyed, probably by the first Aryan invaders. The newcomers built few cities. They were farmers, raising crops of rice, barley, wheat, millet, beans and sugar cane. They had

Fig. 4.1 *A view of a Hindu temple, painted in 1787.*

come with herds of cattle, sheep, goats and donkeys. But the early city craftsmen did not disappear. Between the Indus and the Ganges thousands of small villages grew up where craftsmen continued to turn out fine leathers, metal items, and woven cotton cloth. While the western Africans and the Europeans were still in the Stone Age, these Indian goods were being sold throughout Asia and the Middle East.

The invasions

The combination of industry and agriculture encouraged the growth of a large population. By 500 B.C. the whole peninsula was divided into a number of independent kingdoms. Their rulers were not powerful enough to join the kingdoms into a lasting empire. Nor could they stop wave after wave of new invaders from the west. First the Persians and then the Macedonians, under Alexander the Great, ruled over the Indian kingdoms for a brief while. They were followed by the Scythians and the Huns and a new round of Muslim conquerors from Persia and Afghanistan. Unlike the others, the Muslims did not leave. By A.D. 1400 a line of Muslim rulers, the Great Moguls, had established their capital at Delhi and united the Indian principalities and kingdoms into a loosely-knit, federated empire.

The Moguls

One of the Mogul rulers, Akbar (1556–1605), tried to make India a more manageable centralised state. Working with the native Hindu princes, he set out to build a network of roads which linked all parts of the country to Delhi. Honest governors and royal officials were appointed; the tax system was overhauled and a standing army was created. Akbar's successors were less capable. Most were content to pass their lives spending the empire's wealth on monuments such as the Taj Mahal and the beautiful alabaster palace of the Moguls in Delhi which held a solid gold, gem-encrusted peacock throne. In 1600 several Hindu princes formed the Mahratta Confederacy and revolted against the Muslim Moguls. The Moguls could

Fig. 4.2 *The Mogul Emperor, Akbar, receiving an ambassador from Queen Elizabeth I of England, in 1599.*

not suppress the Confederacy and, by 1700, India was again on the verge of breaking up into warring states.

By the mid-eighteenth century India was again divided into over twenty-five small principalities and kingdoms ruled by local kings, rajahs, sultans and minor princes who obeyed and disobeyed the Mogul in Delhi as it pleased them. The chief mark of Mogul rule was the conversion of many people of northern India to the Muslim religion. Most of their descendants now live in the Muslim states of Pakistan and Bangladesh.

The Europeans in India

Five years after Columbus arrived in the Caribbean, the Portuguese sailor, Vasco Da Gama, was the first European to sail direct to India. Within a hundred years English and French traders had followed and taken over most of the European trade with the Mogul Empire. Both nations set up East India Companies and the Moguls gave them permission to open trading posts, but only around the coast. When Mogul power collapsed in the eighteenth century, the East India Companies began to get a hold on the rest of the country. They built their own forts, coined their own money and signed trade agreements with local Indian rulers.

In 1756 the Seven Years War broke out between England and France. Company officials, like the Frenchman Joseph Dupleix and the Englishman Robert Clive, hired their own Indian sepoy regiments. They were used to fight wars between the Companies and also Indian princes who were slow to grant trading rights to the Europeans.

The French were defeated in the Seven Years War and again in the French Wars. At the same time the British East India Company extended its control over many parts of the Mogul Empire. It forced princes to accept Company officials and tax collectors as the real rulers of their lands. By 1857 the Company had by far the largest army in India, but all its Indian troops were not loyal. British commanders had treated sepoys with little regard for their pride or for their religious customs. Although sepoys outnumbered English soldiers by six to one, few were ever made officers. In late 1857 the sepoy regiments in the Ganges valley mutinied against their British commanders. For a while, British power in north India seemed to have collapsed. However, the mutiny was soon put down as regiments in the south and west refused to join their countrymen.

The 'Indian Mutiny' convinced the British government that the East India Company could no longer be trusted to manage the affairs of the peninsula. A separate department for India was set up in the Colonial Office. The last of the Moguls, who had supported the mutiny, was deposed and replaced by a British governor sent to rule India in much the same way as the Crown colonies in Trinidad and Guyana were ruled. One by one the local maharajahs, rajahs, princes and lesser rulers were bribed, threatened and forced to place their territories under British protection. The system was completed in 1877 when Queen Victoria was proclaimed Empress of India and a viceroy was sent to rule over the local princes in her name. The real rulers of India at every level from the viceroy down to the district officers in charge of a few villages were officials or soldiers born and educated in Britain. With few changes the Empire of India remained intact until the end of British rule in 1947.

Recruitment

Recruiting in India

It was not the planters but the island governments who recruited Indians. Guyana, Trinidad and Jamaica each appointed immigration agents to work from Calcutta. Most immigrants came from the overcrowded villages on the plain of the River Ganges which flowed, with many lesser rivers, through the United Provinces, Bihar and West Bengal. The population of the Ganges plain was rising while traditional village industries such as weaving and iron work were destroyed by competition from English factory-made goods. Hundreds of thousands of villagers left their homes to seek work in other parts of India. Recruiting stations were set up to attract these desperate unemployed people to emigrate to the West Indies.

Each station had a sub-agent in charge. He paid recruiters a shilling for every able-bodied person they brought into the station. The sub-agent was responsible for explaining the conditions of the indenture and seeing that it was legally witnessed by a magistrate. He then sent the new recruits on to Calcutta. Many of the recruits would not have understood clearly what they were told. For each signed contract the sub-agent collected about £3 for a man and £5 for a woman, from which he had to pay all his expenses. Higher fees were paid for women to try to attract them to the West Indies where by far the greatest number of indentured labourers were men. In Calcutta the emigrants were medically inspected and their contracts were again gone over by an English official. If all was in order, the emigrants were sent to barracks to await passage to the West Indies.

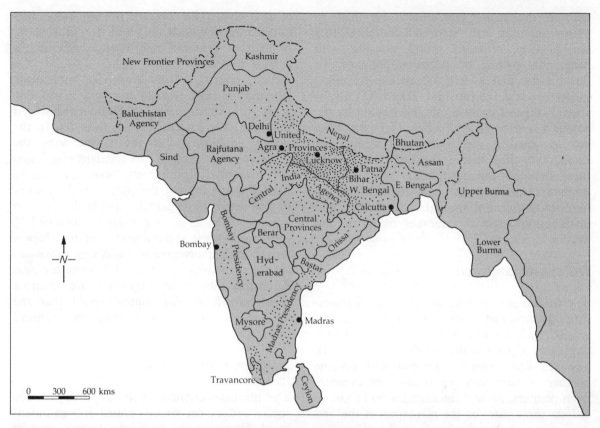

Map 3 *The main homelands of Indian indentured labourers. Each dot represents between 150 and 200 recruits.*

For a time immigrants were also recruited by agents at Madras. But the number of indentured labourers from the south was tiny compared with those from the Ganges plain. In Trinidad the languages of southern India almost disappeared as the few thousand Madrasi immigrants found it necessary to learn Hindi spoken by the northerners.

The voyage

The first immigrants were allowed less than one and a half square metres deck space. These were very cramped quarters for a journey that lasted from 93 to 113 days and death rates were very high. In 1858 the *Salsette* from Calcutta to Trinidad landed only 199 passengers; 124 had died of cholera, dysentery and sea-sickness. Such high mortality rates led to new regulations in 1864. Each immigrant was to be allowed at least two cubic metres below decks, with no more

than one adult for each bunk. Other regulations checked the deadly out-breaks of cholera and dysentery. Each ship had to carry a medical officer, a dispenser, supplies of drugs, warm clothing and adequate provisions. By 1868 the mortality on immigrant ships had dropped to about 5.45 per cent.

Indentured labour

The immigration department

When immigrants landed in a Caribbean colony they came under the control of the local immigration department. It was headed by a protector of immigrants, who was sometimes called Agent-General. Each year planters sent in requests for labourers, and the immigration department divided the arrivals among the estates. It was then the protector's task to enforce the many regulations. He had to prevent families being separated and check that the planters provided sound housing with water-tight roofing and adequate drainage. To do this he had a staff of clerks, travelling inspectors and interpreters. There was also a special corps of medical officers, headed by the colony's surgeon-general. These corps had been set up when it was found that many new immigrants died within the first year. Every three months the protector's staff had to prepare a report on each plantation, listing the number of days lost through sickness, all fines on labourers, and the number of births and deaths.

Indenture contracts

The British government insisted that all indenture contracts had to state clearly the length of service, the number of hours to be worked each day, rates of pay and the conditions for a return passage. The terms of the contracts became harsher as time went on because of pressure from planters. At first, immigrants had to serve at least three years on the plantation of the first indenture and then to remain in the colony for another two years before claiming their return passage. The Trinidadian and Guyanese planters thought that a five-year residency was too short. In 1862 they succeeded in having the contracts lengthened to five years on the first plantation plus an additional five years' residence. The planters still objected to the free passage home, and from 1895 this was given only to the sick and disabled. The others had to pay a quarter of the fare and in 1898 this was raised to a half. Women paid a sixth in 1895 and a third in 1898.

To encourage labourers to settle near their estates some planters in Trinidad and Guyana sold them small plots of land when their indenture ended. The immigrants were often not allowed to sell the land for years. By 1893 about 32,000 immigrants had bought land in Guyana. Between 1869 and 1881 immigrants in Trinidad were allowed to take up five acres (2.02 hectares) of Crown land (government land) instead of their passage home. However, many immigrants preferred to buy plots on the land of their choice. By the time the last Indian had finished his indenture only a quarter of all those brought to Trinidad and Guyana had taken a passage home.

Most contracts laid down that indentured labourers should work a five and a half day week with Sundays and public holidays off. At first the daily hours of work were ten in the factory and seven in the fields; soon the contracts were changed to a standard nine hours for everyone. Immigrants were to receive weekly wages even if the planter had no work to give them. Most colonies had fairly standard wages of 24 or 25 cents per day for men and 16 cents for women and children over ten. Newly arrived immigrants were supplied with provisions for some months at a rate of 8 cents per day. After this they were responsible for securing their own food. All contracts said that the masters had to supply housing and medical care.

Immigration ordinances

The immigrants found that they had to obey special ordinances which applied only to indentured labourers as well as abiding by the contracts they signed in India. These special ordinances generally favoured the planters. Indentured labourers could not leave the estate without written passes from the owner or the overseer. They could not drink liquor in estate housing, use disrespectful language or make insulting gestures to those in authority. It was illegal to congregate outside the plantation to discuss grievances or to refuse 'reasonable' orders. If the owner was not satisfied with work it had to be done again in the labourer's own time. Breaking one of these ordinances could lead to a fine or a fine and a jail sentence. At one time a labourer could spend 14 days in jail or be fined $4.50 (two and a half weeks' wages) for playing sick. In Trinidad leaving an estate without a pass was punishable by a £5 fine and two months in jail. Time spent in jail had to be made up to the planter in the labourer's free time.

Immigration department officials were often harassed if they tried to see that the ordinances were carried out fairly. This happened in Guyana in the 1860s to the Agent-General, James Crosby, a magistrate, William Des Voeux and the Chief Justice, Joseph Beaumont. All three tried to enforce the ordinances and the governor, Sir Francis Hicks, quickly showed them that they should not interfere with 'planter privileges'. He had Des Voeux transferred to St Lucia. He made it difficult for Crosby to do his job by stopping his travelling allowance and ordering that his sub-agents could only pay two visits a year to each plantation.

In 1869 Indians rioted on the Leonora plantation in British Guiana. From St Lucia, William Des Voeux wrote to the Colonial Secretary in London. He stated that riots were inevitable when the ordinances were so often broken and gave examples from his time in Guyana. Doctors often ordered labourers back to work before they were fit. Planters illegally stopped wages or underpaid labourers and magistrates sided with them. The letter led to an enquiry which confirmed the truth of what Des Voeux had written. The British government wrote new regulations which laid down a fine of $24 if the labourer could prove that the planter had broken his side of the contract. Fines on labourers were cut from £5 to £1.

Very few planters were fined and they continued to make the magistrates' courts work in their interests. They summonsed labourers for

Fig. 4.3 *One of the small groups of indentured Indian labourers who worked on the cocoa plantations in Trinidad.*

poor work or some other offence which would mean a fine or time in prison if they were found guilty. Just before the magistrate came to hear the summons the planter often withdrew it and made the labourer pay the costs. In 1870 a quarter of all indentured labourers in Guyana were summonsed and half the charges were withdrawn. In 1906–7 there were summonses against 37.8 per cent of all labourers in the colony. In Trinidad, planters charged more than one in five labourers between 1898 and 1905 for absences, desertions, vagrancy and idleness.

Exploitation

The immigrants were exploited in other ways. Planters often withheld wages or unfair piecework was given which made it impossible for labourers to earn the minimum wages stated in their contracts. Housing was usually substandard. Most estates supplied barrack housing which by law had to contain rooms not less than three metres by three and a half. This was said to be enough space for a married couple and their children or three single adults. Few planters bothered to provide their barracks with cooking facilities, sanitary conveniences, or regular water supplies. In 1888 Mr Robert Guppy, Mayor of San Fernando, described the barracks in his district as:

> . . . long wooden buildings eleven or twelve feet wide [about two and a half metres], containing perhaps eight or ten small rooms divided from each other by wooden partitions not reaching the roof. The roof is of galvanised iron, without any ceiling; and the heat of the sun by day and the cold by night take full effect upon the occupants. By standing on a box the occupant of one room can look over the partition into the adjoining one, and can easily climb over . . . Comfort, privacy and decency are impossible under such conditions.

The hospitals which each plantation had to supply were little better. Many of the first were holdovers from the days of slavery when they had doubled as lockups. Labourers in Trinidad hated them so much that authorities had to pass an ordinance laying down a three-month jail sentence for running away from hospital.

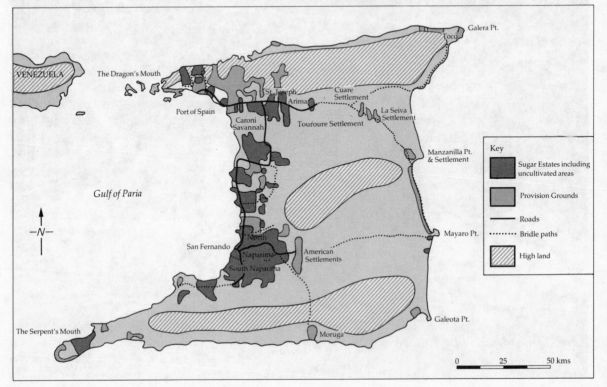

Map 4 *Trinidad in 1850.*

The hospitals did nothing to check the poor general health of the immigrant population. In 1911, 24,000 cases of illness were reported for the 10,000 registered immigrants on Trinidadian plantations. There were over 8,400 cases of malaria and 7,100 cases of diseases caused by parasites, such as hookworm and ground itch. Most of them could be traced to poor diets and insanitary living conditions around the barracks.

Education

From time to time the immigration departments issued ordinances for immigrants to send their children to the few schools that were available. In many cases the Hindu and Muslim parents objected to sending their children to the local church schools. But they were almost never encouraged to set up their own schools. The attitude of the Immigration Agent-General for Guyana in 1880 was typical. He argued against the need to educate immigrant children on the grounds that:

> . . . large gangs of little children . . . are often employed in light work, such as carrying earth, ashes and manure and this is not only a benefit to their parents but also a source of pleasure to themselves . . . in this country, where their work is as much pastime as labour and is conducive to the promotion of health and vigour, both of body and mind, the necessity of such a restriction as going to school does not appear to me to exist.

Thirty years later his successor was still arguing against 'any steps which may tend to the withdrawal of a single individual from the soil'.

The most important exception to this neglect of Indian education was the Canadian Presbyterian Mission in Trinidad. By 1911 they had opened sixty-one free primary schools for Indians as well as two high schools and a teachers' training college.

'The New Slavery'?

In 1871, Sir Joseph Beaumont had left his post as Chief Justice in British Guiana. In England he wrote a pamphlet called 'The New Slavery', which claimed that indentured labour was little more than slavery by another name. Like Des Voeux's letter it was important in leading the British government to write new regulations, but was it true that indentured labour and slavery were the same?

The ordinances made the indentured labourer into an inferior class of citizen but he was not the private property of his owner like the slave. He was paid wages, even if they were unfairly low, while the slave was not paid. The slave codes and police laws gave the planters far more power over their slaves than the ordinances did. A slave could not give evidence against his master in court while a labourer could, even though he found it difficult to use the English language and understand the workings of English courts.

Slavery could only end if the master set the slave free while indentured labour stopped when the contract ran out. Once he had finished his contract the indentured labourer was often a second-class citizen because he was poor and unskilled but there were no laws which restricted him in the same way as free blacks and free coloureds. The indentured labourer was free to go back to India when his time was up. No one sent slaves back to their African homeland. Slavery in any case was hereditary as a slave's child was automatically a slave. This was not true of indentured labourer's children.

Another important difference was that the British government showed a real concern about labourers' welfare while it had shown little for the slaves until the nineteenth century. In many ways indentured labour was more like apprenticeship than slavery itself. It certainly worked in favour of the planters but only because they had enough wealth and social position to break the ordinances as the planters had done to the apprenticeship regulations.

A fully free society was slow in coming to the West Indies. The slaves were emancipated in 1834 only to find themselves bound to serve apprenticeships for another four years. In 1838 they became fully free but, in the two newest colonies, their place as servile labourers was taken by the indentured immigrants from China and India. Only in 1917 did the end come to the long story of enforced immigration to the Caribbean.

Ending indentured immigration

Indian nationalist complaints

By 1885 nationalist organisations in India were beginning to object to Britain's absolute rule. One of the first abuses they attacked was the indenture system. The Indian National Congress, which was mainly Hindu, and the All India Muslim League joined in calling the system unjust, exploitative and an insult to their countrymen's dignity. In 1893 the great Congress leader, Mohandas Gandhi, went to South Africa and was soon leading the Indians there in a campaign to obtain full rights. In 1910 the chance to end indenture came when the British government allowed a few Indians to join a council to advise the Viceroy on future laws. At the first meeting, Gopal Krishna Gokhale asked the Viceroy to consider ending emigration by 1912. The Viceroy refused but agreed to send a Commission of Enquiry to examine the condition of indentured Indians in the West Indies and Fiji. In 1913 the West Indian Commission went back with a report outlining the unhealthy conditions and unfair treatment given to immigrant labourers. After a second Commission reported on Fiji in 1916 the Viceroy suspended indentured emigration and then, in 1917, stopped it for ever.

Support in the West Indies

Many West Indians welcomed the end of indenture. Cocoa and copra producers had complained for a number of years that the indenture system was unfair to them. Only about 5 per cent of the indentured servants were sent to their estates but they paid heavy taxes towards the cost of their indentured immigration. They were supported by some progressive sugar planters, who thought that cheap labour led to backward methods of production and wastefulness.

Some public officials worried that cheap, semi-free labour was holding back the social and moral development of the colonies. In 1897 the Mayor of Port of Spain, Henry Alcazar,

complained that the use of indentured servants kept the educated propertied classes 'at the moral level of slave owners'. Spokesmen for the black freemen also complained that indentures kept wages artificially low for everybody. In 1904 Prudhomme David, one of the first blacks nominated to Trinidad's Legislative Council, protested at the renewal of government subsidies for immigration. He argued that there was no longer a shortage of labour and that more immigrants would only reduce wages further and drive more blacks to look elsewhere for work. David's case was supported by the facts. Between 1901 and 1917 about 84,000 West Indians emigrated in search of better paying jobs on the Panama Canal, Costa Rican banana plantations and Cuban sugar estates. During the same period, West Indian governments had paid subsidies to bring in 24,260 East Indian labourers. Clearly indentured immigration could no longer be justified on the grounds that there was a labour shortage.

The Indians in Caribbean society

The Indians and sugar

Indian immigration provided the labour which the earlier attempts to recruit Madeirans, Europeans, Chinese and free Africans had failed to do. In Trinidad exports of sugar increased five times between 1833 and 1896 and nearly all the field labour was done by East Indians. In Guyana, too, the development of the cane fields went hand in hand with immigration as the following table shows:

Period	Hectares under cane	No. of immigrants	Population per hectare
1852	17,927	15,392	0.86
1861	20,738	31,933	1.53
1871	30,681	50,321	1.64
1884	32,118	63,055	1.96
1885–87	30,719	68,977	2.24
1894–96	27,367	72,097	2.63
1903–04	29,488	72,793	2.46

The table makes it clear that there was a steady increase in the hectares under cane up to 1886. This would not have taken place without the flow of immigrants. After 1884 the sugar industry was in depression, but the flow of indentured Indians continued at a time when their labour was no longer needed.

The cost to the Indians themselves was heavy. The indentured population of Trinidad and Guyana in the nineteenth century was very unhealthy as the result of disgraceful housing, little sanitation and unnecessarily hard work for masters who made no effort to make cultivation easier or more efficient. Labourers on the plantations were, at best, only half free. Most did not have even the chance of factory work as an alternative to toiling in the fields. Most plantation artisans were Africans, but very few would work alongside Indians in the field-gangs with their hateful reminders of slavery.

After indenture

When their indentures were finished and they left the plantations, the Indians often could only find work in poorly paid jobs. They were marked out by their different speech and clothing and despised as 'heathens'. Those who drifted into the towns usually found that there was nothing but 'coolie' work as porters and sweepers. Efforts were made to prevent Indian communities building homes in the towns. One settlement in Port of Spain was burned by the police to force the Indians to trek back into the countryside.

For such reasons most free Indians were reluctant to seek work in the towns after indenture. Besides, for most their only real skill was in agriculture. They preferred to take up small farming on Crown lands or on the margins of the plantations. In this way they made a great contribution to the development of Trinidad and Guyana. Free Indians took the lead in showing that the combined field and factory system of the plantation was not the only way to produce sugar. By the end of indenture there were many Indian farmers in Trinidad selling their canes to be milled in large central factories. After 1906 these Indian farmers outnumbered the creole smallholders. Indians were pioneers too. They showed that it was possible to grow rice in paddy fields in the wet low-lying areas. They helped clear the forests of the northern and central ranges in Trinidad where cocoa was grown.

Community life

The growth of Indian villages in the interiors helped the immigrants to preserve many features of their traditional societies. About 85 per cent of them were Hindu and 15 per cent Muslim. A few had been converted to Christianity in India but very few changed faith in the West Indies. Indians kept their respect for their religious and social leaders, the Muslim *mulvis* and the Hindu Brahmin priests. Although Hindu and Muslim marriages were not recognised by law until well into the twentieth century, the people themselves respected them and refused to register them with the civil authorities.

The Indians kept their languages alive, both the various Hindi dialects and the Urdu spoken by Muslims, which is a form of Hindi with a different script. Other signs of success in preserving their traditional society were mosques and temples and the small coloured triangular flags or *jhandis* which appeared outside houses built in Indian style. They celebrated the Hindu festivals of Holi and Divali (the festival of lights). Even more important was Hose (or Hosein or Hussay). This was a festival of one group of Muslims but all other Muslims and Hindus soon joined in. Almost from the start some creoles added their drumming to the Hose celebrations which became the liveliest of all Indian festivals.

Important for the future well-being of the Indians was the firm structure of family life in which all relations supported each other. In the early years of indenture this had seemed under threat because families were divided between those who stayed behind and those who came to the East Indies. By the 1870s, however, East Indian life was once again built around close family loyalties.

Assignments

1 *Research Mini Project*
Recommended time: three to four weeks for preparation.

Select one of the territories Guyana, Trinidad or Jamaica and write an account of the East Indians in that territory from the time of arrival to the end of indenture, under the following headings:

a) *Reasons for coming – problems in India;*
              – problems facing West Indian planters.
b) *How and when they came. (Include a time chart if possible.)*
c) *The region in which they worked.*
d) *The conditions under which they worked.*
e) *Reasons for returning to India and reasons for remaining in the West Indies.*
f) *The effect of their coming on the territory in the time of indentured labour and into the twentieth century.*

2 *The following two questions are taken from the CXC examination papers of June 1986:*
Basic Proficiency
a) *Give TWO reasons why India became the MAIN source of indentured labour for the British Caribbean during the second half of the nineteenth century.*
b) *List TWO terms of a contract of indenture.*
c) *Describe the hardships East Indians faced as indentured labourers.*

General Proficiency
a) *Why did India become the MAIN source of indentured labour for the British Caribbean planters during the second half of the nineteenth century?*
b) *How was the scheme financed during this period?*
c) *List FOUR terms of a contract of indenture.*
d) *(i) Why were Agents-General appointed? (ii) Do you think they did a good job?*
    Give two reasons to support your answer.

3 *List reasons for and against the opinion that slavery and indentured labour were really very similar.*

5 MIGRATION IN FRENCH, DUTCH AND SPANISH COLONIES

The French search for new labour

After emancipation

Slaves in the French colonies were freed in 1848. The ex-slaves were the only ones in the Caribbean – apart from the few in Danish colonies – who were not forced into some kind of apprenticeship after emancipation.

In French Guyana this meant that ex-slaves immediately turned their back on estate labour. There was plenty of land to occupy and farm. Indeed many slaves had done so before emancipation. After March 1848, most of the remaining labourers left the plantations. They returned to work for short periods when they needed cash to buy tools, clothes and other small items to carry them over until their own farms produced crops for sale.

In the two main sugar islands, Guadeloupe and Martinique, there was a large population of black ex-slaves. Their chances of moving from the estates was much smaller than the French Guyanese. The islands already had many 'small whites' and coloureds who were small farmers, traders and craftsmen. It was difficult for blacks to compete with them for land and work. Even the fact that there was no apprenticeship worked against the blacks. Apprentices on the British plantations had had four years to earn and save enough to buy tools, a trader's pack or a tiny piece of land. The French ex-slaves did not have these savings and it was several years before they could begin to leave the estates in large numbers.

The search for new labour

The Guyanese planters were short of labour before emancipation and this shortage deepened in 1848. They took the lead in looking for new workers. About ten years later they were joined in the search by planters on Martinique and Guadeloupe.

The French planters had the same failures as the British: Europeans did not want to settle in the Caribbean. A few Madeirans and Chinese were brought but showed themselves to be unwilling estate workers. The French had more success than the British in bringing labour from the West Coast of Africa. But it was not truly 'free' labour. Most of the 17,000 Africans were prisoners captured in French armed expeditions into the Congo where they later built a colony. They were given their 'freedom' when they landed in Martinique or Guadeloupe.

Like the British, the French then turned to India. France still owned trading stations in south-east India and the planters first tried to recruit in that area. But, as you saw in Chapter 4, it was much easier to recruit Indian people from the overcrowded northern plains. So, in 1861, the French came to an agreement with the British government to recruit there.

In 1876 the British government refused to allow more indentured Indians to be sent to French Guyana. In 1886 they also banned recruitment to Martinique and Guadeloupe. The reason was that the French had not set up immigration departments to supervise the treatment of Indians. The death rate was higher than it was in British territories after the new regulations of the 1870s. By these dates nearly 70,000 Indians had gone to the islands and only about 20,000 to French Guyana.

The numbers had been too few to solve the Guyanese planters' labour shortage. The schemes had also been expensive. It was reckoned that the colonies' earnings from sugar between 1860 and 1870 paid for only one third of the costs of recruiting even such cheap labour. The French government then tried to help with even cheaper workers. It stepped up a scheme begun in 1852, which transported prisoners from France to work. Between 1852 and 1939, 70,000 convicts were brought to French Guyana. But the planters found them to be poor field workers so that the colony's agriculture still lagged behind that of Martinique and Guadeloupe.

Immigration into Dutch territories

Surinam

Holland freed 45,275 slaves in 1863 but followed this up with a long period of apprenticeship. Ex-slaves between the age of 15 and 60 had to work for their former masters for ten years at a minimum wage. The long apprenticeship had been demanded by the planters in Surinam who had great difficulties in making their estates earn a profit. They were facing competition from new Dutch colonies in the East Indies where sugar was grown cheaply by 'free' labour. From the middle of the nineteenth century there was also competition from European beet. There was also a serious shortage of labour. Like plantations in Trinidad and British Guiana, the Surinamese estates had not been developed before the slave trade was banned.

The search for new labour

When apprenticeship ended, the new freemen behaved in the same way as their fellow Africans in the British colonies. They tried to leave full-time plantation labour and seek work as tradesmen in the towns or become independent small farmers. This created great difficulties for the planters in Surinam. Many had gone into bankruptcy during apprenticeship because they simply could not afford to pay even the minimum wages bill. Now they were forced to pay higher wages to free labourers but, even then, most Africans preferred to do as little estate work as possible.

These changes forced the Surinam planters to copy the attempts made in British Guiana to build up the white population of the colony and to find new cheap labourers for the cane fields. The attempts to attract white settlers failed as

they did in the French and British colonies. Three years before the emancipation, 348 Dutch farmers had been recruited and settled on an abandoned plantation. The scheme collapsed within the year; 189 died from typhus, 56 returned to Holland and the rest abandoned the settlement and moved closer to Paramaribo. Some of their descendants still sell dairy products and vegetables in the city.

The Surinamese had no more success in attracting free field labourers. They turned to the same places as the British and, between 1822 and 1872, 480 Madeirans and 2,502 Chinese were indentured to work in the cane fields. As in the case of British Guiana nearly all left the fields as soon as their indenture ended and became independent merchants, shop-owners or farmers.

However, the Dutch planters noted the use of indentured Indian labour in British Guiana. They asked the British government to allow them to recruit labourers in the same way. The first Indians arrived in Surinam in 1873. In all, 34,024 were recruited before indentured emigration from India was stopped in 1918. About two-thirds of them made Surinam their home after indenture.

The British laid down that the indenture contracts should be almost exactly the same as those in the British colonies. Immigrants were bound to work for five years and received a daily wage averaging 60 cents for men and 40 cents for women. Planters were bound to provide free housing, medical care and a working day of seven hours. When the indenture ran out, the recruits were entitled to a free passage back to India or 100 guilders and a plot of land.

As in the British colonies, the Agents-General found it impossible to protect the Indians from exploitation. For the most part, indentured labourers suffered poor housing, inadequate medical care and police laws weighted heavily in favour of the masters. Yet, the fact that Surinam had an immigration department and officials meant that Britain allowed the Dutch to go on recruiting after they banned the French.

The Dutch planters also recruited labourers

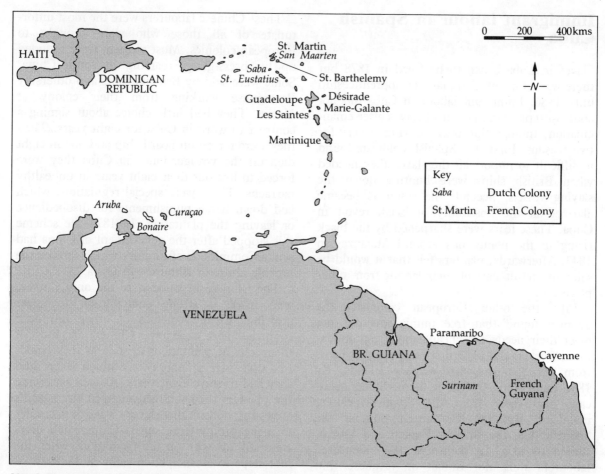

Map 5 *The Dutch and French colonies in the nineteenth century.*

from their own colony of Java, in the East Indies, under the same type of indenture contracts. Between 1874 and 1931, 32,020 Javanese were indentured. The planters preferred the Javanese because they were generally more skilled at agriculture than the Indians, and only about one in four returned to Java at the end of their contract. After the emigration of contract labour from Java was stopped in 1931, several thousand came freely to join families which had permanently settled in Surinam.

The islanders

The Dutch also owned Aruba, Bonaire and Curaçao in the Windwards along with San Maarten, Saba and St Eustatius in the Leewards. By the time of emancipation, there were very few plantations on any of these islands. The colonists had turned to other ways of making poor livings such as growing fruit, producing salt and ranching.

This meant that the islands had no use for immigrant labour. Like the poorest British colonies, the Dutch islands became exporters of labour. After apprenticeship, black labourers began to travel for seasonal work in Surinam or the largest British and Spanish islands. Most people in the Dutch Antilles earned only a poor living by combining this seasonal work with their own subsistence farming.

Immigrant labour in Spanish Cuba

Slaves in Cuba began to be freed in 1878 but there was a time of 'patranato' or apprenticeship until 1886. Immigrant labour in Cuba did not come to replace the labour of slaves after emancipation. Immigration began during slavery for two reasons. First, the Spanish colonists found it difficult to import all the slaves they needed when British ships were hunting down the slaving vessels. Second, the colonists became alarmed at the possibility of black revolt in Cuba. These fears were sharpened by the black rising in the plantations around Matanzas in 1843. Afterwards, planters felt that it would be safer to recruit part of their labour from other places.

Like the other European colonists, the Spanish found that free immigrants did not meet their needs for cheap labour but indentured workers did. The first large number came from the Spanish-owned Canary Islands. By 1861 there were 41,000 of them. Some Mexicans also came from the Spanish-speaking mainland. But for the largest number the Spanish, like the British, French and Dutch, turned to Asia. In their case the indentured labourers were not Indian or Javanese, but Chinese. Between 1847 and 1874, 142,000 came to work in Cuba.

These Chinese labourers were the most unfortunate of all those who were brought to European colonies. Most of them were rounded up by press-gangs roaming in south China. Some were sold by British agents and others by Portuguese working from their colony at Macao. They had little choice about signing a contract to work in Cuba for eight years. Then they were forced on board ship and one in eight died on the voyage. Once in Cuba they were forced to live out their eight years in unhealthy barracks. There were special regulations which laid down harsh punishments for disobedience or leaving the plantation. In 1874 the scheme was stopped after the government of China had sent a Commission of Enquiry which showed the terrible abuse of labourers in Cuba.

The Chinese in Cuba were the only Chinese who made a strong contribution to sugar growing. In the colonies of other European countries there were fewer Chinese and most of them left the plantations as soon as they could. In Cuba their numbers were much larger and they had to serve eight years. As well as serving the planters they indirectly helped the island's slaves by showing that slavery was not necessary to make profits from sugar. Chinese labourers were still at work on the plantations when the first steps to emancipation came in 1878.

Assignments

1 *What similarities and differences can you find by comparing emancipation in the British West Indian colonies with emancipation in the Dutch and French West Indian colonies?*

2 *How was the ending of slavery in the Spanish colonies different from the ending of slavery in the English colonies?*

6 THE END OF REPRESENTATIVE GOVERNMENT

Two types of government

When full emancipation came in 1838, there were nearly three-quarters of a million free citizens in the British West Indies. They were ruled in one of two ways. In most islands there was the old representative system which went back to their early days as colonies. The power to make local laws was held by the elected representatives in the assemblies. Although all laws had to be approved by Parliament in London the colonies were self-governing in taxation and in matters such as making the eighteenth-century police laws.

Trinidad, British Guiana and St Lucia became British in the early nineteenth century and were straightaway made Crown colonies. In English politics the word 'Crown' is often used instead of 'the state'. Anything which belonged to the Crown such as the army, the post office or the customs service was run by the government under rules laid down by Parliament. Making these territories into Crown colonies meant that they were run by the Colonial Office which was a department of the British government. There were no elected representatives in the assembly to make local laws.

Three reasons were given for making them Crown colonies. First, it was said that there were too few free people for there to be a real choice of representatives to elect to assemblies. Second, the free English-speaking whites were heavily outnumbered by free people of colour and by people from other European groups. The government was not prepared to trust them with the power to elect representatives who made laws for a British colony. Third, the British government wanted to keep power in its own hands to make it easier to enforce the laws against slave trading.

The Crown colonies

The Colonial Office appointed a governor and other officials, including a Chief Justice, a Secretary, a Treasurer, an Attorney General and Collector of Customs. Others, such as a Protector of Immigrants and Director of Public Works, were added later. A small number of the most important officials joined with the governor to make up the executive council which was responsible for the day-to-day running of the colony. There was also a slightly larger body, known as the legislative council, which could advise the governor, and pass local ordinances. The legislative council had equal numbers of officials and 'unofficial' members. The 'unofficials' were chosen by the governor from among the most prominent men in the colony.

In Trinidad in 1831 the legislative council had six official and six unofficial members; by 1898 it had increased to eleven of each. The governor chose all the members and could use a casting vote if the other members were divided equally.

Because of its Dutch background, the government of British Guiana was slightly different. Its executive council was known as the Court of Policy. This was made up of four officials and four 'unofficials' who were elected by an indirect system. Their names were chosen by the governor from a list put forward by a special group or 'college' of electors known as the *Kiezers*. The Kiezers was itself elected by the votes of the wealthier planters. British Guiana did not have a legislative council. Instead, all laws dealing with taxation and government spending needed the approval of the Combined Court. This was made up of the Court of Policy and six financial representatives chosen by the Kiezers.

Fig. 6.1 *A view of the inside of the Assembly House, Barbados.*

Representative government colonies

Each island had a governor and a council which he chose himself; but there was also an assembly of elected representatives. The elected members of the assembly did not represent all people because of the system of property qualification. Only the wealthiest were qualified to stand for election. The franchise – or right to vote – was also restricted. Electors had to own property, or have an annual income, above a certain figure. In practice this meant that only landowners, merchants, lawyers and other professional men could elect the assembly. No women had the vote.

British distrust

After emancipation the Colonial Office did not trust the planter assemblies to create a fully free society which would give all citizens the choice of where they would live and work, the chance to own property and to have their children educated. One of its officials wrote to the British cabinet in 1839 suggesting that they were 'absolutely incompetent and unfit to deal with the new state of things and to provide for the peace and well-being of His Majesty's subjects in those parts.'

James Stephen, the emancipationist who was now the senior civil servant in the Colonial Office, was even more blunt. He wrote that the assemblies during slavery had been 'the worst instruments of tyranny which were ever yet forged for the oppression of mankind'. Now that slavery was over the old habits would remain and make laws passed by the assemblies 'unjust and oppressive towards the African race'.

The distrust of the assemblies was behind the Prisons Act which the British Parliament passed in 1838. It gave governors in the West Indies the power to take responsibility for prisons and workhouses away from local magistrates. The British government feared that the treatment given to freemen would be even more harsh when the number of special magistrates declined after the end of the apprenticeship. The island assemblies immediately protested. In Jamaica, the assembly refused to pass the annual laws which gave the governor the power to collect taxes and keep law and order. In reply, the British Prime Minister asked Parliament to place the colony under the governor's direct rule for five years. However, British MPs felt it was wrong to suspend a legally elected assembly, even though they condemned the action of Jamaica's assembly. Instead, they passed a law which made it possible for the governor of Jamaica to sign the renewal of annual laws himself if the assembly refused for longer than two months.

Changes in representative government

After 1838, the representative system faced problems because of the fall in sugar production, especially following the 1846 Sugar Duties Equalisation Act. In all the old colonies the number of plantations fell. This meant there were fewer planters, attorneys or merchants wealthy enough to have the right to stand for election or to vote. Some became bankrupt; many moved to Britain or the United States. By 1855 St Kitts had only 166 registered voters out of a total population of 20,741. In Jamaica in 1854, only 753 voters elected an assembly which governed 450,000 citizens. At any time between 1845 and 1857 one third of the assembly seats in Montserrat and St Vincent were vacant. The few men who did run for election were described by Governor Pine as 'lacking in property, intelligence and principle' and working for their own interests not for the public benefit.

In some colonies, the places of Europeans were taken by wealthy coloureds. In Jamaica by the 1860s, such men made up two-thirds of the assembly. But this change was not welcomed by the remaining Europeans and it did not bring benefits to the black people. They could only have a political voice if the right to vote was given to poorer people. The Colonial Office did not wish to go that far. Even a firm emancipationist such as Henry Taylor, head of the West Indian Department at the Colonial Office, wrote of the wrongness of giving law-making powers to the 'ignorant and bedarkened masses'. What he and other officials wanted was for the colonies to be governed under the Crown colony system so that what the British government thought best for all their people could be done under the governor's orders.

The Colonial Office's view that assemblies should be abolished was strengthened by their failing to set up much-needed public services. There were only a few exceptions. In Antigua, for instance, the assembly set up a system for poor relief for the sick, mentally ill and very old. It gave responsibility for this work to the parish vestries and funded them with $2\frac{1}{2}$ per cent of the island's customs duties. In 1841 the assembly also opened an asylum for the mentally handicapped and it gave occasional grants to a charity, known as 'The Daily Meal Society', which ran a seamen's and a lepers' hospital and an orphanage. But Antigua's system of poor relief was much fuller than most other colonies and other examples of positive action by assemblies were rare. As we saw in Chapter 2, they cut back on even the small amount of money spent on schools in the first years of freedom. In most cases the only roads for the new smallholders and traders were the tracks they made themselves without the help of public money. Almost nothing was done to improve public health. Cholera killed 30,000 Jamaicans in 1851 and 20,000 Barbadians in 1854.

Some people compared this lack of progress with the improvements made in the Crown colony of Trinidad, especially under Governor Lord Harris (1846–54). Lord Harris improved roads, irrigation, and drainage, although this came too late to prevent thousands of cholera deaths. He divided the islands into wards and collected taxes from the landowners in each ward. The money was used for new services including a police service and, most important, a system of elementary education. Harris said that each ward should have a free elementary school with teachers who were trained at a new Normal School he opened near Port of Spain.

Executive committees

Trinidad, of course, was a far wealthier island. Sugar production was increasing there so the government was able to raise taxes on exports and on imported food and estate supplies. In the older colonies, except Barbados, government incomes had fallen because of the decline in trade. British banks and merchant companies were no longer willing to lend money to these colonies. This gave the Colonial Office the chance to take the first steps to end the representative system. The government of Jamaica actually became bankrupt and the assembly was told that Britain would only help with a loan of £100,000 if it would give up some of its powers. The assembly had no real choice and, from 1854, the island's governor had an executive committee which took over decisions about government spending.

Similar changes took place in the other islands as they, too, fell into financial difficulty. In the few years after 1854, governors' executive committees were set up in most island colonies. Barbados was the only colony ruled under the representative system which did increase its sugar production so that its government could collect enough taxes to pay for social improvement schemes and public works. In fact it did very little more than any other colony to reform social conditions.

In all the islands the assemblies constantly opposed spending money on schemes which would benefit the black population. Yet, without such schemes, nothing could stop mounting unrest and demands for change. In the end it was the militancy of the blacks in Jamaica, not pressure from the Colonial Office, which hastened the end of the old representative system.

'Rising' in Morant Bay

Blacks' complaints

In all colonies the blacks' strongest complaint was against the parish vestry committees and magistrates who used the law to prevent black labourers owning land of their own. The magistrates and men on the vestries were still usually planters or managers and there were many ways in which they could keep labourers off the land. Those who occupied plots which had once been provision grounds on plantations were often accused of trespassing. Some men and women were punished for larceny (an old English term for theft) if they collected fruit from hedges around property or collected wood from commons. In many colonies, especially Jamaica, labourers could see good farmland lying idle on abandoned sugar estates. They claimed such abandoned lands should become 'Crown', or public, lands which they could settle on. Magistrates often refused to accept such claims and vestry commitees deliberately held up the title deeds which gave proof of ownership to those who had bought land. Another grievance was that vestries charged unfairly high fees for using local markets.

All these complaints were noted by Edward Underhill, Secretary of the Baptist Missionary Society, when he came to the West Indies in 1859 for a first-hand look at the Society's missions. The pastors and church members he met also spoke bitterly about the lack of steady work and the island governments' failure to provide schools, orphanages and hospitals. After he returned to England, Underhill described these poor conditions in a book. No-one took any notice.

In 1865, Baptist missions in Jamaica sent a new set of reports to Underhill. This time he wrote directly to the Secretary of State for the Colonies to warn him that conditions had worsened since 1859 and serious trouble might develop unless action was taken quickly. The American Civil War had begun in 1861 and greatly increased the cost of American food and clothing in Jamaica. At the same time planters had cut wages because sugar prices had fallen when Cuba began sending sugar to Britain instead of the United States. In 1862 and 1863 severe droughts had ruined the small farmers' provision plantings and their export crops. Instead of showing sympathy, the magistrates and vestries were prosecuting all those who trespassed on abandoned estate property or stole small quantities of food. Underhill begged the Secretary of State to ask the colonial governors to begin poor relief programmes and schemes to market the small farmers' crops. At the same time, Underhill said, they should reform the local governments, checking the great powers of the magistrates and lowering the amount of property needed to qualify for the vote.

Edward Eyre

The Secretary of State sent Underhill's report to the governor of Jamaica, Edward Eyre. Since his arrival in Jamaica in 1862, Eyre had relied on the support of the Country Party in the assembly. This was the party of the large landowners. The opposition Town Party was made up of independent merchants, many of them coloured. The Town Party was usually supported in the assembly by a few elected social reformers, sometimes known as 'radicals'. Eyre stuck by the Country Party and refused to consider changes. He condemned Underhill as a 'meddlesome Baptist' and said the blacks' hardships were due to unwillingness to work regularly on the estates.

While Eyre was dealing with Underhill's report, a committee in Jamaica's St Ann's parish wrote a petition to Queen Victoria. It begged the Queen to order that unfarmed Crown lands should be turned over to their use. The petition was sent to London by Eyre along with his own views on Jamaica's troubles. The Secretary of State wrote the Queen's reply

Fig. 6.2 *Governor Edward Eyre.*

which did no more than repeat the views of Eyre. The petition for Crown lands was turned down. The people who signed were told that they could improve their lot only by working 'steadily and continuously at the time when . . . labour is needed for as long as it was wanted.'

Eyre thought he and the Country Party had won a victory over the radicals and the Town Party. Fifty thousand copies of the 'Queen's Letter' were printed and posted throughout the island. Copies were given to the clergy to read from the pulpits. Many coloured and non-conformist clergy refused to do so, while in every parish blacks met to discuss their next move.

It is clear that Edward Eyre was unsympathetic to the black peasants but it is hard to understand why he did not realise that his policy could easily lead to rioting and bloodshed. The first signs of this came when desperate local people stormed the jail at Savanna-la-Mar and tore down the toll-gates on the road into Falmouth. Eyre took no notice of these warning signs. He continued to give his support to the Country Party and the planters in the old vestries and still refused to have any dealings with the coloured spokesmen for the black country people.

George William Gordon

Ever since he had come to Jamaica Eyre had been the bitter enemy of one of these coloured leaders. This was George William Gordon, the son of a white attorney and a slave who had become a prosperous businessman. He was a Baptist, who did much to help set up country Baptist chapels. He had been a Town Party member of the assembly and in 1861 was magistrate for St Thomas in the East. As magistrate Gordon had complained about the insanitary conditions in the parish lock-ups, the lack of health care and the way the local vestry mismanaged its accounts. The local Anglican clergyman saw Gordon as a trouble-maker and so did the Country Party. Eyre agreed with them and had Gordon removed from his post as magistrate. Two years later Gordon was removed by force from the vestry. Yet he remained active in parish affairs and continued his work as a Bapist leader. Gordon had support from a number of black parsons in the parish. Among them was Paul Bogle, a Baptist deacon who was also one of the few blacks eligible to vote in St Thomas.

The parish of St Thomas in the East

Governor Eyre and the Country Party saw St Thomas in the East as a district which was very likely to give them trouble. There were few sugar estates, so the plantocracy was small and did not have firm control through the vestry. At the same time the black community was well organised. After emancipation many ex-slaves had carved small farms out of the hillsides and rich river valleys. Black Baptist parsons and deacons, such as Paul Bogle, helped to create a feeling of independence and resistance to the island's plantocracy.

The independent farmers were hard hit by the droughts of the 1860s and by the steep rise in prices during the American Civil War. Most of them could not make a living from their smallholdings alone and could not find other work as the parish had so few estates. A growing number were taken to court for trespassing and stealing from fields. Many protested openly when they were sentenced. In October 1865, one court session at Morant Bay broke up in disorder. A man had been charged with collecting wood on land which he claimed was Crown land. The magistrates decided it was an abandoned plantation and sentenced him. A member of Bogle's church shouted out that the accused man must 'pay the fine and not the charges'. Court charges, paid in addition to the fines, were used to pay the wages of clerks and magistrates. The disturbance was a minor one and should have passed unnoticed but the magistrates thought they could use it to put an end to Gordon and Bogle's influence. The following day a summons was delivered to Bogle in his home at Stony Gut. It called on him to appear in the Morant Bay courthouse to answer for the unruly behaviour of his church member.

No normal court of law would have listened to such a charge; and Bogle had good grounds for refusing to come at once. He did, however, agree to attend a vestry meeting on 11 October. The custos, a local official who acted as chairman of the magistrates and the vestry, was afraid that he could not handle the situation. He informed Governor Eyre of Paul Bogle's refusal to attend the court immediately, and called the local militia to be present at the vestry meeting.

The Morant Bay riots

On 11 October a large crowd followed Bogle as he came into Morant Bay for the vestry meeting. News that the militia had been called out inflamed their anger. Fighting started in the square in front of the courthouse. Twenty-eight people were killed. Eighteen of them were members of the vestry including the custos. The courthouse was burned down. The disorders spread through much of the parish in the next few days and four of the most strongly disliked planters were killed.

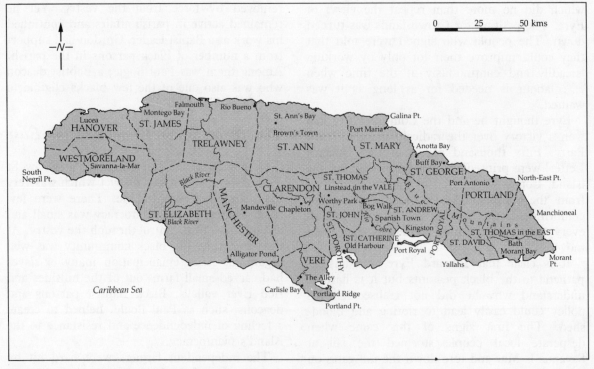

Map 6 *Jamaica at the time of the Morant Bay riots.*

The riot had been serious and violent. But there is no real evidence that it was a rebellion. The black protestors had few arms or supplies and there was no plan behind their actions. Rather than an organised attempt at revolution, the events at Morant Bay were a sudden explosion of frustration and anger. Behind them lay years of drought, rising prices and unsympathetic planters, as well as the persecution of the few men such as Gordon and Bogle who seemed to care about the problems.

This was not how Eyre chose to look at the riot. He decided that it should be treated as a general insurrection or rebellion and declared martial law in all Surrey county except Kingston. The parish of St Thomas was sealed off by troops stationed on all the roads. Eyre called on the Maroons to move against the rioters from their inland strongholds. They had agreed to provide soldiers for the government in the Maroon Treaties of 1739 and 1796. Regular troops were moved to St Thomas from Kingston by sea and reinforcements were called for from the Leewards, and as far away as Nova Scotia. The extra troops never landed, and the inexperienced regulars from Jamaica itself handled the situation cruelly. They were so hasty that no exact records were kept, but more than a thousand homes were senselessly destroyed in their raids on inland villages. Eyre's declaration of martial law gave the troops the right to hold courts-martial of prisoners. Possibly as many as 600 people were executed and the same number flogged. Gordon was made a victim of the same martial law. He was arrested at his Kingston home and should have

Fig. 6.3 *A view of Morant Bay in 1865. On the left is the temporary courthouse used to try the people rounded up in the riot. The accused can just be seen guarded by soldiers.*

been tried by the regular courts which might well have found him innocent of charges of leading the 'insurrection'. Instead, on Eyre's orders, he was shipped to Morant Bay where he could be court-martialled. He was found guilty and executed. On the same day Paul Bogle was arrested. He too was hanged.

The end of representative government

Result of the rising

Eyre never explained why he acted so brutally against the people of St Thomas. It is possible that he did think that the Jamaican labourers were on the point of rebellion and that brutal measures in St Thomas were necessary to prevent an island-wide uprising. It may be that he simply used the riot to settle old scores with Gordon and to destroy the case of other Town Party politicians who had demanded reforms for the freemen. Some historians have concluded that he actually tried to serve the Colonial Office by using the fear of rebellion to frighten the planters into abandoning the representative system.

It is certainly true that he told the assembly in November that 'a mighty danger threatens the land', and that there was a plan to make Jamaica into a second Haiti. Shortly afterwards the assembly agreed to abolish itself and accept a new government by a council of twelve elected members and twelve named by the governor. The fear of black revolt may have been a cause but the planters in the assembly had much more hard-headed reasons for accepting the change. Reducing the number of elected members was a way of keeping coloureds out of the island's government. Most of the council members named by the governor would be chosen from the leading white planters and businessmen. The change would also weaken the influence of the growing number of small and medium farmers who had enough property to be allowed the vote. Finally, the assembly reasoned that when the British took the power to make laws they would have to become responsible for the debts of the Jamaican government.

Once they had agreed to abolish the assembly in their own self-interest, it was difficult for the island's leading whites to object when the Colonial Office decided, in June 1866, that elections should be abandoned altogether and the whole council should be named by the governor. After two hundred years of representative government, Jamaica became a Crown colony.

Eyre himself, however, did not profit from the change. The scale of his actions led to demands in England for an investigation. A Royal Commission came out to Jamaica. It said that the revolt could have spread if it had not been checked but it blamed Eyre for being far too severe and for not giving Gordon a fair trial. He was recalled to England and dismissed from service with the Colonial Office.

Spread of Crown colony government

Jamaica was the largest of the old British West Indian colonies. Her assembly had often given the lead to the assemblies on the smaller islands of the eastern Caribbean. This was true in 1866 when Jamaica accepted the Crown colony system. The small islands had already found that the executive committees had done little to improve their government finances. Now they were ready to follow Jamaica in giving up their representative system altogether. Often behind the decision was the fear that the 'coloureds' would become too powerful in the assemblies and would block firm action if revolts broke out. In most cases, colonial assemblies also needed help with finance. Their goverments were in debt and could not pay their way with the income from export duties and taxation. One way out was to borrow money, usually from private companies. But they would not risk lending to a colony unless the British government guaranteed the loan – by saying it would be responsible if the colonial government stopped making the repayments. After 1866, the British government began to make such guarantees only when an island agreed to closer Colonial Office control of its affairs.

In that year Montserrat and the Virgin Islands turned to a Crown colony administration

Fig. 6.4 *The two Jamaican Assembly houses. The modern building, named after William George Gordon, is used today. The old Assembly House is on the left.*

troops. In the other colonies the move to a full Crown colony system took place in two stages. During the first, the council had a few elected members although the governor always had the deciding vote. This was the arrangement made in 1866 for Dominica, Antigua, Nevis and St Kitts. It was also followed for British Honduras in 1870, Tobago in 1874 and Grenada in 1875. On most islands the second stage was completed by 1878 when all the elected positions were given up in return for loans from the British government. Antigua and Dominica held out until 1898 when they too agreed to replace their elected members with men appointed by the governor.

Only Barbados kept the old representative system. It was the only old colony to increase profits from sugar production in the nineteenth century and managed to avoid the heavy debts which ruined the treasuries of the other islands. Its planter class, too, remained large and confident that it could keep political power away from the black population. To the wealthy classes in other colonies, Crown colony government seemed, after the Morant Bay riots, the only way of keeping power out of the hands of the blacks. As a rule only the most trusted and loyal coloureds were named by the European governors to join the planters on the councils.

with no elected members. So did British Honduras in 1870 when the colony's assembly voted to abolish itself after many arguments with the British government about sharing the cost of an armed steamer and a small force of

Assignments

1 *Make a chart to show the types of government which existed in the British West Indies up to 1962. Explain briefly each type of government you have included in the chart.*

2 *Read the following passage from page 42 and then answer the questions below:*

'James Stephen, the emancipationist . . . wrote that the assemblies during slavery had been "the worst instruments of tyranny which were ever yet forged for the oppression of mankind."'

   a) *Why did all British West Indian colonies have 'assemblies' during the eighteenth century?*
   b) *What reasons would James Stephen have for calling assemblies 'the worst instruments of tyranny'?*
   c) *In which ways did the British see the assemblies as a poor system for governing colonies in the nineteenth century?*
   d) *How did they hope to overcome these problems?*

3 *How do the events at Morant Bay in 1865 demonstrate that colonial society had failed to recognise the legitimate rights of many free citizens?*

7 CROWN COLONY GOVERNMENT

Now that most territories were under Crown colony government, the Colonial Office began to expect its governors and officials to press on with programmes of reform. These would include weakening the power of the planter, the magistrates, the vestry committees and the militias to block improvements in the lives of black people. Public works, such as roads, hospitals and schools were needed. Efforts were to be made to find land and work for more ex-slaves.

All these things were to be done on behalf of the black people of the Caribbean but the Colonial Office did not think they were capable of sharing political power in the colonies. It believed they had to be placed under a 'trusteeship' which would look after their employment, health and education because they were incapable of doing this themselves. This view was not held only about the Caribbean. In the last quarter of the nineteenth century the idea of trusteeship was applied to all the black and coloured peoples of the British Empire.

Whether or not the new policies were carried out depended a great deal on the governors. Many were not forceful in pushing developments forward. Some were too weak to stand up to pressure from wealthy whites. Yet a few brought about great changes which improved the lives of most parts of the population. Two of the most successful came to the West Indies just after the Morant Bay riots. They were Sir John Peter Grant in Jamaica from 1866 to 1874 and Sir Arthur Gordon in Trinidad from 1866 to 1870.

Grant in Jamaica

Law and order

Sir John Peter Grant came to Jamaica after Eyre was dismissed in 1866. In eight years he did a great deal to lay down a model for governors in the other islands which soon became Crown colonies. The Colonial Office believed that the Morant Bay affair had been mishandled and this showed very clearly in the steps Grant took to change the system of law and order. He cut the power of local magistrates and vestry committees by reducing the number of parishes from twenty-two to fourteen. The island then needed fewer magistrates and committee men. Grant got rid of the ones with the worst record of unfairness to the small farmers in their districts. Any person convicted in a magistrate's court was given the right to appeal against the decision to a British judge sitting in a district court.

Grant set up a police force to replace the local militias so much distrusted by the black population. He believed that such a police force under his control would be fairer but could also be trained to be firmer so that disturbances such as the Morant Bay rising would not get out of control. He also undertook to clear up the question of legal ownership of land. Some ex-slaves gained from this but many others suffered. They were farmers who had been working land for many years but who were evicted because they had no document proving their ownership.

Public services

Grant ended an old grievance when he 'disestablished' the Anglican Church, which had shown so little sympathy for the freemen. Disestablishment meant that it was no longer financed by the government but had to find its own funds. The money which earlier had gone to pay Anglican clergy was used for education. In 1863–64 the island had spent only £2,173 on public education; by 1887 the figure was £25,715 and 226 out of the 379 schools in Jamaica received money from the government.

Governor Grant developed other public services. He set up a Public Works Department which built roads from the coast to the interior towns and extended the stretches of railway which had been started in the 1840s. Between

1870 and 1876 it built an irrigation system to bring water to the very dry lands south-west of the Rio Cobre. The most direct benefit from these schemes went to the sugar estates but small farmers and traders did gain from the improvement of roads. The most noticeable improvements were made to the island's capital, Kingston. During the years when sugar plantations were the greatest centres of wealth and social life the towns of the Caribbean colonies had been greatly neglected. Kingston was unhealthy because of the piles of sewage in the unpaved streets, an infected water supply and swamps where malaria-carrying mosquitos bred. Under Governor Grant a beginning was made to give the town its first piped water, a gas works, a fire brigade, a market and many improvements to streets and public buildings as well as a mule-drawn tram service.

These measures provided work for several thousand freemen; they also made Kingston a much healthier place in which to live. Under Grant the island was also first given a government medical service. Spending on medical care increased from £17,019 in 1863 to over £48,000 in 1880–81.

Gordon in Trinidad

The small farmers

Sir Arthur Gordon came to Trinidad in 1866, the year that Grant became governor of Jamaica, and left in 1870. Governor Gordon did not have to deal with the problems of changing over from assembly government to the Crown colony system, but many of Trinidad's problems were similar to Jamaica's. Earlier governors and senior officials had often allowed their policies to be influenced by the white English-speaking Trinidadians. One group with grievances were the French- and Spanish-speaking population. Many of them were cocoa growers and so had not benefited from schemes such as indentured immigration, which helped the sugar planters. Even more serious were the restrictions on small farming by the African people of the island.

On one of Governor Gordon's first trips through the island a bridge broke as his party was travelling over it. It is not surprising that he quickly turned his attention to improving the roads which he described as 'deplorable'. He found the island had had no Surveyor-General for twelve years, so a new one was straightaway appointed to take charge of a programme of road and bridge building. By 1869, thirteen new bridges had been built and the bridle path from Arima to Manzanilla Point turned into a road. The main groups to benefit were the small independent cocoa farmers on the slopes of the northern range. They could not afford to build private roads and tramways to the coast as many sugar planters in the west of the island had done.

Roads were only one part of the help given by Sir Arthur Gordon to peasant farming. Before he arrived, there had been several schemes to sell plots of Crown land to both small and large farmers but no governor had really tried to overcome planter resistance to the idea. Gordon set about encouraging sales by cutting the price in half and by abolishing the rule that small plots could not be sold. As far as possible he tried to see that land was sold in villages laid out by the government. Several villages were planned with shops, churches, a cemetery, school and police station. In 1869, the settlement schemes were extended to include Indians who were allowed to take four hectare plots in place of a passage home after their indenture. Some of the Indians bought isolated plots but most of them were settled in government-planned villages.

One of the many shocking aspects of indentured immigration was the high numbers of deaths among Indians in their first year in Trinidad. Just before Gordon arrived a local ordinance had compelled planters to build hospitals on their estates. Governor Gordon followed this with a feeding ordinance which laid down that masters should provide rations during the first year when new arrivals' provision grounds were not producing. Both ordinances helped to cut the death rate, although ill-health and death remained all too common in the indentured immigrants' barracks.

Fig. 7.1 *A view of a market square in Tobago in 1877. Notice the small stalls and the lack of goods.*

The churches and schools

Like Sir John Peter Grant, Governor Gordon set about ending the special privileges of the Church of England in Trinidad. In 1869 he was given Colonial Office support for a scheme which meant that the Anglican Church no longer took the largest share of government aid. It had only a third as many members as the Roman Catholic Church, supported mostly by French- and Spanish-speaking Trinidadians. In future, government money was to be shared out in proportion to the number of members of each church. Also like Grant, Sir Arthur Gordon turned his attention to the colony's school system. He was so appalled at the state of education in Trinidad that he asked the Colonial Office to send an inspector to investigate the island's schools. The man they sent was Patrick

Keenan, who wrote his report after just seven months. He found that most government elementary schools were run in broken-down and unhealthy buildings, the teachers were poor and in some cases French- and Spanish-speaking children were taught by masters who spoke only English. Gordon immediately recommended a new system in which there should be both government, or 'ward' schools and private schools run by the religious bodies. Both kinds were to be financed out of rates paid by local householders. Gordon had to stand up to the English-speaking Protestants who objected to paying for the 'private' schools which would be mostly Roman Catholic. As we shall see, the elementary schools in both Jamaica and Trinidad remained poor in the amount of government money spent on them and the quality of the teaching.

Social welfare and the Crown colonies

Governor Grant and Governor Gordon made bold attempts to improve the lives of the African and Indian peoples although they shared the common European view that blacks needed to be guided and controlled. Very few other governors did as much for welfare, but all colonies showed some changes along the lines that Grant and Gordon had laid down.

Medical services

The most serious problem of all was disease. Serious illness such as cholera, yellow fever, malaria and typhus were always present. Sometimes they broke out into epidemics like the time when cholera killed more than thirty thousand in Jamaica in 1851. Everywhere infants and children died in terribly high numbers from infection, poor diet, infected water and poor housing. On the estates medical care was sometimes even poorer after slavery than before. Owners closed the buildings which had been used as hospitals and would not call doctors to sick workers. In the days before Crown colony government there were a few hospitals in Caribbean towns, but one English visitor said that the poor conditions and bad sanitation made them less healthy than prisons.

The Crown colony governments were influenced by schemes for public health in Britain. Efforts were made there from the middle of the nineteenth century to deal with some of the main causes for the spread of disease. Towns built sewers and began to lay pipes to bring in fresh water. From the 1860s they built isolation hospitals for people with infectious fevers and asylums to separate people with mental illnesses. Some of these improvements were slowly taken up in the West Indies.

Port of Spain had its first refuse collection in the 1840s and began to build sewers and main water pipes in the 1860s. By then it also had a general hospital. Other islands generally had to wait until they became Crown colonies. Then most copied at least some of the improvements begun by Governor Grant and Jamaica's public medical department. By 1900, for instance, most

Fig. 7.2 *Two views of the railway opened in Barbados in 1882. The top shows the station at Bridgetown and the bottom the arrival of the first train at Carrington Point.*

of the capital towns of the colonies had piped water. All colonies had a medical service and one or two hospitals, which were often small and ill-equipped. The changes did little to raise the general health of people outside the towns. A few districts had dispensaries for free treatment but in most places the countryside occupied by black villagers was neglected.

Communications

The same was true of roads. Most Crown colony governments turned some bridle tracks into roads to link the towns. Few of them reached the more remote villages. The interiors were usually not helped by other new means of communication. In Trinidad the first twenty-five miles of railway track were started in 1876. One of Sir Arthur Gordon's last acts was to order an electric telegraph to be laid between Port of Spain and San Fernando. Other colonies followed this example. At the end of the century, the telegraphs were replaced by telephones. Some colonies were linked with Britain and the United States by underwater cable. These developments helped mostly townspeople with business or professional offices but nearly everyone gained when a system of post offices was opened up. They made it possible for workers to keep in touch with their families and send back money earned in Central America and other places.

Growth of towns

Crown colony government gave towns a greater importance than they had had in the days of sugar and slavery. In many colonies great houses were left empty while new court buildings, libraries, police and fire stations went up in the towns. The number of private houses increased as homes were built for the extra officials from England and those recruited into the less important jobs locally. For a fortunate number of West Indians, most of them coloured, there were new jobs in the government service, as sanitary inspectors and as clerks in the post office or harbour boards. A very few educated West Indians found posts in the civil service. For the uneducated there might be chance of employment in the docks, or building roads or irrigation works. They too could have a home in a town, which would probably be like those described in a 1920 handbook for St Kitts-Nevis, 'Negro huts in back alleys still crowded and insanitary.'

In the twentieth century these new town communities became the centres of opposition to Crown colony government. The lawyers, merchants and writers formed associations to demand a share in government. The dockers and tradesmen formed the Caribbean's first trade unions. Most of these political leaders of the future were educated in schools which were opened in the last thirty or forty years of the nineteenth century. In this time there was a great increase in the number of elementary and secondary schools. By today's standards, nineteenth-century colonial government did nowhere near enough for education but the changes were still important for the future of the Caribbean territories.

Education

Secondary education

Secondary schools generally grew up out of the desire of one social class or religious section to provide education for its own people. This is why Trinidad and British Guiana led the way, for both had European populations divided between Catholic and non-Catholic and between speakers of English and French or occasionally Dutch. In 1844 the Anglican Bishop of British Guiana started a grammar school. Not long afterwards the colony had a Catholic grammar school and two Methodist schools, one for boys and one for girls. In Trinidad, the local government opened Queen's Collegiate School in 1859. Roman Catholics, who already had a girls' convent school, then subscribed to build the boys' College of the Immaculate Conception. This was commonly known as the French College for about half the teachers and pupils were French speaking. In both colonies the governors and school inspectors from time to time recommended that the local government should take over secondary education and make it secular – not restricted to any one denomination. But the Colonial Office always supported those who said that this would be too costly, so only a few secondary schools were paid for from public funds.

In Barbados the main pressure to expand secondary education came from the white planters and merchants who wanted schools for their children. In 1856 the island's assembly had voted for 'a sum not exceeding £300 in any one year in supporting and assisting any school . . . established for the education of the middle classes'. By 1900 the island had more secondary schools than any other colony.

In the new Crown colonies, secondary schools were started only towards the end of the nineteenth century. In many cases they came about by modernising tiny grammar schools intended for a handful of pupils, which had been founded with sums of money given by planters in the 'golden age' of sugar. Now they became secondary schools serving the islands' middle classes. In most cases, as in Trinidad and British Guiana, the religious organisations were active in the secondary movement. A Methodist missionary wrote from Jamaica to his Society in London in 1877:

> We have a largely increasing middle class, black and coloured population, and for girls of this class especially we have no suitable schools in the country . . . The consequence is that a vast number of girls who might, at their parents' expense, have a suitable education to fit them for the position of wives of educated native teachers, and to become teachers themselves, are obliged to be content with the elementary education . . .

This makes clear one of the reasons that the nonconformists had for starting secondary schools. They wished to educate West Indians to become ministers of churches and head teachers of elementary schools. Schools run by the Anglican Church or paid for from colony funds were more often concerned chiefly with the education of the sons of the white creole middle classes and officials serving a time in the Caribbean. There were often complaints about the colour exclusiveness of the system. A report on Trinidad's education in 1869 said:

Fig. 7.3 *Queen's College, one of the grammar schools in British Guiana.*

> The first thing likely to strike a person . . . is the strangeness of the fact that whilst the white population, which is only between 5,000 and 6,000 furnishes 142 pupils to the collegiate establishments, the coloured population, which, exclusive of the coolies, numbers from 60,000 to 70,000, furnishes only 37 pupils.

Elementary education

One of the greatest failures of the old representative system had been in elementary education. In 1861 the Jamaican assembly agreed to give aid worth just £3,700 to elementary schools. This was less than half the amount spent on the island from the Negro Education Grant in 1835. A survey in 1883 found that only 22,000 of the quarter-million black Jamaicans could write. The position was similar in all the colonies, and one of the first aims of the new Crown colony governors was to increase the number of elementary school pupils at the lowest possible cost.

They introduced the system of payment by results, which was copied from Britain and brought first to Barbados and then to the other colonies. The managers of a school were paid a grant which was worked out according to the number of children who attended regularly and the number who passed an examination given each year by the colony's inspector of schools. Payment by results meant that very few schools ever tried to do more than teach just the little needed to win a grant for the next year.

Unlike in Britain, the schools did not need to have satisfactory buildings to receive a grant. Children were crowded into broken-down huts and taught no more than simple writing and reading by poorly qualified teachers, often hardly any older than themselves. Not surprisingly many parents were unwilling to send their children, especially as most schools charged a fee. Often, of course, children could not attend school because they were needed to help in the work and earnings of the family. There were many planters and members of the middle class, too, who did not believe elementary education was necessary. A British Guiana magistrate said that to educate a child was only 'spoiling a good shovelman'.

The cost and the record

Britain counts the cost

By today's standards Crown colony government did nowhere near enough to improve living and working conditions in the English-speaking Caribbean. Yet, in the first years, the new governments spent far more on public works, health and education schemes than the old planter-controlled assemblies had. The increasing costs were noted with alarm and it was not long before Colonial Office officials were working out ways of saving money. One problem they saw was the increased wages bill for colonial civil servants such as school inspectors, medical officers, judges and public works engineers.

The Colonial Office came to believe that the wage bill could be cut by federating the smaller colonies in the eastern Caribbean. They could then share the same officials. The schemes for federation were only partly successful because of the strong objections in many colonies. For instance St Kitts and Nevis did not want to share the funds in their treasuries with Antigua and Monserrat which were both bankrupt. Planters in Barbados resisted a scheme to unite their island with the Windwards. In the end the main result was to join two pairs of islands, Trinidad with Tobago and St Kitts with Nevis. The Leewards and Windwards were each loosely linked under one governor but each island kept its own council and most of its own officials. Little money was saved on wages and the other costs of Crown colony government.

Everywhere, the new schemes for health, welfare and education threatened to collapse for lack of funds. The problem was made worse by the rising population. Between 1841 and 1891 the population of the British West Indies doubled from 863,971 to 1,607,218. In fifty years there were twice as many people needing public services.

In 1882 the British government sent a Royal Commission to investigate the way public funds had been spent in Jamaica, the Leewards and the Windwards. The Commissioners reported that too much money had been spent for a few minor changes in education and medical services. They said that taxes collected for improvement schemes had been wasted on unnecessary officials so there were 'too many useless men in public situations with too high salaries'. They pointed out that small farmers paid most of the taxes and they resented having no say in government. This should be avoided by appointing some coloured and black members to the governors' councils. The 1882 Commission was followed by the Norman Commission in 1897 which recommended the same kind of changes.

The record

The Royal Commissions' reports led to no real improvements. The record of Crown colony government shows that the first efforts to improve education, medical services, road and other public works soon slowed down and in some cases stopped altogether. One reason for this was the lack of money. Another was class and colour prejudice. Too few officials or unofficial members of councils cared much for elementary education. The high rate of deaths among newly born children was blamed on the fact that they were 'illegitimate' rather than on the lack of hospitals, especially in the country districts.

The worst result of Crown colony government was that it strengthened the view that Caribbean societies could be divided into the 'natives' and those sent from Britain to help them. Many books written for the British and American public described the black and Asian people of the West Indies as good humoured and simple-minded but without any ability to take care of themselves. A guide-book to Montserrat in 1886 wrote of the blacks: 'They are a light-hearted, good-tempered race, so accustomed to work in gangs that it is almost impossible to get them to do anything else.' A Scottish-American traveller wrote about British Guiana:

> The Africans and Asiatics have no ambition to distinguish between the right hand and the left, they are not taught, and for that matter, being regarded only as labour-saving beings cheaper to operate than machines, have no need to know more than how to work for and not to steal from white men.

The same writer went on to express a common European fear: 'It is probable that, left to themselves, the negroes and coolies will sink to the level of their brethren on the island of Haiti'.

Such descriptions were not written only about the people of the Caribbean. American and British books of the time contain similar pictures of life in India, Africa, the Pacific Islands and anywhere that colonialism was at work. In the West Indies, they show the strength of the survival of Quashie–backra attitudes inherited from the days of plantation slavery. Sometimes, of course, the idea of the superiority of the white backra over the African Quashie was so deeply rooted that West Indians themselves could not escape it.

Assignments

1 a) *During slavery in the British West Indies what provision was made for the medical care and education of the black population?*
   b) *Between 1838 and the 1860s what provision was there for the medical and educational needs of the black population?*
   c) *What changes and improvements took place in the fields of health and education during the 1860s?*

2 a) *Apart from health and education what other problems did poor people in the British Caribbean face in the 1860s?*
   b) *In which ways did Crown colony governments improve conditions for the majority of the population in the British Caribbean?*

3 *In your territory examine the improvements which took place during the 1860s and 1870s and explain why they came about.*

4 *Make an assessment of the record of Crown colony government up to the end of the nineteenth century. In what ways did the West Indians gain and in what ways did they lose from the activities of these colonial governments?*

8 THE BLACK CHALLENGE TO COLONIALISM

Colonialism in Africa

Already some major black political thinkers had challenged the idea of the superiority of Europeans over blacks and their culture. Among them were Edward Blyden, J. J. Thomas and H. S. Williams. To understand their views it helps to have a picture of European colonialism in Africa, just one of the continents where Europeans had extended their empires in the nineteenth century.

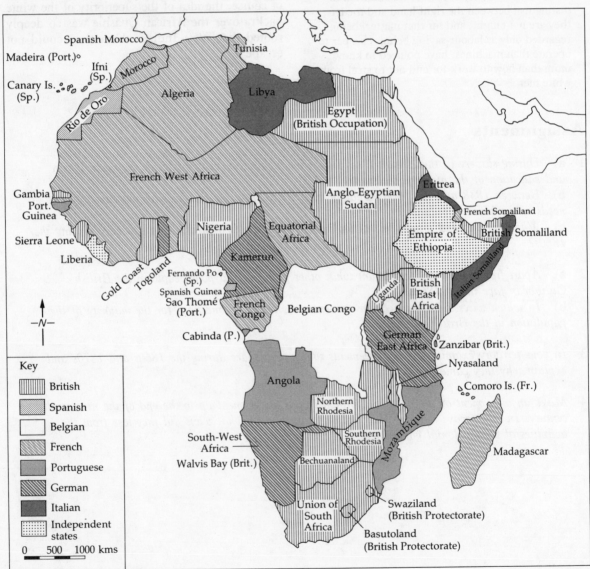

Map 7 *Africa under colonial rule.*

Africans and Europeans

By 1912, only two African states, Liberia and Ethiopia, remained fully independent. Liberia had its starting point in 1822 when it was made into a settlement for freed American slaves. It was a homeland of several African peoples, including the Kru and the Mandingos, although the ruling group were descendants of freed slaves. Ethiopia had survived as a separate state for centuries. In 1896, the Emperor Menelik II defeated an Italian army which invaded his land. Other African armies had beaten Europeans, but the Ethiopian victory at Adowa was the only battle which was not followed by further European invasion. At least, not until 1935 when the Italians under the fascist dictator Mussolini, overran Ethiopia, which was ruled by Menelik's successor, Haile Selassie.

The development of world-wide empires led Europeans to believe in the inferiority of conquered and coloured peoples. They accepted

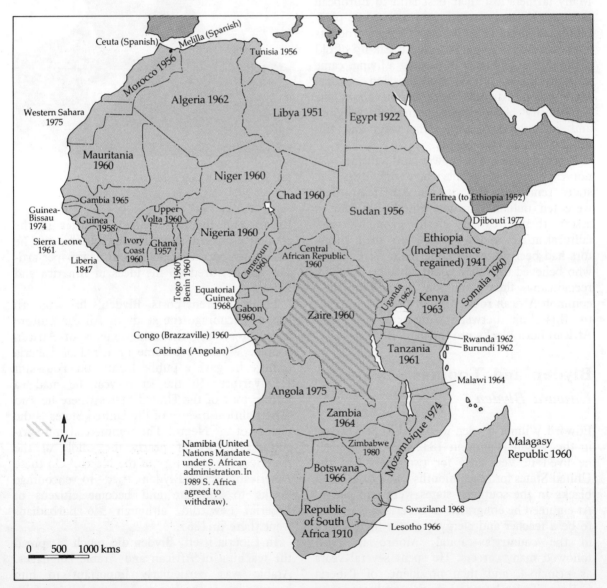

Map 8 *African independence.*

the tales of missionaries and explorers who went into the 'dark continent' and returned with stories of simple-minded heathen people who were said to worship stones and trees and believe in the 'black magic' of witch-doctors. Frontiers between colonies were fixed in Europe. People of the same African community found they had been split between new European rulers.

The Africans were given no opportunity to recover from the shock of rapid colonisation. Many farmers lost their best land to European farmers. Villagers were forced to become plantation labourers or gatherers of forest products such as rubber. Along with the break-up of old communities and ways of earning a living, came new European schools and mission centres. Here young Africans were taught about the 'superiority' of European culture and religion, and encouraged to forget the ways and traditions of their own people.

Resisting European power and culture was not easy in a continent where only two free states remained. But, in the Americas, there were ten million Africans who had begun to assert themselves in social, economic and cultural affairs in the lands where their ancestors had been slaves. Among them were people who believed that they could advance faster by recognising their common race and their common African roots. One of the first to point to this link between American-born and African-born blacks was Edward Blyden.

Blyden and Thomas

Edward Blyden

Edward Wilmot Blyden was born in St Thomas in the Virgin Islands in 1832. As a youngster he lived in Venezuela for two years and the United States for seven months – at a time when blacks in the southern states were still slaves. At eighteen he emigrated to Liberia and trained to be a teacher and clergyman at a high school in the country's capital, Monrovia. Then followed many careers. He spent several years as principal, and then president, of Liberia College. Twice he was Liberia's ambassador to

Fig. 8.1 *Edward Wilmot Blyden.*

Britain and for two years a minister in the country's government. Throughout his life he was a busy writer of books and newspaper articles and lectured on his ideas in America and Britain.

In his different posts, Blyden's first concern was to encourage the study of African culture and history and the achievements of African people. When he became principal of Liberia College he gave a public lecture on Toussaint L'Ouverture. In the same year he made a lecture tour of the United States where he said 'The political history of the United States is the history of the Negro. The commercial and agricultural history of nearly the whole of the Americas is the history of the Negro.' On these American trips, Blyden tried to encourage blacks to emigrate and become citizens of Liberia. Few did, although 346 Barbadians went there in 1865.

In Liberia itself, Blyden did much to spread the teaching of African and Arabic languages. Arabic was particularly important to him because it was the language of the Islamic faith which, he believed, had not looked on the West Africans as inferior peoples as Christianity had done. In 1908, Blyden published his book *African Life and Customs* in which he set out a view different from that commonly held by Europeans. He compared the personality of Africans, with its gentleness and respect for spiritual values, to the Europeans' concern for material goods and ever-faster economic growth. Yet he never rid himself of one idea which was commonly held by Europeans. Throughout his life Blyden accepted the unscientific idea that people of mixed 'race' were inferior to those of 'pure' black parentage. This idea of racial purity was not shared by J. J. Thomas, probably the first man writing in the West Indies to stress the common African heritage of American blacks.

J. J. Thomas

Jacob Thomas was born about 1840 in Trinidad to parents who had been slaves and then apprentices until only two years before. Thus, he was among the first generation of black West Indians to be born into a free society. As a boy he became one of the first to take up a place in one of the government 'ward' schools set up in 1851 by the governor, Lord Harris. From there he went, at about eighteen, to the Normal School, just outside Port of Spain, where ward school teachers were trained. Two years later he himself took charge of a ward school and stayed in this work until 1867.

Another governor, Sir Arthur Gordon, started examinations for the island's civil service to replace the system by which most officials got their posts through recommendation by friends. The new system opened the way into the civil service for at least a few black Trinidadians. In one of the first examinations, J. J. Thomas came top of the list. After three years he was promoted to be Secretary of the Board of Education and to the governing council of the Queen's Royal College in Port of Spain. He stayed in these posts until ill-health forced him to retire in 1879.

Thomas's success in these posts was remarkable for a black Trinidadian of his time, but his importance in West Indian history went deeper. He remained deeply interested in the culture and language of his own people. It was common at that time, as it is sometimes today, for educated West Indians to look down on creole speakers as men and women who could not master the pronunciation and rules of grammar of English or French. By careful study of the spoken language of the people around him, including his mother, Thomas showed that this was not so. The creole spoken in Trinidad had its own rules, and was the result not of ignorance but of a mixing of spoken African and French languages. Today there are many studies of creole language, and all owe something to a book Thomas wrote as early as 1869, *The Theory and Practice of Creole Grammar*. The book was greatly admired in England where Thomas was invited to give lectures in 1873.

Thomas followed this up with collecting creole folk songs. Unfortunately they were not published, so many have today disappeared from memory. He also argued for an educational system which was relevant to the people of the West Indies. He said that schools should not be slavish imitators of those in England but should teach agricultural topics, languages and the history and geography of the West Indies rather than the ancient European world.

By 1888, Thomas was in Grenada, seriously ill and earning a small living by teaching foreign languages. As soon as he was well, he intended to go to England to finish another book on creole language which would include studies from the French colonies and Haiti. But while he was still in Grenada, copies of a new book, *The English in the West Indies*, arrived. The book was written, after a quick tour of several West Indian colonies, by J. A. Froude, a famous English historian. Yet it was not at all a serious piece of history writing. The book was a jumble of prejudiced remarks about two questions: the reform of the undemocratic system of Crown colony government and the future development of the black people.

Froude described the blacks as a simple-minded people, quite uninterested in political affairs. He even went as far as suggesting that slavery had not been altogether a bad thing. Here he is writing about meeting blacks during a stroll in a Jamaican town:

The women smiled and curtsied, and the children looked shy when one spoke to them. The name of slavery is a horror to us; but there must have been something human and kindly about it, too, when it left upon the character the marks of courtesy and good breeding.

But, often enough, Froude contradicted himself and it was not long before he was also writing that the blacks were a political threat. He said there was a dangerously large gap between the two races in the West Indies. Supposing there came a time when blacks had political power: how would colonial governors behave then? To Froude, the answer was clear: 'No Englishman would ever preside over a black council or deliver speeches made for him by a black prime minister.'

'Froudacity'

J. J. Thomas immediately decided to reply to this man he called a 'negrophobic political hobgoblin' and wrote fifteen articles in a Grenada newspaper. He then went to England to turn the articles into a book which was to be called *Froudacity*. It appeared in the summer of 1889 and only then did Thomas begin to finish his new book on creole grammar. Sadly, it was too late. He was already very sick with tuberculosis and died in an English hospital in September 1889 at the age of forty-nine. But he left behind one of the most important books to be written by a black West Indian.

Much of *Froudacity* is taken up with exposing the prejudices and contradictions in Froude's book. One of the striking things about this part of *Froudacity* is that it is fair. J. J. Thomas not only defended his own people against Froude's attacks but also coloured men such as Conrad Reeves, who became chief justice in Barbados, and two governors of Trinidad who had genuinely tried to serve all the people of the island. He attacked other governors savagely. He wrote that one had 'a reputation for vulgar colonial prejudices', another was merely a 'dandy', while another was 'without initiative, without courage'.

Thomas's great contribution to the development of black consciousness runs through the book. It was a belief in the developing strength of the world's African peoples. In the last chapter he surveys their history, and draws attention to their 'soundness and nobility', their ability to survive the horrors of centuries of slavery by supporting each other, and to their rapid progress since emancipation. Over the wide area of the Americas, he wrote, there were ten million people with 'mental and other qualifications which render them remarkable among their fellowmen'. Already he could see signs that American Africans wanted to draw together to carry forward the 'true purposes of the civilised African Race'. Perhaps, he suggested, the American Africans will have a duty to help those in Africa, 'the cradle of our Race, which is probably destined to be the ultimate resting-place and headquarters of millions of blacks in the future'.

H. S. Williams and Pan-Africanism
H. S. Williams

With these words at the end of his book, J. J. Thomas was looking forward to the idea of Pan-Africanism, which at that time meant a combination of people of African descent wherever they might be. With Africa under colonial rule, it was likely that many of the leaders of Pan-Africanism would come from among emancipated blacks in the Americas. And, indeed, it was yet another Trinidadian who organised the first Pan-African movement, just a few years after *Froudacity*.

Henry Sylvester Williams was born in Arouca, in Trinidad, in 1869. Like J. J. Thomas he went to the Normal School and became a headmaster in 1887. In 1891 he emigrated to the United States and then, in 1893, went to university in Canada to study law. From there he moved to continue his studies at London University in 1896. In the next year in London he formed an African Association to:

> . . . encourage a feeling of unity and to facilitate friendly intercourse among Africans in general; to promote and protect the interests of all subjects claiming African descent.

Fig. 8.2 *Henry Sylvester Williams.*

Pan-Africanism

The Association called the first Pan-African Conference, which met in London in 1900. It decided to turn itself into a permanent Pan-African Association with branches in Africa, the Caribbean and the United States. The aims of the Pan-African Association were clearly laid down:

1. To secure to Africans throughout the world true civil and political rights.
2. To ameliorate the conditions of our brothers on the continent of Africa, America and other parts of the world.

The Conference decided to ask the heads of Ethiopia, Liberia and Haiti, the world's only free black states, to be 'Grand Protectors'. Finally the Conference wrote 'An Address to the Nations of the World' which called on countries which had black citizens to treat them fairly and equally with people of other races. 'The problem of the twentieth century is the problem of the colour line', the Address declared.

H. S. Williams became secretary of the Pan-African Conference. In the years after 1900, he worked in several African countries and visited Jamaica and Trinidad to set up branches of the Pan-African Association. He finally returned to Trinidad in 1908. He died there three years later. In these years he had an important influence on other black leaders. One was an Egyptian-Sudanese, Duse Mohammed Ali, who between 1912 and 1918 ran the *African Times and Orient Review*, which was the main newspaper of the Pan-African movement. One man who worked on the paper for a time was a young Jamaican, Marcus Garvey.

Assignments

1 *In what ways do you think colonialism in general and slavery in particular affected black people in the West Indies?*

2 a) *What methods did Edward Blyden, J. J. Thomas and H. S. Williams use to make others aware of race, identity and common problems?*
  b) *How would you summarise the main teachings of these men?*

9 THE FORTUNES OF SUGAR

Sugar in the 1880s

Chapter 2 showed how sugar in the British Caribbean faced a great crisis after the Sugar Duties Equalisation Act of 1846. Some colonies, especially Trinidad and British Guiana, coped with the crisis with the help of immigrant labour, wage cutting, steam machinery and amalgamating estates. But, by the 1880s British sugar was entering a time when it faced new problems. Just how serious they were can be seen from the tables.

Sugar production in Jamaica, Trinidad and British Guiana				
Yearly production figures in tonnes				
	1815	1828	1882	1894
Jamaica	79,660	72,198	36,636	19,934
Trinidad	7,682	13,285	55,327	46,869
British Guiana	16,520	40,115	124,102	102,502

Average prices earned by British Guiana sugar producers	
Years	Shillings per cwt (1 cwt = 50 kg)
1880–84	20
1885–89	14
1890–94	13
1894–99	10
1900–04	9
1905–09	9
1910–14	12
1915–19 (War 1914–18)	22

There were many causes for the loss of production and the fall in prices. The three most important were competition from European beet, the rapid growth of sugar production in Cuba and new regulations which made it difficult to sell British colonial sugar in world markets.

Beet

In 1808 a scientist, Franz Achard (a German with French parents), discovered an efficient way of extracting sugar in Europe's first beet factory on his estate in Germany. At the time the sucrose content of the beet was low and the cost of factories was high because they were used only for a few weeks in the year. Yet the governments of Germany, Holland, Austria, France and Belgium saw good reasons for helping the beet industry. Rotating beet with other crops and cattle grazing helped to enrich the soil and beet tops were a cheap cattle food. Beet gave a few weeks extra employment in the factories. Most important, beet growing meant that European countries need not depend on overseas supplies in time of war.

Government help came in the form of bounties paid to beet producers on all the sugar they exported. By 1884, the German bounty amounted to 60 per cent of the costs of production. Bounties of this size meant that European beet became much cheaper than Caribbean cane and was soon flooding into the sugar buying countries. The pattern of imports into Britain changed like this:

	Beet	All Cane	Caribbean cane
1852	1.9%	98.1%	84.7%
1880	20.6%	68.4%	28.4%
1890	64.1%	35.9%	14.8%
1896	75.0%	25.0%	10.0%

The closing US market

Utter disaster was prevented only because the United States was at that time buying large quantities of British West Indian sugar. In 1895 she took nearly half of Trinidad's crop but that was the first year in which she placed a high customs duty on imported sugar so that she could help the development of American sugar companies in the United States itself as well as in Cuba and in Puerto Rico. Within a few years exports from the English-speaking Caribbean to the United States became unimportant.

Sugar in Cuba

Until 1886 Cuba's sugar was produced by slaves and by Chinese immigrants who worked in conditions of near slavery. By the time slavery ended this one island produced about twice as much sugar as the whole of the English-speaking Caribbean.

At first sight a Cuban slave plantation was very like those in the English colonies before 1834: a stone great house for the planter or his manager, separate homes for the white labourers, a slave compound, and factory buildings. There were few provision grounds, for most food was imported. The differences were in the size of the plantations, usually much larger than in Jamaica and Barbados, and in the factories. Because Cuba did not start large-scale sugar planting until the 1820s, her planters were able to make use of new machinery almost as soon as it was invented. Vacuum pans and steam

engines were in common use in the 1830s and were already said to increase the amount of sugar per slave from 2 to $4\frac{1}{2}$ tonnes per year. Even greater profits could be made from exports when plantations bought the large Derosne steam-driven centrifugal drying machines. These could produce white sugar instead of the old sticky sugar loaf. The increases in production which resulted are shown in this table:

	Exports from Cuba (in tonnes)	No. of factories	Average production per factory (in tonnes)
1792	14,600	473	30
1802	40,800	870	50
1859	610,300	1250	500

The increases were greatly helped by opening railways which were built in Cuba before they appeared in Spain. The first 25 kilometres were

Fig. 9.1 *Sugar cane and processed sugar were carried by the new railways, which were owned by the planters. A late nineteenth-century scene.*

opened in 1837; by 1860 there were 644 kilometres. Most railways were owned by the big planters who used them to bring in cane from the remote parts of the estate and also to carry the sugar to their private wharfs on the coast. Naturally, the railways helped to increase the size of plantations. In the late 1850s Cuba had several which could by themselves produce more sugar than Dominica or Montserrat. Cuba, of course, is larger in total area than all the English-speaking islands.

Sugar production suffered during the ten years of civil war, 1868–78. Then came another blow when the Spanish government began to give bounties to beet growers in Spain. Planters soon found that they could not export any of their sugar to Spain. So, throughout the 1880s, both small farmers and larger planters were forced to sell their estates.

The difficulties of the Cubans became a time of great opportunity for business companies from the United States. There was a huge market for sugar in the United States and American companies moved into Cuba to buy up factories and plantations. A large-scale re-organisation followed. The number of factories was cut from 1,191 in 1877 to only 470 in 1895. New roads and railways linked these monster central factories to the cane fields. Growing and milling were now completely separated. Most of the 'centrals' were in American hands and they could force down the price paid to the growers,

especially if the factory company also owned plantations and rented them to tenant farmers. Sugar production boomed in the early 1890s to reach a million tonnes, four times the total production in the English-speaking Caribbean. But the gain was America's. Both rich and poor Cubans suffered. Many planters gave up altogether. Cuba was prevented from developing a refining industry, which would have given work to thousands, by heavy American duties on refined sugar which meant it was exported in its raw state to be refined by the workers in the United States.

Attempts to revive sugar

Amalgamations

Cuba's sugar industry showed that one key to success was large estates feeding a central factory where the latest machinery could be used. In Trinidad and Guyana the move to amalgamations and central factories had already begun before the crisis of the 1880s and 1890s (see pages 17–18). Usually, the amalgamations meant that plantations were taken over by British companies which often owned plantations and other businesses in many parts of the world. One example was the Colonial Sugar Company which opened the first central factory in the English-speaking Caribbean at Ste Madeleine in Trinidad in 1872. From this time, amalgamations went on steadily and the number of estates fell in this way:

Year	Number of estates
1866	142
1896	52
1936	32

By 1959, five inter-related companies controlled all Trinidad's sugar industry.

Fig. 9.2 *A central sugar factory near Matanzas, photographed in the 1890s.*

In Guyana the Colonial Company had a rival in Bookers, which began as a small Liverpool merchant firm supplying provisions and credit to Guyanese planters. Bookers steadily bought up bankrupt estates or took over planters' mortgages in return for sugar deliveries. In the second half of the nineteenth century, the amalgamations cut the number of estates in British

Guiana from 180 in 1869 to 64 in 1896. The process went on in the twentieth century. In 1976 there were only twelve separate estate administrations. Bookers' controlled ten of these, which were bought by the Guyanese government in that year.

One obvious result of amalgamations was to increase the size of plantations. Towards the end of the nineteenth century, the average estate was 68 hectares in Barbados and 78 hectares in Antigua, compared with 244 hectares in Trinidad and 423 hectares in British Guiana.

Small cane farmers

It cost so much to build a central factory that it would only make a profit by being supplied with more cane than could be grown on even the large amalgamated estates. One way of doing this was to use cane brought in by small farmers. In Trinidad, cane became an important smallholders' crop in places where there was land within a day's journey of a central. The number of small cane growers disproved the nineteenth-century notion that African farmers were unwilling to undertake the hard work and risks involved in private farming.

It was less easy to become a small cane grower in British Guiana. Most of its centrals were built on the low-lying coastal lands which needed pumping stations and drainage works which smallholders could not afford. However in Jamaica it was just this combination of small cane growing and central factories which helped the sugar industry to revive after the steady decline of the plantation system up to the 1880s. Amalgamations were late in coming to Jamaica so that, at the turn of the century, the greatest amount of Jamaican cane was produced by independent farmers.

Farmers often complained of the low prices they received for their cane. They fell even further after the British sugar company, Tate and Lyle, became active in Jamaica in the late 1920s and 1930s. Working through a subsidiary, the West Indies Sugar Company, they bought up a number of properties on the island and started to grow sugar on a large scale.

Because they had their own supplies they could then force down the price paid for smallholders' cane. These twentieth-century amalgamations and the company's price cutting reduced the proportion of cane produced by small growers. By the 1970s it had fallen to less than 8 per cent of Jamaica's crop.

The Royal Commissions

When they had been freed from slavery in 1834 each colony's exports (apart from Belize) were made up almost entirely of sugar. Almost every slave or apprentice did work connected with growing, processing or selling sugar. By the 1890s this was still true of only four colonies: Barbados, where sugar made up 97 per cent of exports, St Kitts-Nevis with 96.5 per cent,

Fig. 9.3 *Cutting sugar cane in the cane fields. A view showing free labourers in Jamaica in the 1880s.*

Antigua with 94.5 per cent and British Guiana with 92 per cent. Trinidad produced much sugar but was large enough to grow other crops and most black labourers did not work in the sugar industry. In the remaining colonies sugar's place had fallen in an even more startling way. In Jamaica it made up only about a sixth of exports and in Montserrat a much smaller fraction. The crop was no longer grown for export on Tobago, Grenada and Anguilla.

The decline of sugar meant that the colonial governments found it difficult to collect the money they needed from taxes. In 1882 the British government sent a Royal Commission to enquire into the state of the finances in Jamaica, the Leewards and Windwards. All were spending more on local government than they were collecting in taxes. The Commission made some suggestions for saving on officials and their salaries (see Chapter 7). But it had few ideas for saving sugar. In fact, its main recommendation was that small farmers should be encouraged to try other crops.

By 1896 the colonies were in even deeper financial trouble, especially as the price of sugar in Britain was tumbling. The British government sent another Royal Commission headed by Sir Henry Norman. Its task was to enquire into West Indian agriculture. In 1897 its report gave a gloomy picture of the sugar industry, saying 'that a serious state of affairs was approaching'. It made a few suggestions for tackling the problem. The British government should press other European countries to end their bounties on beet. It should set up a West Indian Department of Agriculture to help farmers improve crops. There should be government loans to help modernise plantations and build central factories. It also recommended ways of helping small farmers to grow other export crops.

Joseph Chamberlain, the Colonial Secretary, accepted the recommendations, saying 'Her Majesty's Government have no intention of allowing the West Indian sugar industry to be ruined'. In 1899 the Colonial Office paid a grant of £20,000 to start the Department of Agriculture in its headquarters in Barbados. It encouraged research into new varieties of cane which suffered less from disease than those

which had been grown for many years. The new varieties were widely grown from the 1920s onwards. Chamberlain also promised a loan of £120,000 for building central factories in Barbados. Planters here had been slow to amalgamate their estates and the money was to encourage them to do this and cut costs.

In 1903, the European beet producing nations met at a conference in Brussels. They agreed to end the bounties they paid on beet. Unfortunately by that time beet production was improving so that it could still undercut cane even without the bounty.

Imperial preference and world wars

The end of the bounty system was less valuable than the help which came from Canada. In 1897 and again in 1900 and 1907 she agreed to charge lower customs duties on sugar from the British West Indies than from other territories. When German submarines made it difficult to send sugar to Britain during the First World War, Canada became the largest single buyer of British Caribbean sugar. At the same time, the sugar which did get through to Britain fetched nearly double the price it had before the war. Because Britain could not import beet sugar from Europe she set up a government Commission to buy cane sugar in bulk from the West Indies.

In the 1920s Britain took the first steps to end the policy of free trade. By 1931 she had changed to protection – which meant she again put customs duties on imports to protect British industry and agriculture. She had also changed her policy on beet. Between 1925 and 1935 English farmers were paid a subsidy which helped them to produce half a million tonnes of sugar and give work to 30,000 labourers.

Yet, along with protection went schemes for 'imperial preference' which were worked out at a conference in Ottawa in 1932. Imperial preference meant that Britain agreed to import food and goods from the countries of her empire at lower customs duties or none at all. This was important for West Indian sugar. Without imperial preference its sugar would have cost 40 per cent more in Britain and would have

Fig. 9.4 *Labourers in Norfolk, England, in 1913, taking beet from the field.*

suffered heavily from competition from cheaper European beet. Canada also continued to give preference to West Indian sugar.

It is possible to see the effects of all these changes in Trinidad's sugar industry. During the war, production rose from 43,000 tonnes to 72,000 and prices rose sharply too. After the war there was a crisis when Britain began to import European beet again and then grow her own. By 1929 prices were so low that some estates were abandoned, workers either lost their jobs or had their wages cut. Even so the remaining estates had become more efficient. They were now using the new canes as well as more fertilisers. Factory machinery was improved so that more sucrose was extracted from the cane. That meant that when prices improved in the 1930s the island's sugar production rose from its 1928 figure of 81,000 tonnes to 154,000 in 1937.

When the Second World War broke out in 1939, Britain again faced a shortage of European sugar. This time she agreed to buy all the sugar produced in the empire at a price which would be no less than what it cost to produce. Sugar production in the West Indies expanded. In Jamaica, the area under cane rose from 18,616 hectares in 1938 to 26,306 hectares in

1943 and Guyana had very similar increases. In Trinidad, however, production fell in wartime despite the guaranteed price. The reason was that thousands of farmers and labourers left sugar to work at the US military bases which were opened on the island.

After the Second World War

For the first few years after the war there was still a shortage of sugar so Britain continued to buy and resell all Commonwealth crops. But, by 1950, world production had recovered to pre-war levels and prices were falling. In 1951 Britain stopped buying all Commonwealth sugar. Instead, she agreed to buy for her own use a fixed quantity, or quota, from each Commonwealth producer. The price would be fixed each year at a level which gave a 'reasonable' payment. Producers could grow sugar beyond the quota but this would be for sale at world prices.

The West Indians were pleased that some part of their crop would be protected in price but were dissatisfied with their share of the British market. They argued, rightfully, that the generous share offered to Commonwealth producers such as Australia took no account of

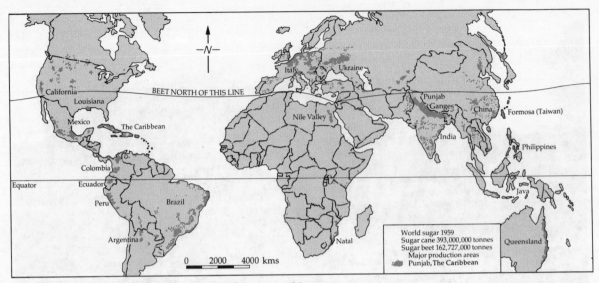

Map 9 *World sugar production in 1959, including sugar cane and beet.*

the special difficulties of the West Indies. Australia was not dependent on sugar exports for her standard of living whereas many Caribbean countries were. West Indian governments sent delegations to Britain to point out that it did not make sense to send aid to the West Indies while forcing sugar producers to sell part of the crop at low world prices. The British negotiators agreed only to increase the English-speaking Caribbean's share by a mere 30,000 tonnes.

In 1953, the Caribbean producers did gain some protection for the sugar which was not part of the quota sold to Britain. The world's producers signed an International Sugar Agreement to control sales on the free market. Each year, each producing country was given an export quota which was fixed so that total sales would be enough to cover world needs at reasonable prices. It was not to be so large that the market would be flooded and prices would tumble. Such agreements naturally do not always work smoothly, as it is difficult to forecast the size of crops or the level of world demand.

An even greater boost for English-speaking West Indian producers came after Castro's revolution in 1958. Canada and the USA refused to buy Cuban sugar, which was sold instead to the USSR. As a result British West Indian producers were granted special tariffs in Canada and were able to enter the United States market for the first time for many years. In 1958 no sugar was exported from the English-speaking Caribbean to the United States, but in 1968 216,369 tonnes were sold there. By then, almost all of the Commonwealth Caribbean's sugar was sold either to Britain, through the quota agreements, or to North America at special tariff rates and at managed prices under the International Sugar Agreements.

After 1962

In 1973 Britain became a member of the European Economic Community. Two years later the EEC accepted the quota worked out between Britain and the Commonwealth Caribbean. The Community also took over agreements between France and her sugar producers. The quotas and special trade deals with North America helped the sugar industry to survive but the West Indies paid dearly. Caribbean producing countries are expected to give preference to imports from countries buying their sugar. They can find themselves obliged to buy goods from Canada, the United States or the EEC when it would be cheaper to buy them on the open market.

For many years, negotiated prices and quotas

protected European interests at least as much as they aided the well-being of West Indians. Until the governments of Trinidad and Guyana bought large shares in their territories' sugar industries, about 92 per cent of the sugar in the Commonwealth Caribbean was controlled by British interests. Most of that control has now gone but governments are still faced with the legacy from colonial times. A single crop was boosted to serve British interests and very little was done to create a stronger and more varied economy in the colonies.

A particular difficulty for the English-speaking Caribbean is that it produces only a small proportion of the total world supply. That means it has little bargaining power in negotiations over prices and markets. In 1972 the English-speaking West Indies' combined total of about 1½ million tonnes came to only a fifth of the 7½ million tonnes produced in the Caribbean as a whole. Of this, Cuba grew about half and the Dominican Republic alone about a sixth. But the Caribbean's 7½ million was only itself a tenth of the world total of 76 million tonnes.

Assignments

1   *Using the table on page 64 to help you, answer the following questions:*
    a)   *Between 1852 and 1896 when did the most significant rise or fall in imports take place in each column?*
    b)   *Where did Britain obtain beet sugar?*
    c)   *Give reasons for the rise in imports of beet sugar into Britain at this time.*
    d)   *What was Britain's source of cane sugar, other than the Caribbean?*
    e)   *Explain briefly how the fall of exports of Caribbean cane sugar to Britain affected the British Caribbean.*

2   *Make a comparison of the state of the sugar industry in the British and Spanish Caribbean territories in the late nineteenth century and the first half of the twentieth century.*

3   *Read the extract from page 67 then answer the questions which follow:*

    'When they had been freed from slavery in 1834 each colony's exports (apart from Belize) were made up almost entirely of sugar . . . By the 1890s this was still true of only four colonies: Barbados . . . St Kitts-Nevis . . ., Antigua . . . and British Guiana.'

    a)   *Why did sugar continue to be the main export crop in the territories named in the extract?*
    b)   *Which British Caribbean territories no longer exported sugar? Why?*
    c)   *Why did alternative export crops develop in other territories of the British Caribbean?*

10 NEW WAYS OF EARNING A LIVING

As earnings from sugar fell it was clear that the future of the English-speaking Caribbean depended on new ways of earning a living. In the nineteenth century, the greatest effort went into new export crops. Little was done to encourage industry or even to expand farming of food for the Caribbean peoples themselves. The new export crops brought more work for some West Indians, but often they were just as much under the control of foreign interests as the workers in sugar.

The new crops developed fastest from the 1890s when sugar production and prices slumped. But they had all been first grown many years before. The largest crops were found in the largest territories where sugar was still important. Yet the different fruits and the cotton grown in the small islands were extremely important to the descendants of the plantation slaves.

Alternatives to sugar

Sugar was the main export from Trinidad, British Guiana and Jamaica. But in each of the three colonies a main alternative crop was developed; cocoa in Trinidad, rice in British Guiana and bananas in Jamaica.

Cocoa

Cocoa had been grown in Trinidad under Spanish rule. After the British seized the island in 1797, Spain continued to be the largest European market for the crop. For the next thirty years there was a steady but small increase in production. The most successful cultivators were immigrants from Latin American territories on the mainland. Many of these 'peons' were descended from a mixture of Amerindian, Spanish and African ancestors.

They were skilled at cultivating cocoa which grew naturally in the tropical rain forests.

After emancipation, some ex-slaves moved from the plantations to squat on Crown lands where they planted cocoa trees. However, it was hard to make a living in this way. Restrictions were placed on the purchase of smallholdings in an effort to keep labourers in the sugar plantations. At the same time, the European market for cocoa was at a standstill. Spain placed crippling duties on imports which came direct from a British colony and Britain bought only small amounts of cocoa.

However, the British demand for cocoa began to grow from the end of the 1840s. A Dutchman, C. J. van Houten, had discovered a way of separating cocoa butter from the beans. The butter could be moulded into blocks of eating chocolate and turned into a liquid or powder for making drinks. Two British firms, Fry's and Cadbury's, first sold eating chocolate in the late 1840s. In 1866, Cadbury's produced their first 'cocoa essence'. The warm drink, made by adding water or milk, steadily became the most popular beverage after tea in Britain. Eating chocolate and cocoa drinks also became popular in the United States, especially in the 1880s when thousands of soft drink bars, or soda fountains, were opened.

At first, Trinidad's exports of cocoa were slow to increase to meet this new world demand. Then, in the 1870s, many sugar plantations fell into the hands of overseas companies who amalgamated estates and built central factories. Many of the plantation owners who sold out to the companies used the money to buy land and started to grow cocoa. Most followed the contract system. By this method of working, the landowner agreed to fell the forest trees and to dig the main drains. He then divided the land and contracted it out to peasant farmers in small plots of a few hectares. The contractor planted the seed and cultivated the trees. While they were developing he was able to plant quicker-growing cash crops such as bananas, plantains, peas, beans and groundnuts. These grew among the young cocoa trees and gave the contractor food for his own use and a surplus to sell at market. When the trees began to bear, the landowner paid the contractor off in cash.

The contract system meant that peasants could build up savings from the payments for their crops and the care of the cocoa trees. The island government was willing to sell them Crown land now that indentured immigrants were easing the sugar planters' labour needs. So, the cocoa holdings came to vary according to what the purchaser could afford. The ex-planters owned the bigger holdings of more than 40 hectares while ex-labourers usually owned between 4 and 20 hectares. But there were many smaller holdings of down to 1 hectare.

The following table shows the steady increase in cocoa exports from Trinidad and the great boost that followed the crisis of sugar in the 1890s.

Average yearly cocoa exports in tonnes					
1800–04	146	1860–64	2,697	1920–24	28,370
1810–14	447	1870–74	3,395	1930–34	20,952
1820–24	674	1880–84	5,055	1940–44	6,567
1830–34	1,027	1890–94	9,389	1950–54	8,067
1840–44	1,416	1900–04	15,872	1960–64	6,003
1850–54	1,966	1910–14	23,654		

In 1920 cocoa made up 43 per cent of Trinidad's exports and in that year nearly 17 per cent of all agricultural land in Trinidad was planted in cocoa trees. By then it had spread into every district in the island, far away from the northern range where the crop had been first gathered. In the 1920s and 1930s cocoa was hit by a double crisis. Prices collapsed as British manufacturers bought from new large plantations in West Africa. From 1928, Trinidad cocoa trees began to suffer from witchbroom disease.

Trinidad's government and the Colonial Office in London stepped in with grants and loans to help the large planters get out of debt and start replacing their trees with disease-free seedlings. Almost nothing was done to help the small peasant cocoa growers or the labourers on the large estates who were laid off or had their wages cut. In the Second World War the British government agreed to buy up to 4,000 tonnes a year at fixed prices.

After 1945, there were signs that the money spent before the war had helped cocoa to survive but it was a less important part of Trinidad's earnings than between the 1890s and 1920s. In those years Trinidad had been second only to Ecuador as the world's largest supplier. Yet no attempt had been made to develop a food or drink processing industry to compete with Britain's or America's. As with sugar, the colonial people had been limited to growing and exporting a raw food product.

Bananas

Bananas had been grown as a locally eaten food in Jamaica for many years before 1868, when an American sea captain, Lorenzo Dow Baker, stopped at Port Morant to refit his clipper ship *Telegraph*. While in port he decided to jettison the ship's ballast of sand and take on a load of bananas. Sixteen days later the *Telegraph* docked at Jersey City where Baker quickly sold the fruit and made a handsome profit. After a few more experimental voyages he decided that there was a profitable regular trade in carrying bananas from Port Antonio on the north coast of Jamaica. In 1872 he officially registered the L. D. Baker Fruit Company.

At first the company drew its supplies from the small farmers around Port Antonio but, within a few years, large proprietors began growing bananas as a plantation crop. Baker himself was one of the largest estate owners with properties in Jamaica, Puerto Rico and Cuba. In 1885 he formed the Boston Fruit Company, which controlled all stages of his banana business: growing, shipping and selling. The Boston Fruit Company made it possible for Baker to overcome competitors who appeared in Central America. One of these was an American railway builder, Minor C. Keith, who began buying up Central American property

Fig. 10.1 *A photograph taken in the mid-nineteenth century, showing a Jamaican family with their home surrounded by banana plants.*

and planting banana suckers. The plantations flourished but he was forced to rely on Baker's Company to sell the fruit through its market outlets in the United States. By 1898 Keith's plantations were supplying about two-thirds of all the fruit sold by the Boston Company. A year later Baker joined with Keith to form the United Fruit Company which controlled over 90 per cent of the American banana trade.

In 1897 the Norman Commission's Report said that the Boston Fruit Company controlled so much of the market that it could force prices down. This was a threat to Jamaica's small banana growers. To help them the Commission recommended that smaller independent companies such as the Jamaica Fruit and Trading Company and the J. E. Kerr Company should

be helped to start a banana trade to England. In 1901 the government in Jamaica and the British government agreed to share a £20,000 yearly subsidy to the English firm, Elders and Fyffes. They would collect bananas from independent Jamaican suppliers and import them into Britain.

Unfortunately competition did not last. In 1903 a hurricane seriously damaged the Jamaican crop and Elders and Fyffes had to buy fruit from the United Fruit Company to meet their orders. The United Fruit Company gladly supplied the bananas but the price was amalgamation. In 1910 Elders and Fyffes, too, became part of the United Fruit Company. The subsidy was stopped in 1911.

The United Fruit Company made bananas a

common part of the American diet. In Jamaica, the number of hectares planted increased from 7,790 in 1896 to over 24,282 in 1906. As for cocoa, the most rapid increase for bananas took place in the years of the greatest fall in sugar earnings.

Both small farmers and large-scale producers could share in the profits of the trade but the monopoly of the United Fruit Company had undesirable effects. It took most supplies from its own plantations and so it could pay low prices for the bananas grown by small farmers. The company plantations were the biggest employers of labour in the banana-growing districts so it was possible for United Fruit to fix wages. In the interests of foreign share-holders these were kept as low as possible. As a multi-national company, United Fruit had naturally no strong sense that it was responsible for the prosperity of any one area. When labour costs, strikes or plant disease drove up production costs in Jamaica, the company directors switched more of their operation to Costa Rica or Guatemala.

This is why the Jamaica Banana Producers' Association was set up in 1929. It paid more per bunch than United Fruit and collected a third of the Jamaican crop, mostly from the small producers. This helped them to continue earning when other small producers, such as Trinidad's peasant cocoa farmers, were giving up because of the fall in world prices. In the 1930s roughly half of the land under bananas in Jamaica was farmed by farmers who worked fewer than 8 hectares.

During the Second World War, Britain did the same for bananas as for sugar and cocoa. She agreed to buy the whole Jamaican crop at a fixed price of £1 million a year. After the war, bananas remained an important part of the Caribbean economy. By the 1960s the industry gave work to about 200,000 people. Bananas were no longer only a Jamaican crop. They were important to the Windwards, Dominica, St Lucia, St Vincent and Grenada. About two-thirds of the earnings of these islands came from exporting bananas.

The post-war industry was still not free from overseas control. This was high-lighted in 1952

when the Dutch firm of Geests contracted to buy all the bananas grown on the Windwards. There followed a 'banana war' between growers on the Windwards and in Jamaica. In reality this was a war for European markets between Geests and Elders and Fyffes.

Rice

Before emancipation rice had often been grown in small quantities in the Guyanese colonies by Bush Negroes in their village strongholds. After the end of slavery, it remained an unimportant crop until the arrival of large numbers of Indian labourers. Most of them had grown rice as a main food in their homeland, so planters imported it for sale to them in British Guiana. After their indentures had been served, Indians were encouraged to settle on smallholdings near the plantations. Rice grew well in the low flat lands and many of them began to cultivate it as a provision crop and for local sale. But until the

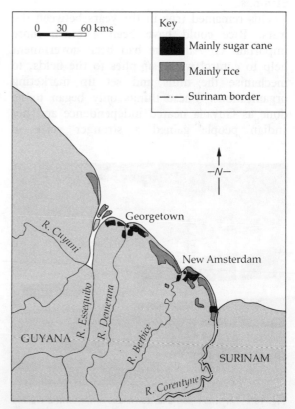

Map 10 *Rice and sugar growing areas in present-day Guyana.*

sugar crisis at the end of the century, far more rice was imported than grown in the colony. Then, the cultivation of rice rose rapidly and by 1908–12 more was exported than imported. By this time it had become a main product of Indians settled in villages in Berbice and West Demerara, away from the sugar districts.

Yearly average in tonnes					
	1898–1902	1903–07	1908–12	1913–17	1918–22
Production (in tonnes)	3,824	10,621	30,006	36,336	28,508
Exports	—	5	3,120	10,710	6,756
Imports	14,693	8,092	2,519	159	72

The exports, however, were not very important in British Guiana's earnings. What was of great value was the almost complete ending of imports and the saving of the cost of buying rice from abroad. This 'import substitution' went some way to shielding the people of British Guiana from the worst effects of the fall in sugar earnings.

This remained true in the years between the wars. Rice could have been a much more important crop if there had been government help to control water supplies to the fields, to mechanise the mills and set up marketing organisations. These things only began to be done as Guyana neared independence and her Indian people gained a stronger voice in

Fig. 10.2 *The new offices and warehouses of the British Guiana Rice Marketing Board in 1953.*

political affairs. Between 1943 and 1960 rice production rose from 75,000 tonnes to 126,000 tonnes. After independence rice became an important export from British Guiana to other territories in the Caribbean.

Crops on the small islands

In the eastern Caribbean small farmers copied the example of the people who grew cocoa, bananas and rice in the large colonies. They turned to other crops. In some cases they were an alternative to sugar. For instance, both Barbados and Antigua made more than 90 per cent of their earnings from sugar but also exported sea-island cotton. In other cases, the new crops almost replaced sugar. This was true in Dominica and Montserrat, St Lucia, St Vincent and Grenada.

Cocoa was grown in St Lucia and Dominica, although limes were more important there. In St Vincent, arrowroot was the chief new crop and Grenada's farmers grew nutmeg. Montserrat farmers specialised in sea-island cotton and limes. Figures for exports from Montserrat in 1920 show just how great had been the changes in an island which once produced little else but sugar, molasses and rum.

Crop	Montserrat Value of exports, 1920 (£)
Cotton lint	168,700
Cotton seed	3,717
Raw lime juice	8,684
Concentrated lime juice	300
Citrate of lime	2,434
Muscovado sugar	7,000
Syrup	434
Molasses	661
Plantain	602
Onions	584
Cattle	1,210

The island's limes were harvested all the year round, taken from the small farms to two central factories where they were sliced and squeezed by water-driven machinery. The juice was then sealed in casks and shipped to Britain. Most of it went to factories in Birmingham or Liverpool where it was used in cordial and sauces.

Fig. 10.3 *Harvesting limes in Dominica in the late nineteenth century.*

Fig. 10.4 *A British advertisement for lime-fruit sauce made by an English firm, which imported a large part of the Montserrat crop.*

Dominica and St Lucia grew the largest Caribbean crops of limes, but they were not always profitable. In 1892 the Montserrat harvest was ruined by scale insects and the blight lingered on until 1899 when a hurricane wiped the orchards out altogether. The fields were replanted but the young trees then suffered from outbreaks of root-wither-tip disease. By 1920, the European market for limes from Montserrat, St Lucia and Dominica was beginning to fall away in the face of competition from fruits grown in the Mediterranean countries and because European chemists had found a cheap artificial substitute for citric acid.

Other small farmers' crops met with similar difficulties. Cocoa suffered from attacks of witchbroom disease. Sea-island cotton crops were often destroyed by pink boll worms and the market weakened as European women's fashions changed. By the 1920s Caribbean oranges and grapefruit were facing severe competition from the same crops grown on a larger scale in Palestine (the modern Israel) and South Africa.

Small farmers and governments

A ground of their own

The new export crops showed that independent farmers could play an important part in the economic life of their countries. Yet in the first twenty or so years after emancipation, most of them had not been given the chance to own anything larger than a provision ground. Planters and local governments had tried to prevent freemen moving from the estates. They used local laws to limit the amount of Crown land they could own. Police laws and parish magistrates dealt harshly with those who tried to farm on abandoned plantations.

In the 1860s the Colonial Office began to encourage local governments to allow black farmers to acquire lands. A major reason for this change of heart was the Morant Bay riots, described in Chapter 6. One cause of the riots was freemen's grievances about being denied land. The governor of Trinidad, Sir Arthur

Gordon, took the lead in 1868 by beginning the sale of Crown land to freemen at low prices.

In British Guiana until 1890 Crown lands could be sold only in lots of 40 hectares at 10 dollars for half a hectare. This put them beyond the reach of smallholders and men who had completed indentures. In 1890, the cost was cut from 10 dollars to 1 and in 1898 land was made available in 10 hectare lots. These new regulations led to the release of what a report called, 'a considerable amount of land along the banks of coastal rivers' to farmers who were to play an important part in boosting Guyana's rice production. Other colonies had little Crown land but small farmers were encouraged to buy waste land from uncultivated plantations.

Where central factories were built, from the 1870s onwards, planters and governments were much more willing for small farmers to buy a few hectares where they could grow and cut cane for the factory. Most of all, colonial governments favoured independent farming where they saw it could help develop new export crops to make up for the loss of profits from sugar. It would also help government funds by increasing the amount of farmed land on which taxes had to be paid.

In Grenada, where sugar production was abandoned, the number of small farms of less than 20 hectares rose from 3,600 in 1860 to over 8,000 in 1910. The smallholders' chief crops were nutmeg, cocoa, cinnamon, pimento and ginger. Similar changes took place in islands such as St Vincent and Nevis. In Jamaica the number of such small farms doubled between 1860 and 1910 and the island developed a great variety of peasant agriculture. Not only was sugar grown for the central factories, and bananas for United Fruit, but small farmers also produced oranges, coconuts, ginger and many other crops, as well as provisions. By 1890 peasants produced three-quarters of the agricultural output of Jamaica.

An important aid to independent farmers were the savings banks set up in most colonies in the 1870s. These made it possible to save money earned from the sale of crops and, perhaps, use it later to buy new equipment or a little more land.

Fig. 10.5 *Pickers in a field of sea-island cotton, taken in the early twentieth century in Antigua.*

Royal Commissions

As we saw in Chapter 7, two Royal Commissions visited the Caribbean in the 1880s and 1890s. In 1882 the Royal Commission came to find ways of cutting the costs of government in the West Indies. They suggested that improved exports could help and made some recommendations. Abandoned sugar lands in St Vincent could be handed over to arrowroot growers. More lime trees could be planted in Montserrat and Dominica. In most colonies, export earnings could be helped by planting coconuts, spices and fruits.

However, the 1882 Commission was concerned with saving money so it did not recommend more spending to help the small farmers. After it left, the changeover to small farms and new crops went on but it was not great enough to save the colonies from falling into deeper debt. For instance, the value of Antigua's exports fell by more than half between 1886 and 1896 while government spending nearly doubled. Many colonies still relied too much on sugar and the price was falling sharply in the 1890s. The British government's method of dealing with the crisis was to send the Norman Commission in 1896. Its 1897 recommendations on sugar are described in Chapter 7.

The Norman Commission

The second part of the Norman Commission's Report turned to the small proprietors. The Commissioners wrote that nothing would give 'so good a prospect for the permanent welfare in the future of the West Indies as the settlement of the labouring population on the land as small peasant proprietors'.

So they strongly recommended that still more land be available to the small farmers. They could not agree on how this should be done but they did suggest ways of making small farming more profitable. One was that every colony should have botanical stations, which would distribute plants and seeds as well as organising courses in agriculture in schools. Another was that shipping lines should be opened between the islands, Canada, the United States and England, so that fruit and other foods could be carried quickly to market.

Small steps were taken to carry out these suggestions. The British government made a grant of £27,000 to help start botanical stations. By the early twentieth century Trinidad, Jamaica and British Guiana each had their own Departments of Agriculture. Most other colonies had botanical gardens which experimented with new varieties of seed and demonstrated new farming methods to smallholders. In 1900 the British made other grants to encourage a regular steamship service between Canada, New York and the West Indies. As we have seen, the Jamaican and British governments each gave £20,000 to Elders and Fyffes to carry 40,000 bunches of bananas to England every fortnight.

Alternatives in other European colonies

The search for alternative crops went on in the colonies of other European nations. Dutch settlers themselves were among the pioneers when they gave up the struggle to produce sugar on their three small Windwards islands. Throughout the nineteenth century, Aruba and Bonaire produced nearly a third of the aloes used in the world. On Curaçao, colonists turned to planting Seville oranges. The dried bitter peels were shipped to Holland, where distillers used them to make a popular orange liqueur drink known as Curaçao.

In Surinam, many sugar plantations had been abandoned by the end of the nineteenth century. Attempts were made to use the land for bananas, cocoa, coffee and tobacco. All failed because of crop diseases or poor world prices. Surinam's only agricultural success was with rice. It began when Javanese labourers turned to growing the crop when their indenture was over. Success was slow in coming. In 1916 Surinam imported 16 million kilograms of rice. But by 1939 she was able to export 19 million kilograms. Rice remained an important export crop after the Second World War. Like Guyanese rice much of it was sold to other territories in the Caribbean.

Alternative crops were not as important to the earnings of French-speaking islands of Martinique and Guadeloupe where nearly half the land was still planted in cane in the 1960s. But they were important to the small farmers of these islands. By far their most important crop was bananas, followed in the 1960s and 1970s by pineapples.

On the Spanish islands in the nineteenth century, alternative crops began with small European farmers who did not wish to try to compete with the large sugar plantations in the west of Cuba. In the east of Cuba and on Puerto Rico, these small planters developed a variety of crops including maize, cotton, rice, coffee and tobacco. In Puerto Rico coffee was grown on 40 per cent of the farmed land up to 1898. In the twentieth century it suffered from competition from the large plantations in Brazil and Central America. Tobacco remained an important crop for small farmers on both Spanish-speaking islands. In the 1950s there were new programmes led by Fidel Castro's government in Cuba and the US government in Puerto Rico to find more alternatives to sugar. They are described in Chapters 21 and 22.

Emigration

In 1841 the population of the British West Indies was 863,917. In 1891 the census recorded a figure nearly twice as high – 1,607,218. The changes in agriculture came nowhere near to providing work for all the additional people. Nor was it possible for all of them to turn to other trades and crafts. Although some road and railway building took place it was on too small a scale to provide a great deal of employment. For many West Indians, there seemed better prospects from emigrating to an area where work was more plentiful.

Central America

Large-scale emigration began in the 1870s, when several thousand British West Indians worked as labourers for American contractors like Minor C. Keith, who were building railways in Central America. In the 1850s, 2,000 West Indians mostly from Jamaica worked on the railway across the isthmus of Panama. When the lines were completed, many stayed on to work in the sugar, coffee and banana industries which had been encouraged by the opening of railways. By 1900 there were large West Indian communities in Guatemala, Costa Rica, Colombia, Nicaragua and Honduras.

Seasonal work

Some emigration was seasonal. The decline of Cuban slavery and its end in 1886 opened the chance of such work for Jamaicans. Between 1878 and 1914 about two thousand travelled each year to Cuba to cut cane. In the twentieth century they were joined by many Barbadians. In the same way workers from Antigua and other Lesser Antilles islands looked for seasonal work in the Dominican Republic's cane fields.

The Panama Canal

When a French company began digging a canal across the isthmus of Panama in 1881 it provided an opportunity for emigration to work which remained for more than thirty years. The first British West Indians left for Panama in 1881. In 1884 the Registrar-General of Jamaica estimated that 34,852 people emigrated there each year. Recruitment came to a halt in 1888 when the French company went bankrupt. It began again in 1905 when the Americans decided to finish the canal. Their Isthmian Canal Commission opened recruiting offices in the Caribbean, with their main centre in Barbados. Jamaica provided the largest number of workers, but Barbados came a close second. When the canal was finished in 1913, at least 40,000 British West Indians were on the American pay roll.

Fig. 10.6 *A view of the Panama Canal in 1913. Two of the parallel locks at Gatun can be seen under construction.*

The USA

A smaller number of British West Indians made their way to the United States and Britain. Britain attracted mostly professional workers. Labourers usually went to the United States. It was easiest to find field work in the cotton and tobacco plantations of the south but some played their part in building railways through the western states. Others preferred to go to the northern industrial cities and take jobs in the factories and service trades. In 1924 a new American immigration act restricted the entry of West Indians, but by that time they had established communities in New York, Chicago, Boston, Philadelphia and Washington. For many West Indians, emigration gave a chance to learn trades and skills which they could not follow at home because of the depressed state of the islands under colonial rule.

Effects on population

Emigration was least important in Trinidad and British Guiana. Estate work was generally available and ambitious small farmers could usually find land at a reasonable price. Indeed, through both the nineteenth and twentieth centuries these two countries received immigrants from the smaller islands. In Jamaica emigration helped to limit the harsh effects of a great rise in population. Most of it was short-term or seasonal emigration. In Barbados and the Leewards emigration had an even greater effect. The population of these colonies remained more or less the same or even declined between 1896 and 1921. This was chiefly due to emigration.

Colony	Population in		
	1896	1921	1936
Jamaica	695,000	858,000	1,139,000
Trinidad & Tobago	248,000	367,000	448 000
British Guiana	279,000	298,000	333,000
Barbados	186,000	166,000	188,000
Windward Islands	146,000	162,000	210,000
Leeward Islands	131,000	122,000	140,000
British Honduras	34,000	45,000	56,000
Total	1,719,000	2,018,000	2,514,000

Remittances

As well as keeping the population from rising, emigration made an important contribution to the incomes of those who stayed behind. The remittances sent back to relatives by emigrants often made up the largest foreign earnings of the colonies from one year to the next. Jamaicans spoke about their 'Panama money'. Government figures of the time stressed the importance of these remittances. In 1903 the Colonial Office reported:

> The increase in the amount of [money] orders cashed was especially noticeable in the presidency of Montserrat, the excess of order paid in 1902 over 1901 being £3,882. This is attributable to the remittances sent by the large numbers of the labouring classes who have emigrated to the neighbouring islands and to the United States.

The Annual Reports of the Barbados Post Office show the large sums received in money orders and cash between 1900 and 1910. By 1910 the island's emigrants sent back more than £120,000, but this was not as large a sum as

Remittances received through the Barbados Post Office, 1900–10					
Money orders in £ from					
Year	Canal zone	United States	British colonies	Total (includes others)	Estimated value of money (in £ sent in registered letters)
1900		2,954	21,222	27,208	
1901		4,010	23,702	31,347	9,722
1906	7,508	16,665	13,745	41,870	28,251
1907	46,160	19,323	14,758	89,924	30,189
1909	66,272	14,006	10,962	96,907	32,389
1910	66,102	15,078	12,518	93,361	34,766

Barbados lost each year by spending more on imports than she earned from her exports. For Barbados and other colonies, emigration could do no more than remove the harshest distress for the people of the colonial British West Indies.

Emigration between the wars

Patterns of emigration depend on two forces: conditions at home and opportunities in other countries. Up to about 1925 these forces often came together for the people of the Caribbean. Jamaica's large population could not all find work connected with agriculture and the island had hardly any industry. Its busiest time for public works came in the 1870s and 1880s; by the 1890s unemployment was high even among people who had learned some skills in work such as building. Barbados depended on sugar which fell into deep crisis from the 1890s. That explains why so many Barbadians travelled the much longer distances to join Jamaicans in Panama or in Cuba.

Until the mid-1920s the hard times could be matched with opportunities in Panama and Cuba but also in other parts of Central America and in the USA. Then the situation changed for two main reasons. The United States began to be concerned about the growth of its non-European population and closed the door on free permanent immigration in 1924. Secondly, world trade began to fall, beginning with agriculture. As unemployment rose, countries around the Caribbean no longer wanted workers, permanent or seasonal.

In 1924, Cuba stopped immigration. Many British West Indians already in Cuba were sent home. Other Central American countries also began to ban immigration. For the next few years figures showed more people coming in than leaving as workers returned early because they had been told to leave or because they had become unemployed.

For the rest of the time up to 1939 the only major place for emigration were the Dutch oil refineries in Aruba and Curaçao. The first oil was refined on Curaçao in 1918. By 1940 the oil companies in the two islands had more than 15,000 workers. There were thousands more jobs with shipping companies carrying oil from Venezuela and Mexico. The tiny islands could not supply all the workers and the rest were recruited throughout the Caribbean, but mostly from the Leewards and Windwards.

In the Second World War

The Dutch refineries were one of the places where extra work was available when the Second World War broke out. Another was Trinidad, where the United States built military bases. Emigration to these territories rose and in the 1950s it was possible to see the signs in the new houses built with earnings or remittances in Grenada, St Vincent or St Lucia. In Britain, seven thousand West Indians served in the Royal Air Force and others worked in wartime factories. Timber workers from Belize worked in the timber industry in Scotland.

A JAMAICAN SERGEANT AIR GUNNER OF THE R.A.F.

Fig. 10.7 *A wartime poster showing a Jamaican air gunner in the British Royal Air Force.*

Post-war emigration

After the war, the industrial nations went through a boom time in the late 1940s and 1950s and looked overseas for extra labour. The first choice for many West Indians was the United States or Canada. But in 1952 the United States restricted permanent immigration by West Indians to a hundred a year. After that, the only work was seasonal farm work. Later, Canada put similar restrictions on permanent immigration. That left Britain where it was possible for British subjects to settle without restriction.

The first Jamaicans to emigrate booked their own passages on one of the few steamers travelling to Britain in 1948. Some numbers followed whenever there was a ship until the early 1950s. Then travel agencies began to organise emigration on regular services and sometimes lent emigrants the money to pay for their passage. In Barbados, the organisation was even more thorough. The local government (still under British control) provided the loans. It encouraged British employers to open offices to recruit workers for hospitals, the bus and railway services and hotels.

In 1962, the Commonwealth Immigration Act stopped free entry from the black and Asian parts of the Commonwealth. Entry could be only with a work voucher and the numbers of these was limited year by year. A census in Britain in 1966 showed that its population of West Indians, including their children born in Britain, was made up of 273,700 Jamaicans and 180,300 from the rest of the English-speaking Caribbean. Half the population of Montserrat emigrated to Britain in the 1950s.

Advantages and disadvantages

Other surveys of Britain's Caribbean population showed that the emigrants were much more likely to have come from towns than rural areas. They were more likely to be skilled or semi-skilled than unskilled and they were much more likely to have had jobs in the Caribbean than to have been unemployed. This was true of the women who moved to jobs in Britain as well as the men. In the mid-1960s each West Indian household in Britain was sending home about £88 a year.

The surveys show one of the disadvantages of emigration. Although it has helped the Caribbean countries to cope with hard times it has often been the more skilled people who have moved. This was again true when the United States re-opened its doors to West Indian settlers in 1965. In the next ten years more than 200,000 emigrated there. Among them were 17,000 with technical, professional and clerical qualifications which might have played an important part in developing the West Indian economy and public services.

Emigrants have also been the younger people and more often men than women. The main advantage of their leaving has been the remittances which have helped to make life easier for relatives. Yet the story of immigration since the 1890s shows that it is an unreliable way of providing a living. Poor trade or prejudice against immigrants can close the door to movement for work almost overnight.

Assignments

1 a) *Use a blank map of the Caribbean or draw your own. Name the British territories and indicate the alternative crops which developed successfully during the nineteenth century.*
   b) *Choose two of these crops and explain how and why they developed.*

2 a) *What problems faced the development of the cocoa and banana industries in the British Caribbean in the nineteenth century?*
   b) *Explain why alternative crops to sugar developed in the islands of the eastern Caribbean.*

3 *Read this extract from page 79 and then answer the questions which follow:*
'Many colonies still relied too much on sugar and the price was falling sharply in the 1890s. The British government's method of dealing with the crisis was to send the Norman Commission in 1896.'

a) *Which British Caribbean colonies 'relied too much on sugar' in the second half of the nineteenth century?*
b) *Produce a graph or chart to show that the price of sugar was falling sharply in the 1890s.*
c) *Explain briefly what was the Norman Commission and what were its main recommendations.*

4 a) *Draw a map to indicate the areas to which British West Indians emigrated during the nineteenth century.*
b) *Explain why emigrants from the British Caribbean were specifically attracted to two of the areas indicated.*
c) *What were the main results of emigration for any British Caribbean territory?*

11 USING NATURAL RESOURCES

In 1897 the Norman Commission had suggested ways of finding alternatives to sugar. Nearly all their ideas were concerned with new food or raw material exports to Europe. It said little about the possibilities for local industries which would keep wealth in the Caribbean. One of its few suggestions was that the pitch lake in Trinidad could be developed. In fact this had begun earlier. In 1886 the Trinidad colonial government had allowed an American businessman, A. L. Barber, to take asphalt from the pitch lake in return for a payment on each load. His company had done this until 1925 when the government gave the rights to the Trinidad Lake Company in return for higher payments

per load. By that time the district around the pitch lake was the centre of a far more important industry, oil.

Oil

Beginnings in Trinidad

In 1857 an American company drilled one of the first successful oil wells in the world in Trinidad. The company was short of cash and there was a poor market for oil, thirty years before motor cars were invented. So it soon went out of business. The same happened to two other companies in the 1860s. After 1869 no more oil wells were sunk until 1902. By then there was a growing demand for petrol for cars. An Englishman, Randolph Rust, borrowed money from a Canadian company and sank a well near his estate at Guayguare. Eight more wells followed in the next five years.

Rust had shown the possibilities for Trinidad oil. The British government was interested because it had plans to change its navy from coal to oil. A British-owned company was set up in 1910 and began bringing up oil and refining it. In 1913 two larger companies joined in. By the end of the First World War, there were several more companies. Between them they had built five refineries, connected by pipe lines to the wells inland from the coast. Ships were calling to refuel at Point-a-Terre/Port Fortin and in 1914 the first tanker had called to take 6,000 tons bought by the British navy.

Between the wars

Between the wars the industry's growth became slower because oil prices fell in the world slump around 1930. The weaker companies collapsed and sold out to three large companies, Trinidad Leaseholds Limited, (TLL), the American-owned APEX and United British Oilfields of Trinidad (UBOT) which was a subsidiary of

Fig. 11.1 *Pitch lake workers in Trinidad in the 1930s.*

Shell. Yet even slower growth led to a steady increase from the 1.9 million tonnes of oil produced in 1919. By 1938 it had become 20 million.

Oil changed the face of south-west Trinidad. Forest, bush and deserted plantations were cleared to criss-cross the area with roads and railways. Labourers cleared the trees with axes. Men with shovels and women carrying trays of earth on their heads moved hundreds of tons of earth to make cuttings and embankments. Along the coast new ports and oil works were built. Behind grew modern towns such as Fortin which had been a settlement with a few huts when the first oil was drilled.

At first it was in roads, railways and building that black creoles had their best chance of work connected with oil. Most skilled jobs in the oilfields and refineries were taken by the British, Americans or Europeans. Blacks did begin to be trained for skilled work in the 1920s but many left to work in the Venezuelan oil fields. In Trinidad the work force was racially segregated and black workers were paid less for equal work. In Venezuela status and pay were equal.

The Second World War

The Second World War brought another boom for the industry. The British Empire needed oil for its ships, aircraft, tanks and other war vehicles. Trinidad's oil shipments could be protected by British and American forces far more easily than Middle Eastern oil. One year before the war, Trinidad provided 44.2 per cent of British Empire-produced oil. By 1946 it had risen to 65 per cent. New refineries and plants to produce aviation fuel had been built. In the middle of the war, 80 per cent of Trinidad's earnings came from oil. Even so, the industry gave work to about 15,000 people compared with the 40,000 who had jobs connected with sugar.

Post-war developments

After the war, the number of cars and aircraft in use world-wide rose steeply. Trinidad's oil production rose too. An important cause of the increase was the shift from drilling on land to offshore oil fields under the sea. The largest of these was the Soldado field discovered in 1954. By 1961 it was Trinidad's major oil field. Another reason for the increase was that Trinidad became an important refiner of crude oil from other parts of the world. TLL built a new refinery plant in the early 1950s. By 1956 it was refining 80,000 barrels a day. In that year Texaco bought TLL. By 1965 the company was refining 345,000 barrels a day. Some came from nearby Venezuela and most of the rest was brought in by Texaco. Trinidad was ideally placed to refine crude oil from Texaco's Middle East wells and pass it on as gasoline or other products to the USA and countries in the Caribbean.

Refining helped to balance out the fact that Trinidad's oil fields are small and poor producers by world standards. Even in the 1970s a Trinidad well produced about 30 barrels a day as compared with an average of 4,000 barrels for a Middle East well. The total output from Trinidad made up only 0.45 per cent of world production. Refining gave the country's oil industry extra value and extra earnings. Another importance of refining is that it leads to chemical by-products used as fertilisers or detergents and for making plastics. In the late 1960s, Trinidad was able to sell chemical products to seventy different countries. Altogether her various oil industries accounted still for 80 per cent of the island's exports. Yet it was not easy to pass on this advantage to the majority of Trinidadians. In the 1960s only 5 per cent of the country's workers had jobs in oil, at a time when unemployment among other workers was around 15 per cent.

Only a few foreign-owned companies had the funds to build the new refineries, chemical works and harbours for new huge tankers like the five which called each day at Port Fortin. In the 1950s and early 1960s this meant that the smaller companies sold out to BP (British Petroleum), Shell and Texaco. Between them they produced 98 per cent of Trinidad's oil. After independence the Trinidad government began to repatriate much of the oil industry and bought a large part of the shares in BP in 1969.

In 1975 it nationalised the Shell Company in Trinidad and renamed it Trinoc.

Dutch oil

Trinidad's oil fields lay in the same rocks as Venezuela's eastern oil fields. The Dutch colonies of Aruba and Curaçao lie offshore from the western oil fields. This explains why a major refining industry grew up there. It began when Shell, a Dutch company, first drilled oil around Lake Maracaibo in 1913. The company did not want to risk building a refinery in Venezuela because it thought the country's politics were unstable. It was also difficult to get ocean-going ships through the shallow coast waters.

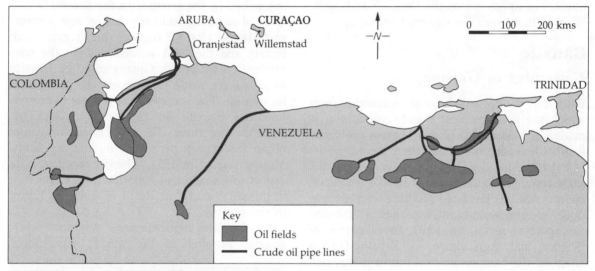

Map 11 *Aruba and Curaçao are well placed to refine oil from western Venezuela. Trinidad takes oil from the eastern oil fields.*

Fig. 11.2 *The oil refineries at Curaçao.*

The two Dutch colonies seemed safer in politics and more suitable for shipping. So, from 1918 Shell shipped the crude flat-bottomed boats to a refinery they built in Curaçao. By 1940 there were refineries, storage depots and oil factories on both Curaçao and Aruba. The industry employed about 15,000 workers. This was roughly the same as in Trinidad, but a large number of employees on the Dutch islands were West Indians from the eastern Caribbean.

Bauxite

Beginnings in Guyana

Bauxite is the ore which contains alumina from which the light stainless metal, aluminium, is made. In 1868 and 1873 government geologists in British Guiana noted that there were deposits of bauxite along the Demerara River. About the same time, geologists found it in the 'red earth' countryside in Jamaica. Nothing further was done because aluminium was then a new and unimportant metal. In 1910, the Director of Science and Agriculture in British Guiana analysed the bauxite ore and found it was rich in alumina.

Five years later an American, George Mackenzie, began buying up large areas of land, saying that he wanted to grow oranges. His real aim was clear when he started the Demerara Bauxite Company in 1916. A year later he exported the first ore from British Guiana. The Guyanese bauxite seams run under the border into Dutch Surinam. In 1922 the Surinam Bauxite Company exported its first ore.

There are three main stages in making aluminium. First, the bauxite is mined by scooping it from the ground with mechanical shovels. Then there comes the extraction of 1 tonne of alumina from every $2\frac{1}{2}$ tonnes of bauxite, by crushing, dissolving in caustic soda and drying into a fine powder. Finally alumina is smelted into aluminium, using great quantities of electrical power.

The ore that Mackenzie exported set a pattern. For the next half century most of the extraction and all the smelting was done in North America. Mackenzie's Demerara Bauxite Company was a subsidiary of ALCAN, the Aluminium Company of Canada which itself was a subsidiary of ALCOA, the Aluminium Company of America.

The Second World War

Production of Guyanese ore developed slowly in the inter-war years while Jamaican ore lay untouched in the ground. In the Second World War, aluminium suddenly had a new importance. It was vital for parts of the aircraft which Britain and the USA needed to fight the war. Production in British Guiana rose. In Jamaica surveys were made to pinpoint the best places for mining. The surveys came too late to provide Jamaican bauxite for the war but ALCOA, ALCAN and three other American companies began buying up properties on the ore fields. Mining started in 1952. The ore was taken for export to Canada and America from Ocho Rios in the north and Port Esquivel and Port Kaiser in the south.

By the late 1950s Jamaica was the largest bauxite supplier in the world, exporting 5

Fig. 11.3 *Bauxite mining in Jamaica.*

million tonnes per year. Surveys had shown that her reserves could amount to 600 million tonnes. At the same time, Guyana ranked fifth in the world and had reserves of about 500 million tonnes. A little further east, bauxite was the most important export from Surinam.

The value of bauxite to the West Indian countries was far less at first than it might have been. The companies paid royalties – an amount per load – on the value of the ore they exported. But ore is worth only a quarter as much as alumina after extraction and only a twenty-fifth as much as aluminium after smelting. Employment and profits from these processes were reserved for America and Canada. Mining in Jamaica and Guyana used advanced machinery so it created very few jobs against the large areas of land which were torn up. In Jamaica, most of the mining takes place on cattle raising land. The government insisted that it was turned again into pasture once the bulldozers had finished ripping out the bauxite.

Increasing the Caribbean share

Even more valuable to Jamaica's income were the negotiations that the government started with the companies over extracting bauxite in the island. At length, the companies agreed to open two small alumina plants on the island. In 1961 they did the same in Guyana. The plants brought more employment and higher royalties but the gains still seemed unfairly small. Even by 1975 when there were five alumina plants in Jamaica, their total exports were 2 million tonnes compared with 15 million tonnes of raw bauxite. Guyana had even lower proportions of bauxite to ore.

In the 1970s both Jamaica and Guyana took stronger measures. Guyana nationalised the Demerara Bauxite Company in 1971 and Reynolds Metals in 1974. In that year Jamaica nationalised the Reynolds Metal business and raised by five times the royalties on bauxite.

Tourism

The tourist's vision

Sun, clean beaches and clear water are important natural resources. To the people of the countries of the industrialised world they are also scarce. In the years after the Second World War the countries of North America and Europe were enjoying a post-war boom leading to higher incomes and longer holidays. These came just at the time that aircraft improved enough to open regular and cheap airline services.

In North America that also meant that many shipping companies turned their liners into cruise ships so holiday-makers had two ways of reaching the Caribbean. In Europe only the wealthiest could afford the time and expense of a cruise across the Atlantic. Yet, as Europe's air services grew so did its tourist industry. Travel agents linked up with airlines to offer package holidays where the flight and the hotel were booked together. Cheap packages changed European holiday-making habits. In 1951 only two million Britains spent their holidays abroad. The number had risen four times by 1971.

Of course, most tourists from America and Europe did not make for the West Indies. Caribbean holidays gained a reputation for being in a superior class. They were taken mostly by those who could afford a holiday in winter when Europe and much of North America is cold and wet. Tourists also set out with romantic visions of the Caribbean.

Many Americans and Europeans thought of themselves as going to the islands of Captain Morgan and the buccaneers, lands where rum flowed freely and smuggling ended only yesterday. They expected to sit under palm trees and watch limbo dancing and carnival processions. From 1959, Americans who had gone to the casinos and clubs in Cuba were no longer welcome after Castro's revolution. They looked for similar holidays either in the Bahamas and Bermuda or in the countries of the Commonwealth Caribbean.

The Caribbean response

Tourism was a great economic opportunity especially for the small islands which had no bauxite or oil, very few small industries and populations who could not all find work in agriculture. Island governments captured an important share of the new international tourism for their people. They did this by offering incentives to hotel companies who were usually North American and sometimes European. The incentives were financial advantages. There might be a tax 'holiday' for the first few years of a business. Import duties on building materials, furniture and food were lowered or dropped altogether. Sometimes there were government money grants.

In return the island people had the chance of jobs in the hotels themselves, although rarely as managers or senior staff. Outside the hotel there was extra work for the people who worked on new airports and roads. There was a boom in service trades supplying food and drink, driving taxis or attending beaches. New forms of work came in handicrafts and the shops which sold the goods to tourists.

The balance sheet

For an island such as Antigua, tourism was an important step in breaking through the disadvantages of centuries when livings could be earned only from sugar and sea-island cotton. The island's government had money for schemes of social development and health improvement. Its people had at least some choice of employment as well as a new airport and a deeper harbour. The same was true in Barbados where 6,000 people worked in hotels alone in 1972. In Jamaica, the tourist industry developed along the beaches of the north coast. In 1961 over 20,000 tourists visited the island and spent an estimated £13 million – nearly four times the country's earnings on bauxite royalties.

Many West Indians believed that tourism also had severe disadvantages. A large part of the profits went overseas to foreign shareholders in hotel companies. Local agriculture did not gain much because large amounts of foreign food were imported to suit tourists' tastes. The new employment did not lead to many opportunities for local people to gain valuable new skills. The most senior and skilled work – and the best paid – was often reserved for foreigners.

The industry could not even rely on its earnings staying the same. A change in prosperity and employment in America and Europe can lead to a dramatic fall in the number of tourists and the amount they spend. This happened in the world recession of the mid-1970s. However, tourism has made a major contribution to improving the living standards of people on many islands.

Timber

From the days of the earliest settlements British Honduras had exported logwood, for making dyes, and mahogany for furniture. Logwood cutting was ruined when Europeans developed artificial aniline dyes from coal in the 1860s. On the other hand demand for mahogany rose in the nineteenth century when it was used for fitting out railway carriages. Yet the industry remained in a backward condition with harsh conditions for workers until well into the twentieth century.

In the early twentieth century there was no road outside Belize City. Timber was cut by fellers who moved out of the town to live in wretched conditions in camps through the cutting season. The greatest distance a tree could be cut from a river was about eight kilometres. A waggon or 'camion' drawn by up to 16 oxen could manage to carry it that short way to the river bank where it had to wait until rains lifted the water level enough to float the trunk down to the sea. There it was loaded, unsawn, on to ships bound for Europe. In working conditions, transport and technology it was an altogether primitive way of developing a natural resource.

Changes before 1945

The first improvement came in 1905 when work started on blasting away granite outcrops and deepening parts of the Belize River. Log transport by water became easier and steam launches could travel upstream to take workers out to the camps. But there was much more to be done. A major problem was that timber was cut in an uncontrolled way with no thought about helping replacement trees to grow for future use. In 1922 a Forest Department was set up to supervise replanting. In the 1920s, too, came the first use of tractors and short tracks of railway to move timber as far as 64 kilometres from the river. This opened up new areas but they were still linked with water transport which discouraged schemes for building the roads which the colony so greatly needed. An important improvement came in 1933 when at last a sawmill was opened at Belize City. For the first time the timber could be loaded on to ships as planks not as whole trunks and logs. The mill also brought a little additional employment.

Post-war changes

After the Second World War, the changes were on a greater scale. Heavy trucks and bulldozers cleared the first all-weather roads which meant that timber could be carried swifty and cheaply all the year round. Fellers no longer had to spend a season in the forests finding their own trees, building a platform clear of the roots and then bringing them down with an axe. Instead chain saws were used to clear the jungle growth and to cut through the trunks. By 1965 the country had twenty-six sawmills in operation and many of these were set up near the cutting operations so that the timber made its overland journey in the form of logs. There was one disadvantage to these mechanical improvements. They meant that increased timber production did not mean extra jobs. In fact the number of workers in the forest industries fell by 700 between 1940 and 1965.

At the same time the Forestry Department was developing more ways of replanting, including growing mahogany saplings among corn grown by Indian farmers. After three or four years the farmers were ready to move to a new site and the trees were ready to push their own way upward. Even so, there were large areas of northern forest where timber had been cut unwisely. Smaller landowners had cut only the largest and most profitable trees leaving the rest to struggle for space. Where this had been done it would be difficult to encourage new growth of first class timber for the end of the century.

In 1940 the government of British Honduras began to look seriously at the country's wealth in pine forests which cover about an eighth of the country. A programme of cutting pine area by area and sawing it in temporary sawmills was started. Cleared areas were replanted with pine to take advantage of the fact that a tree is mature in about twenty-five years.

Assignments

1 a) *In which British Caribbean territories did the following industries develop up to 1962: i) oil; ii) bauxite; iii) timber; iv) tourism?*
   b *Take two of these industries and for each account for its growth and development up to 1962.*
   c) *List two advantages and two problems faced by the development of any one of these industries in any one British Caribbean territory.*

2 a) *Explain the part that foreign companies played in developing: oil, bauxite, timber and tourism up to 1962.*
   b) *What benefits did the British Caribbean territories derive from the development of the above named industries?*
   c) *What further benefits do you think the British Caribbean could have gained from the development of these industries?*

12 CLASS, POVERTY AND CROWN COLONY RULE 1900–45

Classes in West Indian society around 1900

At the end of apprenticeship in 1838 most colonies had a strong white plantocracy as an upper class and the masses of ex-slaves as a labouring class. Almost all this labouring class was connected with plantation work or domestic service. In between the upper and labouring classes there was a small middle class of clerks and petty traders who were mostly coloured.

By 1900 the white upper class had shrunk in numbers. The middle class had grown much larger and had people with many different occupations. The labouring class had grown because of the rise in population. But it too had become more varied. Alongside the men and women who still worked in agriculture there were large numbers in different town occupations. This new social order of the early 1900s was the background to the political changes of the next forty years.

The upper and middle classes

Upper class lives

In the small colonies the white plantocracy had often become very small, especially where sugar had become less important or abandoned altogether. Whites were also very few in numbers in mainland territories such as Belize and Guyana. In Barbados and Jamaica there was still a large English creole upper class living either in great houses or in large town houses. In Trinidad, there was also a French creole class of fifty or so families who owned a large part of the island's wealth and had great power in some districts.

Life for upper class whites had changed much less than than it had for the other classes. Most lived a life of leisure supported by many servants. One way they had of measuring their social position was the number of specialist servants such as coach drivers, cooks, household servants, personal maids and children's servants. They ate English-style meals and gave dinner parties and receptions for each other. Apart from that their lives were often quite empty. A few men sat on the governor's councils, but many did little more than supervise their estates. The women had even less to do. Their social position meant they could not be seen doing any household work or caring for children. In any case children were often sent to England or France for their education.

Racism was often strong. People in this group would not mix socially with black or coloured people, however wealthy. In England their wealthy cousins would take an interest in the affairs of a village, its church and its school. Planters' wives could not do anything like this because it would mean caring for the black descendants of slaves.

Middle class lives

The middle class had been helped to grow by the changes brought in the early years of Crown colony government described in Chapter 7. Towns had become important and so had simple social services such as the elementary schools and some medical dispensaries. Town people needed doctors, druggists, shopkeepers, tailors and civil servants. Town businesses required managers, clerks, and warehousemen. The local governments needed teachers, civil servants, post office clerks, harbour supervisors, school inspectors and building engineers. Newspapers started and there were jobs for journalists and printers. Private citizens and businesses used solicitors for their business deals.

The key to a middle class job was secondary education. Secondary schools charged fees and it was often a struggle to scrape the money together. Norman Manley's mother made great sacrifices when her husband died penniless leaving her a run-down property.

> Mother had one great fixed determination in life – to see that her children, two boys and two girls, got a good education. Belmont was a hard place to manage. It was quite undeveloped and like so many of the old derelict places in Jamaica it carried on as best it could with a little of everything: logwood, sold after being cut into lengths of heart wood with the bark and sap chipped off; a few cattle; a few tenants; a little cocoa. Single-handed she managed all these things and even found time to persuade the authorities to allow her to open a post office at Belmont itself which we took charge of. She made all our clothes, made jellies when guavas were in, kept a small chicken farm . . . When night came she disappeared to her own room to write letters to her few remaining friends, nearly all of them deserted her when she married a near black man . . .

Whatever the struggle, it was usually whites and coloureds who had the best chance of getting a secondary education. Blacks could rarely afford the school fees and were often anyway kept out of secondary schools by rules against admitting children of unmarried parents. But in all colonies there were a few blacks who made their way into the middle class either through education or by success in farming or trading.

It would be wrong to think of the middle class as a single group. There was a range of earnings and types of occupation. At one end were owners of large businesses in Port of Spain, Kingston and Bridgetown whose earnings matched the wealth of the white upper class. Next in earnings and social position came people such as the best-known doctors or lawyers and the head teachers of the most famous secondary schools. Success for these often started with winning an island university scholarship at secondary school. This paid for them to go to study in England. Norman Manley did this and so did Grantley Adams, a future prime minister of the West Indies Federation. He won the Barbados scholarship and read law at Oxford. Eric Williams left the Queen's

Royal College in Trinidad to begin six years at Oxford where he was a brilliant student of history. It was more usual, however, to study law or medicine which were two professions open to creoles.

Towards the other end of the middle classes the jobs were humbler but just as important to the new society that was slowly growing in the colonies. Perhaps the largest single group were the elementary school teachers, who were far more poorly paid than they would have been in Britain. Teaching in elementary schools became one of the first careers open almost entirely to local born men and some women. Living at around the same level were many storekeepers and clerks. In between them and the wealthiest businessmen and busiest lawyers and doctors were all sorts of civil servants, journalists, managers, health and school inspectors.

Living standards in the middle class varied as much as earnings. The richest businessmen were really part of the white upper class. Sometimes they shared the same prejudices. In Trinidad, for instance, most large commercial businesses were owned by white members of the middle class. They preferred to employ white creoles or men from Britain as junior partners and managers, rather than coloured workers who usually rose no higher than clerk. The poorer paid 'white-collar' workers went through a life-long struggle to keep a small house, decent clothes and perhaps a domestic servant who was very badly paid.

Middle class politics

In 1899 an Englishman described a public meeting in Jamaica, saying: 'One's gaze travels over hundreds of brown faces and it is only here and there that sight is caught of a darker skin.' He went on to say that the black working class and peasant farmers were satisfied with the benefits given to them by Crown colony government. This was far from the truth but it does remind us that the middle classes were most active in campaigns for political change around 1900 and shortly after.

One thing that united the middle classes especially in Jamaica and Trinidad was the belief that they should have some say in how their colony was ruled. In 1900 this was very limited. In Jamaica there had been a legislative council since 1884. It had power to pass local ordinances and to advise the governor. The majority of men on the council were official members appointed by the governor. Then there were fourteen elected members, one for each parish. There was a handful of elected council members in some other colonies. There were six in the Leewards and twenty-two in British Guiana (eight on the Court of Policy and fourteen on the Combined Court).

The right to vote for these few men was fixed on a wealth basis. Voters needed to have a regular salary or to own land or buildings. The wealth qualifications for being a candidate were even higher. The result was that the majority of the elected members were planters or the wealthiest businessmen. They were not the sort of people likely to disagree with the decisions of the governor or his officials.

This did not satisfy the new middle class and opposition to Crown colony government grew. In Trinidad it was especially strong because there were no elected members on the legislative council. The only body with elected members was the Port of Spain borough council. This became a centre of middle class opposition to the governor and officials.

Agitation in Trinidad

In 1897 the governor and his officials put forward a scheme to make the borough council pay for drainage, lighting and tramways in the new districts which had grown up on the edge of the town. The money was to come from increasing the rates on properties in Port of Spain. The borough council protested at being forced to charge these extra rates. The Colonial Office forbade the governor to give any help to the council unless it agreed to have its financial affairs inspected by a government official and to charge higher rates. The council refused to agree and its powers were handed over to a committee appointed by the governor.

This meant the end of the one body in Trinidad which gave people a say in government and the way that money was spent. The sense of grievance against the Crown colony system

Fig. 12.1 *Crowds gathering in Port of Spain, 1903, during the protest against the water charges. The large building on the right, the Red House, was burnt down later that day.*

increased. In 1903 it broke into the open when the government decided to make Port of Spain householders pay more for their water supply. Riots broke out and sixteen people died, mostly from bullets fired by the police. A Commission of Enquiry said that the leaders of the agitation against the government were:

> . . . certain coloured lawyers, some of whom have studied law in England, coloured tradesmen doing a substantial business and some less reputable persons, while a few persons of English birth, including the editors of two newspapers, have thrown their lot in with them.

Thus in Trinidad, as in other colonies, the opposition to Crown colony government came most strongly from traders and professional townspeople. They sought a share in government and the right to vote – but only for their own class. Most middle class agitators refused to join up with black and working class organisations. Some spoke of their fear that the leaders of black organisations would teach the 'uneducated' working class that 'demands can be enforced by terrorist methods.'

Legislative reform associations

In Trinidad, the middle class opponents of Crown colony government formed the Legislative Reform Committee in 1901 and called for the right to elect some members to the legislative council. Similar groups were set up in other colonies, such as the Representative Government Association which T. A. Marryshow started in Grenada in 1914. Others sprang up in 1921 when the news leaked out that the British government was sending the Under-Secretary of State for the Colonies, Major Wood, to investigate the working of Crown colony government. All the associations demanded that there should be some elected members where there had been none and that elected members should have a share in day-to-day government.

The Wood Commission

Wood's Caribbean tour has been called the greatest non-event of the century. He and his team listened carefully to all the Representative

Fig. 12.2 *The Wood Commission in Jamaica, 1921. Major Wood is the tall man in the centre. Two members of the commission are on the far left. The others are island officials, including two police officers on the right.*

Associations' proposals but little was done to give the West Indians a more 'effective voice' in government. The British government was not prepared to give up the governors' 'reserve' powers to overrule the councils in matters which they thought were of 'paramount importance'. As an excuse for doing very little the British were able to point to the many divisions of opinion in the colonies.

For Jamaica, Wood proposed that the number of elected members should be increased to give them a majority of four over the nominated members. The leading opponent of Crown colony government was a lawyer, J. A. G. Smith. He and his supporters refused to accept this small change because the governor was to keep his power to overrule the council. As a result no changes were made to the Jamaican constitution.

In some eastern Caribbean colonies a few minor changes were made. The council in Grenada was given its first elected members and three additional elected members were placed on the councils in St Lucia, St Vincent and Dominica. In Montserrat, St Kitts and Antigua nothing was done because a few prominent planters and merchants argued that to have more elected members would increase the power of uneducated blacks.

In Trinidad, the merchants and businessmen asked for strictly limited changes: only a few elected members, with the right to vote restricted to wealthier people. They did not want to see popular movements such as the Trinidad Workingmen's Association or the Young India Party gain political power. To established businessmen, these organisations smacked of socialist or even Bolshevist politics. They claimed that if such people were given a political voice foreigners would not invest money in the island's new oil and asphalt industries.

Wood also found the East Indian opinion divided. Some supported the Young India Party which wanted candidates to stand for election in any district whatever the ethnic group to which they belonged. Other East Indians feared that their separate identity and culture would be swamped by the black vote and asked for their 'communal' representatives. After listening to the arguments, Wood suggested only very slight changes to the Trinidad constitution. The legislative council was given its first seven elected members but they were outnumbered by twelve official and six nominated members. The elected members had to be wealthy, with an income of at least $1,920 and the right to vote was given only to men earning $300 a year or owning expensive property. Only one out of every five Trinidadian men of voting age qualified. A few women could vote provided they were wealthy and over thirty.

In British Guiana the Combined Court had a majority of elected members and the power to decide all matters concerning finance and taxation. It asked Wood to give it stronger powers and the right to pass laws on certain non-financial matters. Wood refused but said it would be a mistake to take away the financial powers of the Combined Court as the Guyanese system of government had 'special historical traditions behind it'.

This advice was ignored four years later when there were complaints that the colony was heading for bankruptcy and a Royal Commission arrived to investigate. The Commissioners blamed poor planning by the elected members of the Combined Court which included men from all communities: African, East Indian and Portuguese. In fact, the shortage of money was due, as usual, to falling world sugar prices, but the Commission still recommended that more power be given to the governor.

A local Commission was set up to work out the details with only one Guyanese, E. G. Woolford, allowed to take part. It reported that the development of British Guiana was held up by the many deadlocks between the governor-controlled Court of Policy and the elected Combined Court. It recommended that the two courts should be replaced by a single Governor's Council of sixteen appointed and fourteen elected members. This meant that the power of elected Guyanese politicians to control finance was abolished. E. G. Woolford refuse to sign the Commission's recommendations but the British Parliament passed them in 1928.

The working classes

The largest social group in the West Indies was made up of the black descendants of slaves and the indentured Indian labourers. In some places there were also small numbers of poor whites such as the 'redlegs' of Barbados.

The single biggest occupation was agriculture, either as a plantation labourer or as a smallholder with fewer than 4 hectares. But as sugar had declined and the West Indian population rose, many labourers had moved to other work. Some found it as petty traders or road labourers in the country districts but very many made their way to the towns. Workers who moved to other colonies usually went to the towns too. There were a large number of these migrants in and around Port of Spain where a quarter of all the people in Trinidad lived. The other great magnet for people seeking work, mostly from Jamaica itself, was Kingston.

In the towns the labourers looked for jobs in the ports and warehouses, in public works and building. This was unskilled casual work. A few were able to take skilled work, perhaps as printers, carpenters in a furniture making business or as a superior type of tailor. Their numbers were far smaller than those who did domestic work in the houses of the upper and middle classes.

Women often played a full part as wage-earners, although they were paid less than men. In the countryside they did much of the field work on plantations and smallholdings. In towns they worked in domestic service or took in washing. Many were porters loading coal or bananas or shifting the earth for new roads in Trinidad's oil fields.

Poverty: housing, diet and health

There is poverty in the West Indies, as everywhere else in the world, today. From 1900 and up to the 1930s poverty was part of the lives of nearly all working people and their families. In 1936 a British professor summed it up in this way:

> A social and economic study of the West Indies is necessarily a study of poverty.

What he meant was that the colonies were not rich enough to give everyone regular work, decent housing, education and health care. The reason was that European thinking about the

Fig. 12.3 *Labourers' homes on a plantation in Jamaica.*

97

right sort of economy for the Caribbean had not really changed since the days of slavery. Then the colonies had exported sugar and imported almost everything else including large amounts of food. When the Royal Commissions came in 1882 and 1897 they could only suggest that the colonies varied the foods they exported. They did not even recommend that they should try to grow and process more of their own food instead of importing so much. Still less did they think about starting local industries which would give work.

Housing

Housing conditions were one of the clearest signs of poverty in all colonies. Sixty years after emancipation, large numbers of labourers still lived on plantations. Most planters put these workers into barracks, lines or ranges. These were likely to be long wooden buildings with iron roofs divided into a series of single rooms. Each room was home for a family or for three or four single men. Labourers who had their own huts on the plantation or their own smallholding did little better. Almost everywhere huts were single rooms with walls of wood or bamboo packed with mud and roofs made of palm branches or cane trash. It was only the more successful peasants who could be sure of a wooden-roofed cottage with a porch.

Town workers' housing was often just as bad. For workers who had moved to a large town, such as Kingston, where land was scarce, housing could be worse than in the countryside. Only a skilled worker with a regular job could afford the rent for a home of his own. The rest would have to take a room in a 'range' which gave no more room or privacy than a plantation barrack. Conditions could be unhealthier because the ranges were packed together in areas without pavements or drains. Hundreds of people shared a few latrines and water from a few taps or wells.

Diet

The lack of sanitation, fresh air and clean water was a major cause of bad health. Another cause was poor diet. In many places people went hungry at times, but everywhere their diet was always short of essential proteins and vitamins. Throughout the West Indies there was a shortage of fresh milk. This was serious for adults. For children it was often fatal. If a mother's health was poor she might not be able to feed her baby with her own milk and there was no supply of cow's milk. In most places there simply was not enough protein. People near the coast might have fresh fish. In other places some imported codfish was an occasional luxury.

The average amount of meat eaten by all classes in Kingston was a pound per person per month, which included the much larger amounts eaten by the better-off. Daily meals varied from place to place, but almost everywhere the largest part was a starchy food such as rice, yams, cassava or corn. Beans were eaten widely but bread was often not available. Coffee might be drunk by itself or with a splash of condensed milk, but many people drank no more than sugared water.

The poor quality of Caribbean diet was a man-made problem. The West Indies has the soil to produce fresh foods, milk and meat but the land was given over to export crops or lay undeveloped. Trinidad supplied Europe and North America with sugar and cocoa and yet 80 per cent of everything eaten on the island was imported. Jamaica supplied Europe and North America with sugar and bananas but 25 per cent of her imports were foods. She even exported salt (from two of her small islands) to Canada for curing the saltfish she imported.

Health

It is not difficult to understand the effects on health of poor housing, bad sanitation, filthy water supplies and poor diet. There was a terrifying list of common diseases. The single most important cause of death in adults was tuberculosis which is due to damp and overcrowded housing. Malaria, yaws and venereal diseases were widespread. Hookworm disease affected people in every district. In parts of Trinidad the victims numbered between 79 and 98 per cent of the population. Hookworm bred where there was poor sanitation but it was caught mostly by children and adults who had no shoes.

The worst thing about malaria, yaws and hookworm was that they led to weakness which could last for life. Some surveys showed that hardly anyone among the working population was free from such weakness. Second-rate health was a fact of life. Children and infants did not escape either. An official enquiry among schoolchildren in Georgetown in 1918 found that over half had parasites in the stomach, four out of ten had skin diseases, three out of ten were undernourished and a quarter had worm parasites in the skin. Like most children of labourers in the West Indies they did not know what it is to feel healthy and vigorous.

One of the most terrible facts about health even as late as 1938 was the infantile mortality, that is death rate of children who were born but did not live to their first birthday. It varied from 120 per thousand in Trinidad to 216 per thousand in Barbados. Even these figures were an improvement on forty years earlier. In Jamaica the infant death rate had fallen to 137 in 1938 from 175 in 1897.

Three things were needed to tackle the health problem. The first was better public health measures to improve sanitation and water supplies, and introduce vaccination against diseases. The second was simply better housing and diet. The third was medical care. The astonishing fact is that large numbers of West Indians simply never saw a doctor. Most doctors did not want to live in the rural districts. Even in towns the labourers could not afford their fees. Only those who had no chance of earning anything at all were given any medical help. But they paid a price because they had to go into the infirmary of a poor house. One writer described them in 1936:

> All I saw were also overcrowded, yet always with a long waiting list of human wrecks to fill the beds as soon as they had become vacant.

As with so many things, the poor house infirmaries were copied from England but there most had become public hospitals long before.

Education and employment

Elementary schools

The start of elementary education under Crown colony government is described in Chapter 7. Up to the 1930s most children were taught by 'pupil teachers'. These were older pupils, generally between 14 and 18. They spent four hours teaching during the daytime and studied at night under the head teacher. In the countryside, he too would most likely have been a pupil teacher, although a few town head teachers had been to secondary school themselves. At the end of this time, the pupil teachers could take an examination for the teacher's certificate. Only a small proportion passed and many of these did not stay in teaching. The pay was extremely poor, so many ex-pupil teachers looked for jobs as clerks or storemen.

Britain gave up the pupil teacher system in 1902 and, from then, all her teachers had to pass through secondary school and training college. These improvements were not brought to the Caribbean. In 1938, a report had this to say of West Indian education as it was after sixty or seventy years of Crown colony government:

> Teachers in the West Indies are inadequate in number and in training, especially in the smaller islands. Too great reliance is placed on the pupil-teacher system, too little effort is made to attract into the profession those who have received a secondary education.

Other reports in the 1920s and 1930s described the shortage of teachers and books, and the poor school buildings which were often semi-ruins. They noted that many children did not go to school. In the large colonies 80 per cent were enrolled, but in St Vincent it was only 46 per cent. Even enrolled children did not always go to school. Some were often sick, and diseases were easily caught in insanitary school buildings. Others were at work. Planters were keen to use their cheap labour and some families were so poor that their wages were important. A Barbadian school inspector wrote in 1891:

> Children of tender age are toiling in factory, workshop and field, at the expense of their physical growth, their intellectual development and their moral welfare.

In the same year, the Barbadian assembly admitted that it spent one-third of the island's education funds on 500–600 scholars in secondary

Fig. 12.4 *A Jamaican primary school in the 1920s. Pupil teachers can be seen watching the pupils at work. The man on the left is probably the head teacher.*

schools and that two-thirds went to the 23,000 pupils in elementary schools. In Barbados and all the colonies some of the money was spent on 'industrial schools' or 'reformatories', which were grim places where parentless children or those convicted of 'vagrancy' or petty crime were kept at boring tasks.

Teaching and learning

The lowest school attendance was among Indian children in Trinidad and British Guiana. This was mainly because parents were reluctant to send them to schools run by Christian churches or to government schools where the language and culture were different. The result was that Indian children led the tables for illiteracy. In 1911, 97 per cent of them could not read. But illiteracy

was widespread everywhere. In the 1930s it was 43 per cent for all children in Trinidad, 63 per cent for those in Guyana and 30 per cent in Barbados. Some schools were so poor that children ended up semi-literate.

It is difficult to blame parents who did not send children to school when the curriculum did little to help them. Education had been made compulsory in St Kitts, but in 1917 still only 46.2 per cent attended regularly. In that year the subjects in the island's sixteen elementary schools were:

Obligatory: Reading, Writing, Arithmetic, Needlework for girls. Moral Instruction and Tropical Hygiene.

Optional: Elementary science, Geography, Singing and Dancing. Only two optional subjects may be taught, and on condition that the work in the obligatory subjects is sufficiently good.

Like nearly all elementary schools in the British West Indies, teachers in St Kitts were expected to concentrate on the 'three R's'. They were not told to start courses in subjects such as agricultural science, domestic science, mechanics or crafts, which would have helped pupils to go on and earn independent livings.

Secondary schools

Secondary schools charged fees. Most of their pupils went to them after a few years in private fee-paying primary schools. The fees excluded most children of black working people. By the 1930s just a few secondary school scholarships were open to children who had been to public elementary schools but few succeeded. Children in rural elementary schools usually did not have a sound enough education to pass.

The secondary schools were also criticised for having a curriculum which was unsuitable for the needs of the West Indies. The main emphasis was on European literature, history and geography, mathematics and often Latin and Greek. These were the traditional subjects for people taking white-collar jobs in England. They were of very little relevance to life and work in the West Indies. In Britain, secondary schools had also started courses in science and modern languages. Other young people could study engineering and commerce in technical colleges. The people who ruled the West Indian colonies did not see the need for such courses.

Employment

The most important fact behind family poverty was that most men and women workers were only semi-employed. In agriculture this came about for two reasons. On estates most work was seasonal and there would be none in the off seasons. If a family had a smallholding it was most likely to be less than 4 hectares and that was not enough to keep family members busy all year.

It was the same pattern in the town work. Dockers and porters were paid only when ships were in dock. Small craftsmen, furniture makers and people in the building trades could only work when there was a job to do. Even people who did the better paid and more dangerous jobs, such as the wood cutters in Belize and Guyana, had work for only six or seven months in the year.

No wonder that an official enquiry in British Guiana in 1930 said that the majority of manual workers were casual workers. It went on to say that this was partly the result of employers' policies, especially on the plantations:

> The policy of the estates has been to maintain, or even to increase slightly, the number of persons employed, while reducing the total amount paid in wages and the number of days work per week allotted to each labourer.

The report was describing the system of rotational work. Instead of taking on a worker for five or six days or for a whole season a planter took on two workers for two days each. Instead of giving work for a whole season he gave a fortnight each to workers in turn. By doing this he could save on wages. He could simply pay for fewer hours and it was also easier to pay lower rates to a casual worker who was grateful for a short spell of employment. Even without rotations and under-payment, wages were poor. They ranged in sugar from around 1/- for planting to 2/- for cutting, with more for factory and shovel work. Women worked in large numbers but they earned only about two-thirds of the wage for the same job.

The figures mean little to us today but what is important is what wages could buy. One example was given by the Nevis Agricultural and Commercial Society in 1938:

> the minimum requirements for a labourer amount to one shilling and threepence per diem, as shown below:
> Breakfast – Bread 2d., sugar 1d.
> Dinner – Meal or flour 2d., potatoes 1d., meat or fish 2d., lard or butter 1d.
> Supper – Rice 2d., peas 1d., meat or fish 2d., lard or butter 1d.
> In the above estimate there is no provision made for house repair, clothes or for protective nourishing foods such as milk or eggs. Nor is allowance made for household necessities such as oil, matches, soap, starch etc or for church and society dues, provision for sickness, medical fees . . .

The chief industry that gives employment for a period of a few days per week for two or three months in the year is cotton. Sugar-cane cultivation provides very little employment under the present system. Men who are fortunate in getting employment earn one shilling; the women sixpence per diem.

The survey shows how low wages led to all the other aspects of bad social conditions in housing, medical care and diet. Even when the man and wife had a full day's work they were only 3d in hand. It is interesting to try to work out which items should be dropped from the diet on days when between them they earned 1/- or only 6d. What would they do when neither man nor wife worked?

Poverty in the Spanish-speaking islands

The problem of poverty was not limited to the English-speaking Caribbean. In the Spanish-speaking and French-speaking territories poverty was a way of life just as much as it was in the British West Indies. In the Spanish-speaking territories, the real causes were the same. Cuba, Puerto Rico and Dominica were all prevented from developing their own agriculture and industry because of the way the islands concentrated on export crops. The two differences from the English-speaking Caribbean were that sugar was still the outstanding export and that American business had a very strong hold on the economic and social lives of the Spanish-speaking peoples.

Sugar exports and food imports

American sugar companies' money created huge estates which supplied cane by rail to a small number of central factories. In Puerto Rico there were laws which forbade corporations to own more than 243 hectares. They were ignored and by 1917 four American companies owned 477

Fig. 12.5 *A scene in the main street of a small town in Puerto Rico, 1923.*

estates larger than this. In Cuba, the Cuban American Sugar Company owned 20,250 hectares and there were half a dozen companies with similar holdings. In Dominica the spread of American-owned sugar companies meant that the export of sugar grew ten times between 1903 and 1939.

The rise of sugar meant ruin for small farmers growing other crops. Many were forced to sell land after falling into debt. There was a drastic fall in the amount of food crops grown for the local market. The small farmers had to compete with a flood of cheap food from large mechanised farms in the USA. Before 1898, Puerto Rican farmers had grown all the island's rice, which was the main food of the poor. They had also exported large amounts of coffee. In 1934, $6\frac{1}{2}$ million dollars worth of rice was imported from the United States and Puerto Rico was also importing coffee. 80 per cent of the food eaten in Puerto Rico was imported. In Cuba, tobacco fell from being 40 per cent of exports in 1902 to only 10 per cent in 1939.

Employment and wages

As land turned over to sugar, fewer and fewer peasants were able to remain smallholders. If they did, their tobacco and fruit earned them very low incomes. Most became agricultural labourers and then they shared all the problems we have seen in the English-speaking Caribbean. Plantation labour was seasonal, and by 1930 nearly a third of Puerto Ricans were unemployed in the out of crop season. It was also low-paid. Nearly two-thirds of Puerto Rican sugar workers earned less that $100 a year to feed an average family of six. In Cuba, the daily rate for a sugar labourer was 80 cents – and he was reckoned to need 38 dollars a year for his own food.

Just as in Kingston and Port of Spain, workers moved to try their chance in towns such as Havana and San Juan. For some there was seasonal, low-paid work on the railways and docks and in domestic service. But there was another form of work. The large numbers of unemployed and semi-employed workers attracted smaller American companies. They brought work over to be done by cheap labour. Puerto Ricans rolled tobacco into cigars for only pennies a day. Women sewed gloves which had been pre-cut in the United States for a few cents per pair; 40,000 young girls worked as embroiderers for 6 cents an hour. Puerto Rico became known as the sweatshop of the United States and with good reason.

Health and education

Low wages and lack of regular work led to poor diet and housing. Most Puerto Ricans lived in unhealthy villages or in settlements like El Fanguito (little mud) built on a swamp outside San Juan. There was little sanitation and hardly any medical services, except in the cities, for those who could afford them. In 1935 half of all the doctors in Cuba worked in Havana. In 1930 it was estimated that 30,000 Puerto Ricans suffered from tuberculosis, 200,000 from malaria and 600,000 from hookworm disease. The average length of life was about forty-five years, almost twenty less than in the USA.

Elementary education was as defective as it was in the English-speaking colonies. In 1933 over half the children in Cuba were enrolled for elementary school but only one in twenty had a chance to spend more than six years in school.

Assignments

1 a) *Find pictures or make drawings which illustrate the main characteristics of each of the classes (upper, middle and lower) in West Indian society around 1900.*
   b) *For each picture/drawing comment on the main features illustrated.*
   c) *For your territory find out the appropriate numbers which comprised each group.*

2 *What were the main changes that took place in the lives and life styles of the upper, middle*

and lower classes between emancipation and 1900? (You can confine this to your territory or write in general terms for the whole British Caribbean.)

3 *Explain why opposition to Crown colony government came most strongly from traders and professional townspeople.*

4 **a)** *Explain carefully the difference between the old representative system of government and Crown colony government.*
b) *What developments took place in Crown colony governments in the British Caribbean between 1865 and 1944?*

5 *What problems faced the working (lower) classes in the British Caribbean in the second half of the nineteenth century in the areas of employment, housing, education and health care?*

6 *What similarities and what differences existed between social and economic conditions in the British Caribbean and the French- and Spanish-speaking territories before 1935?*

13 THE LABOUR MOVEMENT IN THE BRITISH COLONIES TO 1938

The labour movement before 1914

Labourers' protests

The section on 'Middle class politics' in the last chapter showed how the new middle classes formed organisations to press for political change. For the mass of black and Indian labourers around 1900 political change was something they had no chance of bringing about. Their main need was to change their pay and working conditions as a first step to a better standard of living.

The simplest way of trying to do this was by striking. Strikes were not new in the Caribbean. We saw in Book One how Samuel Sharpe tried to call a strike to force Jamaican planters to free their slaves. Estate labourers struck in many colonies when wages were cut in the 1840s. East Indian indentured labourers were forbidden to strike by law but they held at least a hundred short-lived strikes on the Guyanese plantations between 1886 and 1889. East Indians often went on strike in Trinidad in the later years of indentureship. These estate strikes usually had little success. They were not backed by trade unions and employers could easily find other unskilled workers to replace the strikers.

Craft unions

The first trade unions in the English-speaking Caribbean began among skilled craftsmen in towns. Often they began as friendly societies or burial clubs. Members paid a small weekly fee into a fund which was used to help them in times of sickness or to pay for a funeral. Only people with regular work could do this. In time, some moved on to forming small unions with usually less than a hundred members. In 1889 the carpenters, bricklayers and cigar makers

organised the first craft unions in Jamaica and many others were started in the next twenty years. They often collapsed after a short time.

Some organised strikes, hoping that the employers would not be able to replace them as they were skilled workers. However, most strikes ended in failure including the printers' union strike that Marcus Garvey helped to lead in 1907. In Trinidad a druggist Alfred Richards started the Trinidad Workingmen's Association for skilled workers in 1897. In 1902 it collapsed after a waterfront strike failure and the TWA was not restarted again until 1906.

Unskilled men with casual work found it even harder to build unions. But that did not always prevent them taking strike action. In 1905 the dockworkers in British Guiana stopped work and demanded higher wages and better working conditions. They were led by a Bookers' waterfront worker, Hubert Nathieniel Critchlow. The strike had support from men like A. A. Thorne, a Barbadian scholar who lived in British Guiana and supported the improvement of workingmen's conditions. The government, however, sent troops to brutally suppress the strike.

Foreign encouragement

The early West Indian unionists learned much about trade unionism from Britain and the United States, often from workingmen returning from these countries. By 1900 there were over 2 million members of unions in Britain. In 1901 their leaders took the main part in setting up the British Labour Party. In 1906 29 Labour Party MPs were elected to Parliament in London. The American Federation of Labour was formed in 1886 by Adolph Strasser and Samuel Gompers, although the AFOL never formed a political party.

After the Spanish American War in 1898, the AFOL helped to organise union movements in

Puerto Rico and the Dominican Republic, and it was also active in Jamaica. In the eastern Caribbean, the British Labour Party encouraged unions in British Guiana. For several years the Trinidad Workingmen's Association was affiliated to the British Labour Party. One British Labour MP, Joseph Pointer, visited Trinidad in 1912, which gave the TWA a lot of prestige in the island.

Difficulties

These first unions were weak and short lived and met with violent hostility from employers. Many of the salaried middle classes were suspicious of them. At this time there were no laws to protect the unions or give them the right to strike. Colonial officials usually listened to the employers' side in any dispute. Official action against unions in the Spanish islands was even more severe. In 1912, a 'revolt' by Cuban rural labourers ended when, it was claimed, three thousand were brutally murdered.

Action by employers and governments was only one reason why the early unions were weak. It was difficult to organise the largest group of labourers, who worked seasonally on plantations. Until indentureship ended, East Indian labourers were not allowed to join unions or strike. British and American unions were strongest among miners, railway workers and men in large-scale industry but the West Indies had few such enterprises. Skilled craft unions in the Caribbean were small and usually not eager to take up the cause of unskilled workers.

The First World War and the unions

Effects in the Caribbean

In August 1914, Britain and her allies, France and Russia, went to war with Germany, Austria and Turkey. In 1917 the United States joined Britain and the war of 1914–18 later became known as the First World War. The outbreak of war brought a halt for a time to trade union activities in the Caribbean. Special wartime laws forbade strikes because they would inter-

Fig. 13.1 *Jamaican soldiers setting out to fight in the First World War.*

fere with producing or shipping goods needed for Britain's war effort. But, in the end, the war played an important part in strengthening the Caribbean trade unions.

Many British civil servants were called home to join in the war effort so there was a sharp increase in the number of West Indians in the civil service, police forces and public utility companies. British trade with the colonies fell away and Caribbean artisans and craftsmen were able to greatly increase local manufacture of goods. These new industries pushed along the change in West Indian towns from being administrative and commercial centres mainly for the middle classes to being working places for a non-agricultural labour force. These new urban workers were ready recruits for post-war unions.

Black workers and soldiers

As British and American men were called to fight in the armies they left vacancies which West Indians emigrated to fill. In Britain by 1918 there were 20,000 black workers, both African and West Indian. They worked in the munitions and chemicals industries which were vital to the war effort. More than a thousand black seamen helped bring food to Britain in ships which were hunted by German submarines.

For a year, Britain refused to involve black soldiers in the war. Then in 1915 she formed a West Indies Regiment making it clear that this was not part of the British army. They would have lower rates of pay. No non-Europeans could be officers and they were not to fight against Europeans. Despite this discrimination, 15,000 black West Indians went to fight for Britain. Most of them spent the war doing labour services in Egypt or digging trenches and carrying ammunition to British soldiers facing the Germans in the trenches in France. They were only allowed to see action against Turkish troops.

In 1918, just after the war ended, much of the West Indies Regiment were in Italy. Here they were put to work on tasks such as laundry and digging latrines, while they were given segregated canteens, cinemas and hospitals. Some of their officers protested, including the Trinidadian captain, Arthur Cipriani. The protest was dismissed out of hand by the British commanders. But it left its mark on the future of the Caribbean. Some West Indies Regiment sergeants formed a secret Caribbean League to plan for changes in colonial government and working conditions when they returned home.

While black troops were treated shabbily in Italy, their fellow West Indians were suffering discrimination and violence in Britain itself. As the war ended and soldiers returned home, black workers were sacked from their jobs, especially as seamen. The first half of 1919 saw white mobs attacking black settlers in London and other large British towns. There were similar racial riots in American cities at this time.

The West Indian press reported these cases of racial discrimination and violence. Then thousands of black soldiers and workingmen returned from Britain. Their experiences and local feeling about their treatment led to a time of widespread labour unrest in the West Indies. For two or three years, trade unionists and leaders of the movement for black racial pride had widespread support.

1919 strikes and their results

The Trinidad Workingmen's Association did not succeed as a skilled craft workers' organis-

ation, but in late 1918 new leaders were elected. Many were dockers such as its secretary, William Howard Bishop, and the Barbadian brothers, James and John Brathwaite. Under these new leaders it set out to be an organisation for all Trinidad's working people. In 1919 the TWA called on all workers to join in their struggle for higher wages. Soon there were strikes by dockers, railwaymen, city council employees and asphalt lake workers. Then in late 1919 the dockworkers began another determined strike which was backed by other Port of Spain workers. Soon workers were on strike in most of the island's towns. But the unrest did not stop there. Estate workers in Tobago and Indian labourers on Trinidad estates joined in.

The results were mixed. The dock companies gave their workers a 25 per cent increase. At the same time the governor asked for 350 British servicemen. Once they had arrived the government took action against the strike leaders. Eighty-two were imprisoned and four were deported. It took other steps against the workers. Local ordinances said that strike action was not legal until time had been spent on procedures for settling the dispute. Another ordinance gave the government power to seize socialist or Garveyite literature and close down any newspaper it believed was preaching 'sedition' (active protest against the government).

Unrest in British Guiana had begun before 1919. The wartime slow-down in trade led to a rise in the cost of goods in short supply, especially clothing which was usually imported from Britain. Guyana's dockworkers became restless as the cost of living rose faster than wages. Their spokesman, Hubert Critchlow, asked the governor to use his influence with Bookers to have the wages increased and the long working hours reduced. The governor refused and, in January 1917, the dockworkers went on strike. After two weeks, Critchlow was able to negotiate better wages and a nine-hour day. Neither he nor the union members were satisfied so Critchlow then drew up a request for an eight-hour working day. When he refused to back down, Bookers fired him.

This did not stop Critchlow; it simply meant he had time to build a broader and stronger union movement. In 1919 he organised the British Guiana Labour Union which was open to all labourers. Estate workers and craftsmen joined but its strongest support came from the Georgetown dockworkers. The British Labour Party campaigned for the Colonial Office to order the Guiana Court of Policy to pass a law recognising the right of the BGLU to exist. In 1921 this was done and the BGLU became the first legally recognised trade union in the overseas British Empire.

While Critchlow was busy in British Guiana, Bain Alves, a Jamaican cigar maker, was busy building up his earlier labour organisation into the Longshoremen's Union No. 1. He hoped to make this the first section of a general labour organisation, the Jamaican Federation of Labour. With advice from the Colonial Office, the governor forced a law through the legislative council which gave official recognition to unions in Jamaica. In 1922 the Civil Service Association of British Honduras was also officially registered as a union.

Black organisation

One of the reasons for the widespread support for the new unions and the strikes of 1919 was the widespread feeling that black workers needed to unite against racial discrimination and colonial rule. This was helped by leaders of the Pan-African movement whose story up to 1912 was told in Chapter 8.

Felix Hercules

In 1918–19 one of its most active leaders was a Trinidadian, F. E. M. Hercules. He had gone to study in England in 1914 and had become editor of the *African Telegraph*, which was the newspaper of the Society of Peoples of African Origin. In 1919 in England he had played a leading part in protesting against the racial violence against black soldiers and seamen. Then he made a tour of the West Indies just at the time of the 1919 strikes, visiting Jamaica, Trinidad and British Guiana. When he tried to return to Trinidad at the end of 1919, the

height of the island-wide strikes, the governor refused to let him land.

Smith, Yearwood and Briggs

In British Guiana, Randolph Smith helped to organise the Negro Progress Convention. In Central America, James B. Yearwood worked with West Indian workers to set up the Universal Loyal Negro Association. Cyril V. Briggs, who had left St Kitts to look for work in the United States, was shocked at the harsh living and working conditions of most blacks in the northern industrial cities. In 1919 he founded .the African Blood Brotherhood. Two years later it had branches in Trinidad, British Guiana, the Windward Islands and the Dominican Republic. These men all wanted more than an improvement in living standards. They looked for a new society which would give black people a pride of race, a sense of purpose and the power to achieve a quality of life which colonial society denied to them. The most successful of all the organisations was the Universal Negro Improvement Association and Africans' Communities League, later shortened to the UNIA. It had been founded in 1914 by Marcus Garvey.

Marcus Garvey

Marcus Garvey was born in St Ann's Bay, Jamaica, in 1887. At 14 he was apprenticed to a relative who worked at the printing trade in Kingston. Garvey was a quick and capable student and earned the title of master printer in six years. He did not stay long in the trade. In 1907 he led a printers' strike which was quickly broken when his employer imported machinery to do work previously carried out by hand. After the strike, no employer in Kingston would hire Garvey. Like thousands of his countrymen he emigrated. He stopped in Costa Rica to work for a few months as a timekeeper on a United Fruit plantation, then moved on for short stints in Panama, Nicaragua, Honduras, Colombia, Venezuela and Ecuador. Each new country saddened him more as he saw the wretched conditions of the black West Indians,

Fig. 13.2 *Marcus Garvey.*

Fig. 13.3 *Poverty for blacks in American cities took a different form from that in the Caribbean. These are homes in Harlem, New York.*

forced to live in segregated ghettoes.

In 1912 Garvey travelled to London where he met Duse Mohammed Ali, the publisher of the *African Times and Orient Review.* Duse Mohammed Ali talked to him about the richness of African history and its ancient states such as Ghana and Ethiopia. They discussed the need to free all Africa from the European colonial powers and to end white imperialism over the world's coloured races. At that time only Ethiopia and Liberia were fully self-governing black states in Africa.

In 1914 Garvey returned to Jamaica to begin his life's mission; he would work to free Africa so that it could be the black man's true home. This was important for the dignity of all Africans, but especially for the Afro-Americans. Garvey believed they needed a homeland to identify with, and to return to if they wished. Once the richness of Africa was re-learned the indignities suffered by black men living in white

dominated societies would be overcome. The Afro-American must not look to the white man for help but gain new self-confidence by relying on his own skills and resources.

The UNIA

These were the ideas which led Marcus Garvey to start the first branch of the UNIA in Jamaica in 1914. The first results were disappointing. There were disagreements with another new organisation, the Jamaican Federation of Labour. After the First World War broke out public meetings were forbidden in the colony. In 1916 Garvey travelled to the United States to discuss ways of starting separate black business organisations such as the National Negro

Business League begun by Booker T. Washington. Washington died before Garvey could meet with him. Rather than abandoning the project, Marcus Garvey stopped in Harlem in New York and opened a branch of the UNIA. Here he received the first enthusiastic support for his ideas.

By 1917 all the northern industrial cities of the United States had ghettoes of poor black labourers. The ghettoes were stifling but they did allow ideas to spread among people who lived apart from the outside 'white' world. In them the first large-scale black organisations grew up, such as the National Association for the Advancement of Coloured People (NAACP). More militant organisations appeared on the scene, such as Briggs' African Blood Brotherhood, Dr W. E. B. Dubois' Pan-African Congress and Cleveland Redding's Ethiopian Missionaries to Abyssinia. The new movements published their own tabloids and newspapers. In 1916 the NAACP started the *Crisis*. In 1917 Philip Randolph and Chandler Owen began their leftist *Messenger* and in 1918 two black literary and cultural journals appeared, *Challenge* and *Negro Voice*.

The UNIA quickly won widespread support from the West Indian immigrants in the United States. By 1918 membership was large enough for Garvey to buy a small printing press and publish the *Negro World*. New memberships poured in after 1919 when Garvey started the Black Star Line, to build a steamship link for black enterprises around the world and carry those Afro-Americans who wished to return to Africa. In September the first ship, the *Yarmouth*, was bought.

The Black Star Line was only one of Garvey's many plans to unite black men of the world. He also began a network of community centres called Liberty Halls. At weekends they became religious centres and dance pavilions. In the week they were turned over to public meetings or used as information centres where job notices were posted and legal clinics set up. Liberty Halls contained kitchens and dormitories for the destitute but, most important, they became the bases from which black people were drawn into the life of their community. Men and women

Fig. 13.4 *An advertisement selling shares in the Black Star Line, which appeared in a Nigerian newspaper in 1921.*

were drilled for the marching battalions of the African Legion and members who owned vans and trucks were organised into the Royal African Motor Corps. Women were recruited for the Black Cross Nurses. Fire departments were set up, as were youth groups, choirs and marching bands. The Liberty Halls, said Garvey, must be used to give people power of every kind:

> Power in education, science, industry and higher government. That kind of power will stand out signally, so that other races and nations can see, and if they will not see, then FEEL.

Many new enterprises began in the Liberty Halls. Membership dues were used to rent property to open co-operative grocery stores, restaurants, clothing factories and other enterprises ranging from phonograph recording companies to publishing houses. The businesses in the United States were grouped under the UNIA's Negro Factories Corporation. Garvey hoped that the

Corporation would be the grounding for a world-wide economic system, owned, staffed and managed by blacks. The chances seemed good for, by 1921, Liberty Halls had opened in forty countries on four continents.

The Convention

Before then Garvey had organised the first UNIA International Convention. In 1919 invitations were sent to black leaders throughout the world and the *Yarmouth* was sent on a goodwill tour to give a free passage to New York to as many as possible. When the Convention opened in Madison Square Gardens on 1 August 1922 over 5,000 official and 25,000 unofficial delegates attended. The delegates set up an international government for world Africans, although they recognised that the people of the many African states should rule themselves once they had freed their lands from colonial rule. The government was headed by two honorary officers: Mayor Gabrielle Johnson of Monrovia (the capital of Liberia) as Potentate and George O. Harke of Sierra Leone as deputy Potentate. Marcus Garvey was elected President General and Provisional President of Africa.

The Convention then produced a Bill of Rights. Its most important claim was that the world's governments should recognise the UNIA as spokesman for all black men. The Bill went on to demand that Africa be freed from colonial rule so it could become 'Africa for the Africans at home and abroad.' It called for equal treatment of Africans who lived as minorities in 'white' countries. There should be no discrimination against them in employment and they should receive full political rights. The Bill warned that the UNIA would use all its power and influence to right the wrongs done to the world's blacks, even if it meant racial war. It was a ringing announcement that the time had come for change.

Attacks on the UNIA

As the UNIA gained strength the United States government and the colonial powers took steps to check its growth. In Africa it was banned by colonial governments. They outlawed the *Negro World* which was banned in most Caribbean colonies. The British lifted the ban but, by then, the movement had been seriously weakened, mostly by the strong campaign against Marcus Garvey in the United States.

Rumours were purposely spread that he used the money of shareholders in Black Star Line for other purposes. Charges were laid and in 1920 he was put on trial for using the United States mail to collect money by fraud. The UNIA's records were seized and held by the prosecution for their evidence, so it was impossible to defend Garvey properly. He was found guilty and then lost his appeal and was sent to the Atlanta Federal Penitentiary in 1924. He stayed in prison for two and a half years before he was pardoned by the United States President and deported to Jamaica.

Without Garvey's strong personality the UNIA began to fall apart. Disagreements broke out between the West Indians and American blacks and also between those who supported the NAACP, which advised working with sympathetic whites, and those who preferred to be completely independent of them. A serious blow came in 1924 when Liberia refused to accept Afro-Americans wishing to return to Africa. The UNIA asked the League of Nations if they could use Tanganyika as a homeland for dispersed Africans, but the request was rudely ignored. The Black Star Line, too, ran into difficulty. It was restarted, in 1924, after Garvey's trial and a second ship, the *G. W. Geothals*, was bought but its boilers exploded in Kingston Harbour on the first voyage.

Garvey in Jamaica

In Jamaica, Garvey tried to revive the UNIA. New headquarters were opened and an island-wide campaign for new members was started. In 1929 another international convention was held in Kingston. Garvey also played an important part in the development of trade unions in Jamaica. He started a political party to run for the few elected seats on the governor's council. The party had its roots in a labour union, the Jamaica Worker's and Labourer's Association. Garvey ran for a vacant seat on the council and in his campaign accused certain unpopular judges of taking bribes. For this he was arrested. He never won a seat on the legislative council but he was elected to the Kingston St Andrew Corporation in 1929, even though he was serving a prison term at the time. The seat was declared vacant but he won the new election after his release from prison.

Garvey and black consciousness

Throughout the 1930s Garvey tried to keep the UNIA alive against increasing difficulties. When the *Negro World* was forced to close in 1933 he started a new paper, *The Black Man*. In 1935 he moved the headquarters of the UNIA to London where he spent the last years of his life, dying in 1940. By then his organisations had failed but his ideas were ready to be taken up by new men who have continued to make them part of black society in the Americas. Garvey had taught them an absolute pride in race and a new self-confidence rooted in their African heritage. Even after the UNIA collapsed, the Liberty Halls remained as centres of community involvement stressing the practical and cultural strength of black America. The sheer force of his movement meant that white America could no longer dismiss the black as a quashie, an Aunt Jemimah or an amusing addition to a minstrel show.

The unions and politics

Arthur Cipriani

During the 1919 strikes in Trinidad, the TWA was joined by Arthur Cipriani who had returned from the war with the rank of Captain. He had already earned a name for himself in Trinidad by his campaign to help ex-soldiers with their claims for pensions and land to resettle themselves.

Cipriani was one of the first West Indian leaders to call himself a socialist. He was not content to see the Workingmen's Association become simply another union demanding better wages, benefits and hours for the few workers in regular jobs who could afford to pay union fees. It must be organised, he believed, to help all labourers and win political power for them.

In 1923 he became leader of the TWA and turned it into a broad movement, supported by the poorest of labourers, who Cipriani called his 'bare-footed khaki brigade'. It was also open to East Indians just as much as creoles. When Major Wood's Commission arrived, Cipriani and the TWA played a leading part in putting the case for electing members to the legislative council. When the first elections were held, Cipriani won a seat with the backing of the TWA. The following year he also won an election to the Port of Spain city council. From these two councils he became one of the first West Indian politicians to lead opposition to local Crown colony government in the name of the mass of the people. He campaigned for pension schemes, minimum wages and for public control over the electricity and telephone service. He called for higher royalties and taxes on foreign companies taking oil and asphalt from the island. Under Cipriani, the TWA became more and more like a political party. He refused, in any case, to register it as a trade union because the law gave unions such little protection. In 1934 the TWA decided to act openly as a political party and renamed itself the Trinidad Labour Party.

In 1926 Critchlow tried to widen his Guyanese movement by starting the British Guiana and West Indian Labour Congress. He hoped that other unions in the West Indies would join the Congress although it received little support until after 1938.

Set-backs

Despite all the gains made by Critchlow, Cipriani, and Alves in Jamaica, the West Indian trade union movement remained weak throughout the 1920s and up to the mid-1930s. One reason was that the laws still did not give full protection to the unions. Employers could sue a union for damages or losses caused by a strike. It was still illegal to picket a workplace to persuade other workers to join in the strike. The authorities were still ready to use violence against union demonstrators.

In 1924 workers from Critchlow's union in British Guiana organised a peaceful march to support labourers striking on several of Bookers' plantations outside Georgetown. The march was broken up and thirteen of the demonstrators were killed. In Trinidad, planters and merchants formed vigilante platoons to disrupt labour demonstrations. In all colonies, unions wanting to register as legal organisations had to pay a fee which was made high to discourage them. Combined with high levels of unemployment and continuing emigration abroad, these difficulties kept unions weak, although the groundwork had been laid for a surge forward in the late 1930s.

The great depression

The great economic depression of the 1930s was world-wide. In the industrialised states, factories closed and unemployment came to millions of workers. Between 1929 and 1932 world production fell by a third and world trade by two-thirds. The depression was felt hardest in places like the West Indies which depended on one or two major export crops. Governments lost their spending money as the income from export duties slumped. So they suspended public works programmes which had always given work to many part-time labourers.

In the past, the governments of the poorer colonies had been granted small British loans, but in 1931 the Colonial Secretary ordered a complete freeze on colonial spending. Remarkably, Trinidad turned the tables and made a grant of £5,000 per year for five years to the British government! The colony could hardly afford such generosity. Although oil production continued to rise, exports of both asphalt and agricultural goods slumped. Asphalt production fell from 187,142 tonnes in 1927–31 to 83,000 tonnes in 1932–36. In 1928 Trinidad's agricultural earnings had been nearly £3 million; by 1935 they had fallen to only £1,696,423.

The depression came at a time when it was already becoming more difficult for West Indian workers to emigrate. In 1924 the United States had passed the Restrictive Immigration Act to block workers' entry. In 1927 the Act had been extended to prevent labourers from the English-speaking Caribbean, apart from British Guiana, taking jobs in Central American and Caribbean countries where American business interests were strong. Cuba, the Dominican Republic and the Central American states began to round up and deport British West Indian workers. The round-up was especially brutal in Cuba where some parts of society had never welcomed black immigrants. Over 20,500 Jamaicans were ordered home between 1930 and 1935. To these numbers were added emigrants to the United States who began to return when they lost their jobs as a result of the depression.

Unrest in the early 1930s

The migrants' return meant an end to the flow of money through the post which had been so important to many families. It also led to a rise in the numbers of unemployed and that made it easier for employers to cut down wages and the number of days' work they gave. The result in the early 1930s was a rise in the number of strikes. There were several on the Guyanese sugar estates in 1931 and 1932. In 1933 the Trinidad oil field workers organised a hunger march to draw attention to their suffering. The next year there were strikes and riots in the island's sugar belt. Local officials and middle class politicians could do nothing about the social and economic conditions which were leading to the unrest. The workers were taking matters into their own hands. The strikes and marches were the beginning of a process which would bring the fall of the British Empire in the West Indies.

Riots, strikes and new leaders, 1935–38

St Kitts, St Vincent, St Lucia

The demonstrations first became violent in the smaller territories where the hardships were greatest. In January 1935, sugar workers in St Kitts laid down their tools and demanded better wages. Some of the strikers planned to march from plantation to plantation calling on their fellow workers for support. The magistrates reacted too quickly and too harshly. Police were armed and sent in to break up the march; a British warship was called to stand by. Three of the workers were killed and eight injured.

In October a riot broke out in St Vincent following an announcement that the government planned to increase customs duties. This would lead to higher prices and more hardship for labourers who were already finding it difficult to keep their families clothed and fed. Again the police were armed and at least three demonstrators were shot dead.

A few months later, a strike broke out in St Lucia among the stokers who worked at the naval yards in Castries. They were joined by some unemployed urban and rural workers. The strike was quite peaceful but the governor decided on a show of force. The local militia was called out, a warship was summoned into Castries harbour and marines patrolled the streets rounding up suspected troublemakers.

The governors of these islands had all been quick to make a strong show of force with warships, marines and armed police under British commanders. Yet nothing was done to solve the problems which caused the unrest. So, although 1936 was a year of uneasy quiet, new and more violent outbursts took place in the larger colonies in 1937.

Trinidad and 'Buzz' Butler

When the sugar and oil workers had started strikes and hunger marches, Cipriani advised them to call them off because the governor and council had agreed to pass a law for a minimum wage. Yet, when the law was passed in 1934, it did not give the workers what they expected. It was left to the governor to decide when an employer would have to pay the minimum wage. He refused to do this for four years even though the price of goods rose by 20 per cent. The oil companies even cut labourers' wages in 1937 and yet paid a higher dividend to shareholders.

Cipriani's advice led to a split in the TWA. He had tried to stop the strikes and marches because he believed the Trinidad Labour Party

Fig. 13.5 *Uriah 'Buzz' Butler, photographed in the 1960s.*

should work for gradual improvements rather than organise demonstrations. By 1935 this had lost him the support of many workers who were turning to a new leader, Tubal ('Buzz') Uriah Butler.

In 1935 it was 'Buzz' Butler who led 120 people from the southern oil fields on their own hunger march into Port of Spain. Unlike Cipriani, Butler was himself a labourer, born in Grenada in 1891. He was more outspoken than Cipriani and believed that the workers must struggle themselves and not wait for their leaders to win improvements by slow negotiations. The disagreement was followed by Butler being expelled from the Trinidad Labour Party. In 1936 he founded his own organisation, the British Empire Workers' and Citizens' Home Rule Party.

Butler won wide support because of his strong personality and his forceful way of speaking. As well as being a unionist, he was the leader of a pentecostal church and his meetings were like religious crusades. He called himself 'God's Appointed' and 'Chief Servant of the Lord' who had come to lead the suffering black workers from the 'wilderness of colonialism'. He did not speak of his followers as a barefoot brigade but as working class 'warriors'.

Throughout 1936 and early 1937 growing numbers of oilworkers gave their backing to Butler as he demanded higher wages. He was clearly anxious to avoid a strike because of the suffering it would cause his followers but the governor and employers still refused to listen. As a last resort he called a general strike for June 1937, stating that he and his warriors had heard too much of 'Ignore the Nigger, those blacks only bark, they cannot bite.'

On 19 June every single oilworker laid down his tools and the strike then spread quickly to the cane workers and some labourers in Port of Spain. On the first evening of the strike, police were sent to arrest Butler while he was speaking to a meeting. The crowd attacked the police and, during the battle, Butler was able to slip away into hiding. The police and troops fired on the crowd, a police corporal was burnt to death and the governor sent for troops and a warship. Bursts of firing at strikers and demonstrators went on for several days and fourteen people were killed, twelve of them civilians. Butler remained in hiding until he felt he would have a fair hearing before a Royal Commission.

Barbados: Payne and Adams

The next riots broke out in Barbados, the only colony where lawmaking was still in the hands of an elected assembly. The property qualifications to vote or become a member of the assembly were so high that the island was governed in the interests of the most privileged. A writer who supported the cause of the masses of Barbadians wrote about the assembly in 1920:

> There is no sense of duty to the individuals of the island as a whole. There is no sense of responsibility for broad and reasonable treatment.
> There is only a sense of class.

The sense of class was most obvious in the countryside. Barbados was still a land of large and medium sized plantations with labourers working for low wages in the cane fields overlooked by the great houses. Ill-health and near-starvation were widespread. A report of 1939 said that many children had no regular meal from Wednesdays to Saturdays. The only relief came with emigration and that ceased with the fall in world trade of the 1930s. Throughout 1936 there was talk of coming violence. In January 1937 a young lawyer, Grantley Adams, pleaded for something to be done to ease the suffering of Barbadian labourers. He wrote in the Barbados *Observer*, pointing out the 'crying necessity for the coming together of every man of goodwill who believes that life is not intended to be selfish pursuit of individual comfort, happiness, or worse still, luxury.'

The plea came too late. While it was being written, Clement Payne, born of Barbadian parents in Trinidad, was leaving for Barbados. As a young man he had joined the Trinidad Youth League and later Butler's British Empire Workers' and Citizens' Home Rule Party. He arrived in Barbados calling himself Butler's minister of propaganda. In the famous 'Seventeen Consecutive Meetings' Payne called on the Bridgetown labourers to unite into clubs, unions and workingmen's associations to force employers to improve wages and working conditions. Like Butler and Garvey, Payne told the black Barbadians to have a new pride in their race and to work together. He had no patience with those who served the white authorities; to Clement Payne, black policemen were 'dogs of the capitalists'.

The Barbadian authorities waited for Payne's meetings to end, hoping he would return to Trinidad. When he showed no signs of leaving they served him with a deportation order claiming that he had falsely told immigration officers that he had been born in Barbados. Payne took the case to court. After much hesitation, Grantley Adams agreed to be his lawyer. Adams won the case for Payne but the governor decided to deport him anyway. When the news reached his followers in Bridgetown that he had been placed on board a ship, rioting broke out. The official report later said:

> The mob then spread through the city in bands smashing motor cars and electric street lamps.

When the police tried to stop these outrages the mob rained showers of stones and bottles on them.

The following day, 27 July, rioting spread to the countryside. The official report gave several reasons for this:

> . . . hunger or the fear of hunger coupled with the news of the disturbances in Bridgetown were the chief causes of the outbreaks in the country districts.

The police were armed and in the skirmishes which followed at least 13 people were killed, 47 wounded and over 500 imprisoned. An uneasy peace then settled over Barbados.

Grantley Adams spent many months defending people accused of rioting and became outspoken in his attacks on the restricted right to vote and the island's undemocratic government. In 1938 he took the lead in organising the Progressive League which had strong support from the new Barbados Workers' Union. By 1941 Adams was president of both organisations.

Jamaica: the 1938 riots

The Jamaican riots were similar to those in the eastern Caribbean but at first there was no strong leadership such as that given by Butler and Payne. The disturbances began in January 1938 at Sterge Island, just a few kilometres from where Bogle had set out on his march to Morant Bay in 1865. Cane cutters had demanded an increase from 10½d to 2/- per tonne. When the management refused, 1,400 workers blockaded the factory. Police were sent in from Kingston and injured 34 rioters and arrested 60; 21 were later fined or sent to prison.

The second disturbances came at the other end of the island at Frome, near Savannah-la-Mar, where the workers marched on the pay office of the West Indian Sugar Company, demanding better pay and fewer deductions from wages. The unrest continued for several days, until 2 May, when the police fired into the crowd and charged with fixed bayonets. Four workers were killed, thirteen injured and over a thousand arrested. But the disturbances continued to spread, first to St Ann's Bay and then to Kingston where the waterfront workers walked out on strike. On 20 May, the streets of Kingston were filled with over 6,000 demonstrators. Before order was restored, six more people lay dead, two hundred were wounded and another seven hundred arrested.

Bustamante

A new working class leader, Alexander Bustamante, believed like Butler and Payne that the labourers could be organised to force the colonial governments to undertake political and economic change. Bustamante had been born William Alexander Clarke on 4 February 1886. He had worked in Jamaica as a store clerk and junior overseer on a small property before emigrating to Cuba. There he worked for an American tramway company. In a few years he was promoted to traffic inspector and sent to the company's Panama branch. By 1920 he was back in Cuba, this time as a member of the police force. Twelve years later he migrated to New York where he trained and worked as a dietician.

In 1934 he returned to Jamaica and, at the age of 50, opened a small money-lending business in Kingston. As a moneylender, Bustamante came face to face with the hardships and sufferings of the Kingston labourers. From the beginning, he upheld their right to unite in unions and self-help programmes. He wrote:

> Hungry men and women have the right to call attention to their condition and to ask of people fulfilment of promises made to them, as long as they do so without using violence or behaving disorderly.

Fig. 13.6 *Alexander Bustamante leads a march of workers during the riots in Jamaica.*

Bustamante wrote regular letters to the press on behalf of workingmen and was soon accepted by other labour leaders. He began to share speaking tours with Allen George Coombs who organised the Jamaica Workers' Trades Union (JWTU) in 1936. Coombs' union was not limited to people with trades; it also tried to work on behalf of the unorganised agricultural labourers. Bustamante did not stay long in the JWTU; he was expelled in 1937 when he refused to support the leftist policies of its general secretary, Hugh Buchanan.

This did not turn Bustamante from the workingmen's movement. He teamed up with a leading Garveyite, William Grant, to back the estate strikes in 1938. The two men travelled to the site of the riots to give the strikers support. Then they went on to take part in the Kingston demonstrations. Bustamante could draw huge crowds to hear his ringing speeches. One listener commented 'that man is the uncrowned king of Jamaica for the next ten years.' Bustamante was arrested and charged with holding unlawful meetings and obstructing the police.

Jamaica: Bustamante and Manley

It was at this point that Bustamante's cousin, Norman Washington Manley, won for himself a place in the labour movement. Manley, brought up by his widowed mother, had become a leading Jamaican lawyer. He arranged for Bustamante's release and the two men negotiated a settlement between the strikers, their employers and colonial officials. The success of the negotiations brought support for Manley and Bustamante from many workers who were dissatisfied with the JWTU. This gave Bustamante the chance to form his own Bustamante Industrial Trades Union, which had a large following in Kingston and even more support from the sugar workers.

The importance of the union grew when it gave its support to the People's National Party, led by Norman Manley. The PNP had been formed from an alliance of several middle class reform groups, such as the Jamaica Progressive League, and readers of the *Public Opinion* newspaper. The support of the BITU gave it the chance to become one of the first mass parties in Jamaican history. Until their split in 1943, Bustamante and Manley worked together to make the labour and political movements speak out for the cause of Jamaica's working people.

Assignments

1 a) *How did trade unions develop in your territory?*
   b) *Which factors assisted and which hindered the development of the movement in your territory?*

2 a) *What provision was made for the interests and well being of labourers in the British Caribbean i) during slavery? ii) between 1838 and 1900?*
   b) *How did British Caribbean labourers begin to took after their own interests after 1900?*

3 *What did the strikes and riots which took place in the British Caribbean between 1919 and 1940 have in common?*

4 *Give examples of black organisations in the British Caribbean in the first half of the twentieth century.*

5 a) *Make a chart/diagram to show the main leaders who emerged in each British Caribbean territory in the first half of the twentieth century.*
   b) *State briefly what you think were the main achievements of each leader.*

14 THE TURNING POINT 1938–45

The trade unions end British ignorance

British ignorance

Until the riots of the 1930s the British people had usually been ignorant about widespread distress in the Caribbean. Sometimes they seemed to prefer to believe in myths. One very strong myth was that life in the West Indies was very easy. According to this English view, Caribbean people enjoyed such a climate that they could want little in the way of clothes or shelter, and ample food lay on the ground waiting to be picked up. Another myth was that the local governments had helped large numbers of peasants to become successful small farmers.

The truth was very different, as one writer discovered when he took the trouble to investigate. He found that smallholders were settled on only 67 of the 344 square kilometres in Grenada, where much of the land is unsuitable for agriculture anyway. They could use less than one-tenth of the area of Jamaica. In Barbados three-quarters of the smallholders owned half a hectare or less and in St Kitts they had little more than gardens. No wonder this man put at the beginning of his book:

> When I went to the West Indies I was told by men of all shades of opinion that I should find everything ideal and I fully expected to. My doubts when I returned were received coldly . . . In fact the root of the trouble lies in the lack of knowledge and of sympathetic imagination in the British public responsible for imperial policy.

The commissions

The riots brought a sharp end to British ignorance about the Caribbean. Her alarmed government sent a series of commissions to enquire into their causes. Unlike earlier commissions they wrote blunt and outspoken reports. The Deane Commission's view that the Barbados riots were caused by stark poverty was just a start. Shortly after, the Colonial Office sent Major Orde-Brown to report on the position of working men and their organisations. His report was called 'Labour Conditions in the West Indies' and it said bluntly that they were 'absolutely deplorable'. Orde-Brown gave details of low wages, the large amount of casual and part-time work and the lack of proper social services. He pointed out that the riots could have been avoided if trade unions had had the same rights as they had in Britain and if they had been allowed to negotiate freely with employers and the colonies' local governments.

An even fuller picture of the West Indies came from the Moyne Commission which was sent here to study social and economic conditions throughout the English-speaking Caribbean.

Fig. 14.1 *A street scene in Kingston, Jamaica, in 1938.*

The Moyne Commission at work

Lord Moyne and his team travelled through the West Indies for fourteen months, from August 1938 to November 1939. Unlike earlier commissions, they listened to people from all walks of life, and asked very sharp questions about details of every kind: profits, wages, working and living conditions. In every colony the views of labour and union leaders were listened to carefully. One of the British commissioners was Sir Walter Citrine, the Secretary of the British Trade Union Congress. He used his long experience in the labour movement to cross-examine witnesses. Here he is questioning members of the Barbados Sugar Producers' Association about reasons for delay in passing a Workmen's Compensation Act.

Sir Walter: Do you have a Workmen's Compensation Act?

Mr Coke: So far as I know the Bill has not been passed.

Sir Walter: It is rather extraordinary that there is no Workmen's Compensation Act in an island like this?

Mr Pile: . . . the urgency for it is very much less than in neighbouring countries.

Sir Walter: You think the industrial worker is better off here than he is in another island which has the Workmen's Compensation Act?

Mr Pile: More important things occupied the time of the House [the Barbados Assembly]. That is they seemed important to the majority of the members of the House . . . Most of the members of the House of Assembly are entirely agreed that a Workmen's Compensation Act should be passed. At the same time there is no urgent necessity for it in this particular island.

Sir Walter: You said that the matter is not regarded as one of great urgency . . . Is it not a fact that the Secretary of State for the Colonies has communicated with the government here a long time ago asking that legislation of this kind should be enacted?

Mr Pile: I believe so.

Sir Walter: He would regard the matter as one of urgency?

Mr Pile: He doesn't know local conditions as well as we do.

Sir Walter: He may be as fully aware of local conditions as you are.

Mr Pile: The delay has nothing at all to do with any opposition by any members. It was delayed because of more important things.

Sir Walter: More important to whom?

Every word was heard through loud-speakers by a crowd outside the meeting room. The *Barbados Advocate* published the evidence given and questions asked during the commission's two week stay in Barbados. The paper described it as a record of 'one of the outstanding events during the century.' The commission's visit to each colony gave West Indians some hope that the truth about conditions in the Caribbean would at last be widely known. For once they were not cheated. The final report was a round condemnation of Britain's policies which had allowed hunger, disease, unemployment and suffering to go unchecked.

The Moyne Report: health

The report made it clear that medical services were completely inadequate. 'Serious economic and social problems' were caused by tuberculosis, malaria, worm infestation, yaws and leprosy. The very young and elderly suffered from diseases stemming from malnutrition and poor diet. In many cases to be too old to work meant 'under-nourishment amounting to starvation.' The infant mortality rate was equally shocking. In Barbados, of every thousand live births 217 infants died before their first birthday. This was the fourth highest infant mortality rate in the British Empire. The mortality rate was worse only in Gambia, Hong Kong and Malta. The fifth highest rate was St Kitts with 209 deaths for every thousand live births. In England the rate was less than 58.

The commissioners visited centres for the mentally ill and those suffering from communicable diseases such as tuberculosis and leprosy. All too often they found 'dark and crowded huts in which no education is provided and no facilities exist for any form of recreation.' Yet even such poor centres were not found in the country districts. The colonial governments simply lacked the funds to provide proper medical and social services. In the commission's words the unhealthy state of the population arose from 'poverty of the individual, of the medical departments and the governments.' It recommended that the entire medical service of the English-speaking Caribbean be re-organised under one central authority, which would provide long-term measures to prevent disease and train medical workers through a new school of hygiene.

Housing

The commissioners were appalled at the housing they visited.

> It is no exaggeration to say that in the poorest parts of most towns and in many of the country districts, a majority of the houses are largely made of rusty corrugated iron and unsound boarding . . .; sanitation in any form and water supply are unknown in such premises . . . Such is the pressure of poverty that when a second room is available, it will often be sublet for the sake of a few shillings . . .

The commission blamed these conditions for the spread of disease, the breakdown of family life and the high crime rates. It supported the call of local leaders for a public works programme of slum clearing backed up by building suitable low-priced housing.

Education

Education was seen as being just as poorly developed as health and housing. The region had not enough school places and was short of equipment of all kinds. Buildings were often in a 'chronic state of disrepair and insanitation'. The report spoke of a 'great need' for more teachers trained in secondary schools and colleges to replace the underpaid pupil teachers. It spoke up for the views of many West Indians when it called for an end to methods of teaching and syllabuses which had been given up in England. The report called for sources 'more closely related to the life and experience of residents in the West Indies.'

Labour conditions

The blame for poor working conditions and low wages was laid squarely on the shoulders of the colonial governments, which had failed to make laws against the use of unsafe machinery or the exploitation of women and children. The report showed that, in the worst cases, city shopgirls worked for wages of less than 20/- a week and female domestics worked seven days a week from 6 a.m. to 9 p.m. for as little as 6/-. When food was provided the wages were reduced to about 1/6d per week! No laws had been passed to insist on standard allowances for sick leave, annual holidays or time off. Many women did hard manual labour work for a few shillings a week. Some weeded and manured fields, others loaded and unloaded barges with sand, coal or heavy banana stems. The poorest broke stones or worked at road building for as little as 9d a day. The need to investigate working conditions was emphasised while the commissioners were in the Caribbean when a labour dispute on Plantation Lenora in British Guiana led to four deaths.

New approaches in the Moyne Report

The Moyne Commission recommended that the British government should take steps to tackle the root causes of the shocking poverty and the widespread discontent in the West Indies. They underlined that this was a British responsibility and said action was needed in three main areas. They were laws on labour conditions and the rights of trade unions, help to improve the West Indian economy, and steps towards more democracy and self-government.

Moyne on trade unions

The report criticised the lack of legal recognition for the trade unions and described how governments and employers were hostile to them. Workingmen's leaders had asked for laws which would allow unions to picket peacefully and which would protect them against being sued by a company for the money it had lost during a strike. British unions had had these rights for thirty years and the Moyne Report said that the

West Indian unions should have them too without delay. It said that the colonies should also immediately set up workmen's compensation schemes, unemployment insurance and guidelines for minimum wages. There should be factory inspectors to see that workplaces were safe and healthy. The colonial governments should have labour departments to see that these improvements were carried out and to protect the rights of trade unions.

Moyne and the economy

The commissioners agreed with the people who told them that more jobs had to be created. Yet they found it difficult to make recommendations for major changes. Increasing export crops was not the best answer because of the poor overseas markets. Instead the commission suggested that the West Indian territories try to build up their internal manufacturing industries, using locally grown products wherever possible. For instance, it recommended that governments look into the milling of cornmeal, which could provide factory work and a larger market for locally grown maize. The coconut industry might be encouraged by manufacturing soap, margarine and lard substitutes locally. The possibility of building a condensed milk plant in Jamaica was discussed along with the opening of a plant which could sell cement to public works programmes for new schools, hospitals, public housing and sewage. For British Guiana there was talk of making wood-pulp for high-class paper from wallaba trees.

The commissioners realised that these schemes would not be enough. The proposed cement factory, for instance, would give work to only 100–200 men. Still, they pointed out that 'the growth of urban unemployment is so serious that even small contributions to its solution should not be neglected.'

The commission made an important suggestion for a new way of providing the funds for schemes to improve health, housing and welfare and to start new industries. In the past the British government had offered only loans which had usually meant that the colonies had fallen into even greater debt. This time, the report said that a special welfare fund should be set up for the region and the British government should pay an annual grant into it of £1 million for twenty years.

Moyne and self-government

Trade union and labour leaders made self-government one of their demands to the Moyne Commission. In the eastern Caribbean they called for the territories to be allowed to form a self-governing federation. Everywhere Moyne heard demands that the people of each territory should elect their own assemblies by adult suffrage – which meant that every man and woman would have the right to vote.

On the other hand Moyne heard opposition to the idea of adult suffrage, self-government and federation from many businessmen, planters and officials who did not wish to see the ordinary men and women have an influence in government. In the end, however, the Report recommended a slow movement towards the goals of the union leaders. It called for a 'cautious extension' of the franchise and eventual self-government and said that federation of all the colonies was an 'ideal' development which should be worked towards despite the many difficulties.

The Second World War: the economic impact
Britain's response to Moyne

When the commissioners returned to England in November 1939, their country had been at war for three months. In September Britain had declared war on Hitler's Germany in a bid to stop the dictator's conquest of Europe. By June 1940 Britain stood alone. Her allies and sympathisers – France, Belgium, Holland, Denmark, Norway – had all been overrun by German armies. All the British could hope to do was survive with the help of her overseas empire and wait for the day when the United States and possibly the USSR joined the war against Germany.

The government feared that the empire's war effort might be weakened if it became known that Moyne had agreed with the West Indians and blamed the Colonial Office for not acting against

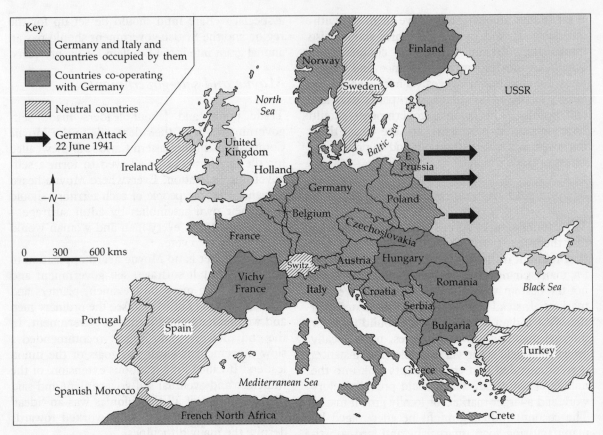

Map 12 *Early June 1941: Germany and Italy occupied or controlled most of Europe.*

hunger, disease and unemployment in the Caribbean. Especially while Britain stood alone against Germany, she depended on supplies and men from her empire, so she dare not publish a report which might strengthen the anti-British feeling in the colonies. So the full report was not published until victory was in sight, at the end of 1944. Meanwhile just a summary of Moyne's recommendations was issued in 1940. At the same time, two proposals were acted on straight away. One dealt with trade unions and the other with economic development. Both showed how Britain was anxious to keep the colonies quiet and producing the food, raw materials and manpower which she needed to survive.

Trade unions

Orde-Brown and Moyne had agreed in their reports that steps must be taken to protect the rights of working people and unions. In 1939 the British government sent instructions to all governors in the West Indies telling them that laws must be passed to recognise and register trade unions and to protect workers. It told the governors that 'harmonious relations' between workers and employers were absolutely essential 'during the war . . . and the critical period likely to follow it'. This was particularly true in Trinidad whose oil was extremely important for Britain's warships and planes.

The colonial governments obeyed the orders. Local laws were passed so that unions could be registered at lower fees. Unionists were given the right to picket peacefully during strikes. Employers lost the right to sue them for business losses caused by a strike. Some colonies had their first schemes for workmen's compensation in cases of injury, unemployment insurance and minimum wages. A very important step was that colonies' governments set up labour departments. Their officials were responsible for employment conditions and for helping unions to negotiate with employers on an equal footing.

The new labour leaders helped the trade unions to firm up the strength they had gained in the late 1930s. Before the riots, craft unions had often counted their members in hundreds and general unions for all workers had been easily crushed when employers and the government took action against them. As unions registered under the new laws it was seen that they had begun to outgrow this early weakness. The Barbados Progressive League claimed 23,000 members, the Antigua Trades and Labour Union, 12,000, and the Manpower and Citizens Association in Guyana said it had 4,000, mostly estate workers.

In 1939 only twenty-eight unions were registered. By 1945 there were another forty or so and the West Indian unions had around 100,000 members. Yet there were still problems. Many unions still had fewer than a thousand members. It was still difficult to organise seasonal workers, people with part-time employment and those who travelled to work. Domestics were the most difficult of all to bring into unions although they were often the most exploited of all workers. All unions suffered from the fact that even small membership fees were too much for many lowly paid workers. However, some workers supported unions and their leaders without becoming dues-paying members.

Labour conditions after 1945

The difficulties that unions had in organising showed the importance of laws which protected all workers whether they were in unions or not. This is why the labour departments were so important. Their staff set standards for factories so that machinery was made safe and there were arrangements for sanitation and first aid. Labour departments set up the tribunals which could assess how much a worker should be paid in compensation if he was injured.

The pressures for improved labour conditions began during the war but it took many years to carry through the changes. Some were only possible when political parties which grew out of the labour movement had a share in government. They were behind laws which gave workers pay while they were sick, holidays with pay, redundancy payments and some government pension schemes. By the time of independence these laws had done much to remove some of the worst aspects of working life.

Colonial development and welfare

The second step taken by Britain to follow up the Moyne Report came in 1940 through the Colonial Development and Welfare Act. This set up a special fund to help economic and social schemes in all the poor parts of the empire. The West Indian share was about £1 million a year, the figure suggested by Moyne. The Caribbean headquarters of the Colonial Development and Welfare Organisation (CDWO) was set up in Barbados. It was the first major institution to treat the whole of the English-speaking Caribbean as one unit with common problems. Its work continued after the war, for, in 1945, the British government promised £15½ million to the West Indies over ten years.

The CDWO in Barbados was often criticised for its methods of work. T. A. Marryshow, of Grenada, said in 1945 that he would not believe in it until he saw a West Indian on its executive committee. There were certainly far too many British and too few Caribbean people on its expert staff. The work was slowed down because every scheme had to be sent back to London for approval. Some critics said that too much of the money was spent on minor schemes which would not have any effect on the real problems of the Caribbean such as the lack of industries. There is much truth in these criticisms but the CDWO's work did have some value for the future.

Public works programmes, including building roads, bridges, reservoirs or a new jetty in Barbuda, gave some work at the time and helped future development. This was also true of the few new schools and medical centres which were provided from the funds. Some of the money went on training schemes for people such as nurses, or on agricultural research to find new and better crops or farming methods. Another value of the CDWO's work was that it encouraged local governments to study their country's needs and to make planning decisions about the best ways of spending money to lead to economic development. The post-war years saw many such plans which were more far-reaching than those put forward by the CDWO. One example was the Jamaican National Plan of 1947, which started the post-war industrialisation of the island.

The Caribbean economy in wartime

Very little of the fighting in the Second World War came into the American hemisphere, although German submarines often attacked shipping bound to and from Europe and once raided vessels in harbour in Barbados and St Lucia. But the effects of war were felt here. Just because they were usually beyond the reach of Britain's enemies, the Caribbean colonies became important to her war effort as a source of valuable supplies and as naval bases.

The war years were a time of boom for West Indian agriculture. Before 1939, Britain imported cane and beet from countries now in enemy hands or in areas where her navy could no longer protect merchant ships. So she agreed to buy all the sugar that could be grown in the English-speaking Caribbean. But that was not the end of the West Indian contribution. After 1941, the whole of the Jamaican banana crop was bought at a price of £1 million per year. Sea-island cotton was sent to make barrage balloons which were filled with gas and floated above British cities to prevent low-flying air attacks. Bauxite from British Guiana was in great demand to produce aluminium needed in aircraft construction. Rice from the same colony helped feed the people of Britain whose food supplies were strictly rationed.

Of all war materials, oil was perhaps the most important. The Caribbean contribution came from stepping up the output in Trinidad and the Dutch colonies of Curaçao and Aruba. Much of the workforce was recruited among emigrants from the Leewards and Windwards. Other workers from the eastern islands found work in the bauxite industry in British Guiana. Many West Indians went to work in the United States where production of war materials and food

boomed.

Until December 1941, America stayed out of the fighting but gave a great deal of aid to Britain. Then the Japanese attacked the United States naval base in Pearl Harbor and America declared war on both Japan and her ally, Germany. But United States influence was felt in the Caribbean well before that. Early in 1941 came the Anglo-American naval agreement. The United States gave fifty old destroyers to the British navy in return for 99-year leases of land in Antigua, St Lucia, Jamaica, British Guiana and Trinidad. The land was to be used to build bases for the US navy and would bring a great deal of well-paid work for West Indians.

The deal was arranged by the British government in London. It was strongly opposed by West Indian governments, especially by Sir Hubert Young, Governor of Trinidad and Tobago. What troubled the objectors was the fact that the land for the bases was to become American territory. The governors argued that this would lead to future trouble with the nationalist movements when they had become strong enough to take over the government of their colonies. They pointed out that American troops and workers on the bases would not be bound by local laws or currency and customs regulations.

The British need for American support was so great that the agreement was signed in spite of the objections. The largest base was built at Chaguaramas in Trinidad. This was on land which would one day be needed for the development of Port of Spain. However, during the war, it did bring one short-term benefit in providing work for Trinidadians and emigrants from the small islands.

American influence in the Caribbean took another step forward in 1942 when the Anglo-American Caribbean Commission was set up. This was later joined by the French and Dutch governments and became known as the Caribbean Commission, which had its headquarters in Trinidad. Rather like the CDWO, it aimed to encourage favourable feelings to the United States and the European powers by carrying out social and economic development schemes. But it, too, was often criticised for having too many overseas staff and no real intention of helping the

Fig. 14.2 *The US naval base at Chaguaramas, Trinidad.*

Caribbean colonies to stand on their own feet.

As we have seen, the war led to a boom in production for export and in employment in oil, mining and the building industries. But these benefits were offset by the sharp rise in prices. Enemy shipping action and government purchase of materials produced shortages of food and most other goods. The governments made some effort to check the price rises. They appointed food controllers and other war emergency officials. But they could not stop demands for wage increases. In some colonies, Advisory Boards were set up to consider minimum wages in particular industries but wage rises rarely kept up with price increases.

The governors were given other wartime emergency powers. They could control imports and exports and censor private letters as well as the press. They also had the power to intern, or keep in one guarded place, anyone who threatened the war effort. The governor of Jamaica used this power in 1940 against Alexander Bustamante and other labour leaders on the grounds that they had threatened to lead a violent strike of waterfront workers. In Trinidad, 'Buzz' Butler was interned throughout the war on the grounds that he was a threat to the security of the oil industry.

Developing the economy, 1945–62

Wartime lessons

The years between 1939 and 1945 had been a turning point in the way that the West Indies colonies were governed. In the long run, the most important change was the fairer deal for trade unions which helped the growth of the labour movement in politics. Even by the end of the war, union leaders had a voice in the way that many territories were governed. In the next fifteen years their position became stronger throughout the English-speaking Caribbean. The new politicians had no intention of letting the colonies slip back to the poverty which had been so much part of life before the wartime boom.

Fortunately the war had shown that economic and social development was possible. There had been three key changes in government. One was the coming of labour departments which meant that governments had at last accepted that working conditions were part of their responsibility. Another was the growth of many bodies concerned with economic and social development. The CDWO and the Caribbean Commission had too many European and American experts for the liking of most West Indians but each government, especially in the larger colonies, had to build up planning departments to carry out their plans locally.

The third change was a new way of thinking about the economy of the Caribbean. Before the war and the Moyne Commission, foreign money had been used only to increase export crops. The money spent by the CDWO and the Caribbean Commission showed how funds could be used for the development of local industries and welfare services.

Pioneer industries

These lessons were not lost in the post-war years. Both Trinidad and Jamaica soon set up government departments with the task of creating local industries. By 1950, Jamaica's Department of Commerce and Industry had helped to set up a mill for grinding maize, a plant for the manufacture of cattle feed, a sawmill, two lime oil distilleries and a sisal factory with its own plantation. In Trinidad, the Ministry of Commerce, Industry and Labour was also active in creating local projects but concentrated less on industries with an agricultural connection. By 1950 it was overseeing the opening of a glass works, a brewery, a time-recording instruments factory, a textile mill and a box and staple factory.

Steps were taken to encourage local industries and attract new ones from abroad. Developers were offered 'tax holidays' for the first few years when they would make little profit. Other incentives to spend money in the Caribbean were government grants and lower customs duties on machinery and raw materials. In Trinidad there were measures such as the 1946 Hotels Development Encouragement ordinance, the 1950 Income Tax in Aid of Industry ordinance and the 1950 Aid to Pioneer Industries ordinance. In Jamaica, the Hotels Aid law was passed in 1944, the Textile Encouragement Act in 1947, the Cement Industry Encouragement Act in 1948 and the Pioneer Industries Encouragement Law in 1949.

By the mid-1950s Barbados had joined the push to industrialisation. It began with the 1956 International Business Companies Exemption from Income Tax ordinance. This offered exemption from income tax to international companies which did not then trade in Barbados if they placed their head offices in the island. This opened chances for Barbadians to find work as office staff or in the building and supply trades. In 1958 the Pioneer Industries Act offered a seven-year tax holiday for companies who would manufacture some of a wide range of products needed on the home market. Thirty companies took advantage of the Act. The 1965 Industrial Incentives Act encouraged building of local factories by removing import duties on a list of construction goods. In 1969, Barbados set up the Barbados Industrial Development Corporation along the lines of the Jamaica Industrial Development Corporation, or JIDC. Both provided services to possible new industrial developments, including information on the countries' social, political and economic life and advice on factory location and labour recruitment.

By the time of independence the effect of the encouragement to new industries could be clearly seen. In Jamaica and Trinidad there were new citrus canning companies and copra factories which manufactured edible oils,

Fig. 14.3 *Cars being assembled near Port of Spain, Trinidad.*

margarine and soap. Both islands had textile mills along with smaller factories assembling fridges, stoves and cars or making brushes, brooms and matches as well as foods which included biscuits, macaroni, condensed milk, sauces, sweets. The British American Tobacco Company had opened factories in Jamaica along with smaller enterprises in Dominica and Grenada. By 1962, Jamaica had 800 registered manufacturing concerns of which 149 of the largest had been set up under the incentive scheme. Trinidad and Tobago had nearly as many industries with only half Jamaica's population. She also had a larger share of the heavy industries such as automobile assembly.

The new industries helped the balance of payments. In Jamaica, the value of exports of manufactured goods increased from £850,000 in 1955 to £4,000,000 in 1965. However, they fell short of creating the expected number of new jobs in manufacturing itself, because most of the new industries were highly mechanised. In 1972, only about 5,000 Barbadians out of 250,000 were employed in manufacturing. In Jamaica in 1965, the industries started under the incentive programmes employed about 10,000 workers. At the same time the workforce was growing at about 20,000 each year. Up to 1963 only 4,666 direct jobs had been created by the pioneer industries in Trinidad in years when the workforce had grown by 100,000. Yet the new industries provided an unknown amount of work indirectly to people with jobs in selling, transport, repairs and maintenance, building and other service trades.

Welfare

The new industries went alongside the development of oil, bauxite and tourism described in Chapter 11. They also grew when the first serious efforts were being made to develop welfare services in the Caribbean. Like industrial development, the new services owed a lot to the wartime years. The labour politicians pressed for laws for sick pay, compulsory education and so on. The governments set up ministries for health and education. Overseas money was spent wisely. Much of it came from the CDWO but there was help from other international groups such as the World Health Organisation.

Between 1951 and 1960 the number of pupils in secondary school doubled in Jamaica. The large territories had colleges to teach technology and science. The pupil teacher system was replaced by proper training schemes for school teachers. In 1948 a University College was opened at Mona in Jamaica. By 1962 it was a full university with campuses in Trinidad and Barbados and teaching bases in all Caribbean countries.

Since the Moyne Report there have been dramatic improvements in health. The post-war death rate in Jamaica was nearly half that of the 1920s. Infant mortality has fallen by even greater proportions. Much of this is due to better working conditions, diet and sanitation. But there were also developments in medical care. Health centres were opened in the rural areas and new training schemes started for doctors and nurses.

Assignments

1 *What were the main results of the riots which took place in the Caribbean in the 1930s?*

2 *In which ways was the Moyne Commission different from the other royal commissions which had toured the British West Indies?*

3 *What do you think were the most important aspects of the Moyne Commission? Give reasons.*

4 *How did the Second World War affect the British West Indies?*

5 a) *Give examples of pioneer industries in three British Caribbean territories.*
   b) *What steps were taken to encourage pioneer industries?*
   c) *What benefits were gained from pioneer industries?*

15 SELF-GOVERNMENT

The background 1938–47

Britain's wartime policy

The Moyne Report had called for a 'cautious extension' of the franchise and gradual movement to self-government. To many Caribbean leaders this approach seemed half-hearted. The Mayor of Port of Spain called it a 'hoax'. And so it might have been but for the Second World War.

Until June 1941, Great Britain stood alone against Germany and Italy. On 22 June, Hitler's forces attacked the USSR and she came into the war, Britain's first great ally. After the Japanese raid on Pearl Harbor the United States went to war with Japan and Germany. Britain had a

second ally. But she also had a new enemy, Japan, whose forces set out on a triumphant rush through south-east Asia, capturing Dutch, American, French and English colonies almost every week. To Britain, the greatest blow of all was the loss of her huge, well-defended naval base at Singapore on 15 February 1942. By May, the Japanese were in Burma and pressing up to the frontiers of India, the 'brightest jewel in the English crown'.

These events led to changes in British policy towards the empire. The United States and USSR made it clear that they were not fighting to defend British imperial interests. They pressed her to state that she intended to grant self-government to her colonies. The victories

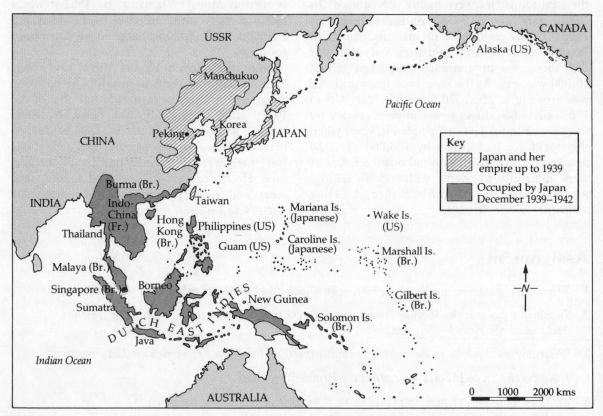

Map 13 *Between 1939 and 1942 the Japanese occupied all American and European colonies in Asia up to the frontiers of British India.*

of Japan, an Asiatic nation, emphasised the fact that the world had changed and non-European peoples would have to be reckoned with. The Indian nationalist movement was quick to press home the point. When Britain attempted to win Indian support for the war effort by promising eventual self-government after the war, the Congress Party turned it down. Its leader, Mohandas Gandhi, described it as a 'post-dated cheque on a crashing bank' and led a campaign of civil disobedience under the slogan of 'Quit India'. The Indians took the lead but there were other nationalist movements: in Egypt, Africa and, of course, here in the Caribbean.

The British government quickly changed the language it used to describe her colonial policy. Before the war, British politicians had spoken of the subject peoples as being under Britain's 'trusteeship'. During the war, they began to talk of 'partnership' between the peoples of the empire. In 1944, the Secretary of State for the Colonies, Oliver Stanley, re-emphasised that the eventual aim was to end the Crown colony system in the Caribbean and replace it by self-government under locally elected governments. Nor was this idle talk. Two important steps forward were taken during the war. In 1943, Britain greatly increased the number of Barbadians allowed to vote for the island's House of Assembly. In 1944, all adult Jamaicans were given the vote.

Britain's post-war policy

Immediately after the war ended in May 1945, there was a British general election. Clement Attlee and the Labour Party won a huge majority in the British Parliament. The new government was sympathetic to the nationalist and labour movements in the empire, especially in India and the Caribbean. In 1947, the wartime promise to India was carried out and British rule was replaced by the two fully independent governments of India and Pakistan. The new Colonial Secretary was a man very different from those who had held the post before the war. Arthur Creech Jones had made a lifetime study of the colonies and was a friend of socialist and trade union leaders in many parts of the empire. In 1939 he had written about the West Indies:

> We carry a grave responsibility for a colonial policy based on cheap labour and cheap raw materials. The facts are out and we can no longer plead ignorance . . . there has been official irresponsibility and the dominance of narrow calculating colonial interests. We can point to years of criminal neglect.

In 1947, as Colonial Secretary, he wrote in a government White Paper:

> The central purpose of British colonial policy is simple. It is to guide the colonial territories to responsible self-government within the Commonwealth in terms that ensure to the people concerned both a fair standard of living and freedom from oppression.

To nationalist leaders in the colonies this statement was welcome as a sign that an important shift in British policy had taken place. On the other hand, some noted that Creech Jones had written about 'self-government' and not 'independence'. The White Paper also showed that Britain still believed that she had the right to 'guide' the colonies towards self-government in the way she thought best.

Patterns of constitutional change

Reasons for delays

The promised self-government did not come until the late 1950s and then not for all colonies. What reasons were there for the slow movement to self-rule? One was that part of Britain's schemes for the Caribbean included setting up a federation of colonies. She was not eager for separate territories to have strong self-government before plans for the federation were well under way. At this time Britain believed that her smaller colonies could not survive as independent states.

Another reason was that there was no overall plan for self-government. Britain never offered changes in advance, although she usually gave way to local demands when they became strong and clear enough. Progress towards self-government depended on how quickly local politicians won support in their own territory. At times, they saw good reasons for not rushing too quickly towards self-rule. It was important to be sure that Britain would not suddenly abandon her responsibility to help the Caribbean overcome some of the economic and social problems which had resulted from colonial rule.

Constitutions

Although there was no master plan for self-government events in the Caribbean did follow a similar pattern of constitutional change. A country's constitution lays down the system of government. Most Caribbean colonies had several constitutions between the 1940s and the 1960s. All were based on the 'Westminster model', which is another way of saying that West Indian constitutions used British ideas about democratic government. Westminster is the district where the British Houses of Parliament and government offices are found. Some obvious signs of the Westminster model in West Indian constitutions remain today. Most states have two houses of parliament or assembly – one fully elected and one only partly so, or entirely nominated. Britain has an elected House of Commons and a non-elected House of Lords. West Indian constitutions usually provide for a 'figure-head' president or governor-general and give the real power to the prime minister, or premier. In Britain the queen, or king, has a figure-head position and the prime minister is the real leader of the government. If West Indian constitutions had been based on an American or French model, the president would be the person with the main powers of government.

The first great constitutional change away from Crown colony government was usually winning universal adult suffrage. Every man or woman then had the right to vote for members of an assembly, council or parliament. But it was possible to have elected assemblies and for all the powers of government still to be in the hands of the governor and officials. So an important step came when elected members were brought into the work of government. Usually they were first chosen to sit on the governor's executive council but without any great responsibility. In time,

such local politicians won the right to be given a 'portfolio' – which meant they took charge of a government department, or ministry. At this stage the governor could still overrule the advice of his executive council.

After some time the executive council became a cabinet. This happened when a majority of the ministers with portfolios were members of the elected parliament and not governor-appointed officials. Governors, at first, kept some powers to overrule the cabinet, but there usually came a further step when they gave up most of these. Full internal self-government came when the leader of the largest party in the elected parliament took over from the governor as chairman of the cabinet. He became the territory's 'chief minister' or 'premier'.

Internal self-government

Internal self-government was not full independence because the premier and his cabinet did not have all the powers of government in their hands. The Colonial Office still kept control over the colony's foreign policy and its defence forces. The governor remained on the spot as Britain's representative. He expected the premier to consult him about cabinet appointments and keep him informed about plans for new laws. In most cases, the governors held some reserve powers which could give them the right to interfere in matters concerning the police, the workings of the law courts and the appointment of senior officials. In cases where British interests were threatened, such as in British Guiana in 1953, the Colonial Office in London would instruct the governor to suspend a constitution altogether.

Reserve powers were one sign that British paternalism did not disappear altogether with internal self-government. There were other signs. Most territories had many British expatriates in the civil service and British police chiefs were common. Nor did self-government end the privileges based on colour. Resident British bankers, engineers and businessmen still had a privileged place in society. Large sections of the economy were still controlled by overseas business interests. Some athletic and country clubs still remained exclusive to whites.

The labour movement in politics

In old colonial society the local politicians who sat on legislative councils had little need to seek support from the people of their country. They were elected by small numbers of the wealthier middle classes. The strong surge of union organisation after the labour riots of the 1930s meant that these politicians were often swept aside by parties which appealed for support to the common man and woman. Many leaders of new political parties were themselves union leaders, while others were middle class professional people who recognised that the future lay, rightfully, with the new mass movements. Of course, the new political parties could not develop fully until the people of a colony had the right to vote.

Jamaica

The growth of the new union-based political parties can be seen clearly in the history of Jamaica. Their origins can be found in the labour movement of the late 1930s. In 1938, the year of the major Jamaican riots, Alexander Bustamante organised the Bustamante Industrial

Fig. 15.1 *Norman Manley in the 1950s.*

Trades Union. Shortly afterwards, the BITU gave its support to Norman Manley, Bustamante's cousin, who was busy founding the People's National Party.

In the Second World War the Crown colony government passed special regulations which limited the rights of trade unions. At the same time, shortages of shipping and supplies led to loss of jobs and higher prices. The BITU threatened strikes and the island's governor used his wartime powers to place Bustamante in internment. Norman Manley took charge of the BITU's organisation until Bustamante was released in February 1942. Also immediately afterwards, the labour movement in Jamaica split into two camps. Bustamante and the BITU broke away from the PNP and formed their own political party, the Jamaica Labour Party. Manley and the PNP kept the support of the other main union organisation – the Trades Union Congress – which was replaced in 1952 by the National Workers' Union.

The differences between the parties were more than a matter of personal rivalry between Manley and Bustamante. The JLP was more concerned with getting immediate improvements in working and social conditions. The PNP placed greater emphasis on long-term changes, to bring about self-government for Jamaica and then to carry out a socialist programme including public ownership of industry and services and government planning of the economy. Both Manley and Bustamante were agreed on the need for universal suffrage so that elections would show who had the support of the majority of Jamaicans. After nearly two years of discussions, the British gave way and announced that all adults could vote in December 1944 for the thirty-two seats in a new House of Representatives. Five members of the largest party in the new house were to be given some responsibility for government departments, although working with a British official.

In the 1944 elections, the JLP won twenty-three of the thirty-two seats and the PNP became the main opposition. As leader of the JLP, Bustamante was head of the government party. The JLP won the next election in 1949, although this time with only seventeen seats to the opposition PNP's thirteen. Both parties pressed the

British to bring in a ministerial system. They did so in 1953 and Bustamante became chief minister. But the next stages in the march to self-government were taken under the leadership of Norman Manley and the PNP which won the 1955 elections. Two years later the PNP carried out the change to full cabinet government and Norman Manley became the island's first premier. British officials still controlled certain departments such as the police, until 1959 when Jamaica won full internal self-government.

Throughout the long years of the struggle for self-government, Jamaican politics were dominated by the two labour-based parties, the JLP and the PNP. No other political parties succeeded in challenging their appeal to the country's electors, although several tried. For instance, the Farmers Party was formed in 1953 and put up thirteen candidates in the 1955 election but not one was elected. Earlier the Jamaican Democratic Party, a businessman's group, failed to win any seats in the 1944 election. The fact that the country had two major parties, each competing for the votes of the ordinary elector, meant that Jamaica quickly developed a two-party system with party leaders putting forward different programmes. This system continued through the 1970s and 1980s with the JLP and PNP forming the government.

Barbados

The beginnings of modern politics in Barbados can also be found in the labour troubles of the 1930s. The 1937 riots were mostly a movement of workers, in Bridgetown and the countryside, who were not organised into unions. Almost as soon as they were over, leaders of the Barbadian working people and Grantley Adams, the lawyer who supported their cause, formed the Progressive League. The League set out to win power in the island's legislative assembly. This was a difficult task. Although Barbados was the only colony with an elected assembly, the right to vote was held by only a small proportion of the population. One of the League's main demands, therefore, was for a wider franchise. It did win six seats in the assembly in 1940, but it was unlikely to do any better until the vote was given to ordinary Barbadian men and women.

Fig. 15.2 *Grantley Adams in 1956.*

The League's greatest strength was its connection with the Barbados Workers' Union which was formed in 1941. Its founder, Hugh Springer, set out to build a general union which included workers from all trades and industries. Grantley Adams was made the union's president from the start. The unity of the Barbados labourers gave them and the Progressive League greater strength in their demands for a change in the Barbadian constitution.

In 1943 the wartime British government agreed that changes should be made in the franchise. Many working men and some women were given the right to vote and stand for election to the assembly. Soon, new political parties were formed to seek the support of the larger numbers of voters. In 1944 the Progressive League and the Barbados Workers' Union set up the Barbados Labour Party with Grantley Adams as its leader. A little later a second party appealing to the new voters was set up, the Congress Party. The first elections under the new system were held in 1946 and the Labour Party and Congress Party each won eight seats out of the twenty-four in the assembly.

The 1946 election destroyed the power of the small groups of wealthy and influential men who had controlled law-making in Barbados throughout colonial times. The Labour Party and Congress Party agreed to form a coalition led by Grantley Adams. This gave them a two-thirds majority in the assembly. The British government soon recognised the new balance of power and ordered the island's governor to hand over the portfolios for some government departments to members of the coalition. These were the first ministers in modern West Indian history and Grantley Adams became the first premier. But the power of the new premier and his ministers was limited. Officials still sat alongside them in the executive council and kept charge of important departments such as police and the civil service.

Grantley Adams and the ministers continued to press for further improvements in the constitution. In 1951 the British granted a full adult franchise. At last every man and every woman would have a vote. They also agreed that assemblymen should be paid, an important step for political parties which put forward candidates who were not themselves wealthy.

Elections were held again in 1954 and this time Grantley Adams and the Labour Party won a clear majority in the assembly. The party was now in a strong enough position to demand that a full ministerial system be set up. Grantley Adams was now chairman of a cabinet of ministers. Colonial officials no longer had charge of any departments. Barbados was well on the road to full internal self-government, although there were still quarrels between the ruling Labour Party and the governor over many important issues.

Before 1954 the island's new political and union leaders needed to be united to press the British for changes in the constitution. Once self-government came, it was only natural that they should disagree about which were the most important and urgent policies. The case for modernising Barbados' economic life quickly was made by a young member of the Labour Party, Errol Barrow. He was a barrister who had begun his career as legal adviser to the Antigua and St Kitts unions. Barrow believed that Grantley Adams was too cautious in introducing new industry to the island and in setting up full welfare schemes. In 1955 he broke away from the Barbados Labour Party and founded the Democratic Labour Party. His party organisation was strengthened by building up a connection with a new labour union, the Transport and General Workers' Union. In 1958 Errol Barrow became its vice-president. In 1961 it was the turn of Errol Barrow to become premier after his party won the election in that year.

The Windwards

In the Windwards, it was again the union-based parties which took the lead in the struggle for self-government. The task was hard, for these islands had almost no industrial workers and few dock labourers compared with the larger islands. There were no sugar estates with large numbers of workers like those who had taken an important part in the union movement in Jamaica. Yet, political parties did arise in the 1940s. In St Lucia the Labour Party grew out of the Workers' Co-operative Union. George Charles was president of both. In St Vincent the Workers' and Rate Payers' Union gave its support to E. T. Joshua, one of the island's first active opponents of the Crown colony system. In Grenada, T. A. Marryshow had a long record of attempts to organise local political movements and to prove that local politicians were capable of taking a leading part in their country's affairs. In the 1950s, a new leader, Eric Gairy, burst on to the political scene. He had returned from the Aruba oil fields in 1946 and set about organising the Manual and Metal Workers' Union which drew its support from poor estate workers. Shortly afterwards, the Union backed Eric Gairy when he started the Grenada United Labour Party.

All the territories gained a full adult suffrage in 1950 or 1951 and all the Labour parties won the general elections which followed shortly. After this, the labour leaders became locked in sharp struggles with the island's administrators. Local politicians were allowed only a few portfolios and the Labour Party leaders usually held the post of Minister of Trade and Production in the administrator's executive council. Even after the British gave way and allowed a form of 'cabinet' government with local chief ministers, they refused to hand over full control over finance.

Throughout the 1950s all the Windwards were given grant aids from Britain and the Colonial Office saw this as a reason for keeping control over government spending. It did not believe that any of the islands could ever have a strong enough economy to become fully independent by itself. Any further steps to self-government would have to wait, in Britain's view, until after federation. So the Colonial Office administrators remained in the colonies. Although some of them were West Indian, this could not alter the fact that the Windwards were not being given any more real control of their own affairs and were being denied the chance to introduce plans for national development.

The Leewards

The Leewards, too, were considered by the Colonial Office to be too small and too poor to move towards self-government. As in the Windwards, the cost of government in the Leewards was partly paid for by British grants-in-aid. However, colonial rule met with vigorous opposition from the labour movements.

In St Kitts-Nevis, the labour movement dated back to the 1930s. By 1940 both St Kitts-Nevis and Antigua had a Trades and Labour Union which shortly afterwards gave support to labour parties. In Montserrat the Trades and Labour Union was first registered in 1946 and it, too, was soon followed by a Labour Party. Universal adult suffrage was won for the Leeward Islands in 1951, followed by Labour Party victories in elections. As in the Windwards, it was some time before the British allowed a full ministerial system. In 1956 some elected members of the legislatures were allowed portfolios and the leading labour politician usually took the post of Minister of Trade and Production. In 1960 the right of each island to have its own chief minister was finally won, but that still did not mean full self-government.

Even these gains had meant sharp struggles against local administrators by the labour leaders, Bradshaw and Southwell in St Kitts-Nevis, Bird and Hurst in Antigua and Bramble in Montserrat. As in the Windwards there were two main issues in these quarrels. One was over the rate of prog-

ress towards government by elected leaders. For instance, in 1958 the administrator of St Kitts reappointed a nominated member of the government after he had been voted out of office by the elected members of the Council. In doing this, the administrator had the support of the Colonial Office. The second issue was over the right of the elected ministers to control finance. Until the late 1950s the Colonial Office insisted that the portfolio for finance, as well as that for police and the law, should be in the hands of an official.

Trinidad and Tobago

In the 1920s and 1930s there was a close link between parts of the Trinidad labour movement and political parties. The Trinidad Workingmen's Association, led by Arthur Cipriani, put forward candidates and a political programme for elections to the island's legislative council. In 1934 it re-organised itself into the Trinidad Labour Party. After the 1937 oil field riots, 'Buzz' Butler used his unions as the base for the British Empire Workers' and Citizens' Home Rule Party.

Universal suffrage came in 1945 but politics in Trinidad and Tobago did not follow the pattern in the other islands where mass parties appealed for support to the new electors. This was because the colony already had many small parties and organisations. Each pressed for the interests of its own group.

There were several reasons for the different development of Trinidad's politics. The councils had more unelected official members than elsewhere. Local politicians who got elected were outnumbered by officials and not able to press for new laws in the same way as Grantley Adams in Barbados or Bustamante in Jamaica. Some quickly accepted their position as part of a tight government circle, which ruled Trinidad as it had been governed for the past 150 years with little regard for public opinion. The divisions in Trinidad and Tobago's society also held back the growth of union-based political parties. The oil industry's workers organised themselves separately and so the labour movement was split between industrial and agricultural workers, and between skilled and unskilled. The population included two major racial groups which made it more difficult for mass political movements to develop.

The result of these racial, social and political divisions was that no party could win a large number of seats in the legislative council elections of 1946 and 1950. This meant that there was no party pressing for rapid movement towards self-government. Five elected members were given some ministerial powers in 1950 but, by 1956, Trinidad and Tobago had developed less towards self-rule than Jamaica or Barbados.

The elections of September 1956 seemed to show just how fragmented political movements were in Trinidad and Tobago. For twenty-four seats on the council there were eighty-nine candidates from eight parties. The main ones were the People's Democratic Party, supported largely by East Indians and led by Bhadase Maraj, who was leader of the Maha Sabha Hindu movement; the Trinidad Labour Party; the Butler Party; the leftist Caribbean Socialist Party and the independent Labour Party. A more conservative organisation was the Party of Political Progress Groups (POPPG) led by Albert Gomez. One new party which many felt had little chance of success was the People's National Movement (PNM).

The PNM had been launched at a public meeting in Port of Spain's Woodford Square in January 1956 by Dr Eric Williams. Dr Williams had been deputy chairman of the research council of the Caribbean Commission. In 1957 it refused to renew his appointment and he left to play his part in the political development of Trinidad and Tobago. He quickly established a new style of political leadership with his lectures in the 'university of Woodford Square', where he spoke to tens of thousands about the background to their territory's problems and the solutions he offered. The PNM broke with traditional politics in Trinidad and Tobago by calling for a national movement, which it described as 'a rally, a convention of all and for all, a mobilisation of all the forces in the community, cutting across race and religion, class and colour'.

Dr Williams made it clear that he favoured an integrated state educational system to replace

Fig. 15.3 *Dr Eric Williams.*

the denominational schools which had catered separately for Catholic and Protestant, Hindu and Moslem. He took policies from both left and right. The socialists were told that the PNM was not against public ownership if it was in the interests of workingmen and for the national good. Business interests heard that foreign investment should be encouraged if that would help the development of Trinidad and Tobago. The PNM won approval from many sections of the population by its promise to end corruption and graft in their government and by its determination to press for faster progress towards self-rule.

Those who doubted that the PNM would succeed were wrong. The party won thirteen of the elected seats on the Legislative Council. It was the first time any party had won a clear majority of the elected seats. But it was not an overall majority as five members of the council were still nominated by the governor. Dr Williams immediately demanded that, as leader of the largest elected party, he had the right to name two of the nominated members so that the PNM would have a true majority in the Council. The governor hesitated, but the Colonial Office soon ordered him to agree to this demand. From then on, Dr Williams was in a position to guide Trinidad and Tobago through the stages of ministerial government, cabinet government and finally to full internal self-rule in 1959.

British Guiana

Like Trinidad, British Guiana's modern politics began with many sectional divisions between local leaders and groups. As in Trinidad, Crown colony government in British Guiana gave no real opportunity for the development of a mass political movement in the 1930s and 1940s. Local pressure on the governor's executive council came from the middle class business interest groups in Georgetown and the position of the Bookers' sugar empire was an added obstacle to Guyanese control of their own affairs.

However, in the late 1940s two young nationalist politicians came home to British Guiana and launched the movement which was to begin the long, and often unhappy, struggle for full independence. In 1947, Dr Cheddi Jagan returned with his American wife from the United States where he had trained as a dentist. The two Jagans quickly entered the trade union movement and were especially active among the rice farmers and the sugar estate workers, both mostly East Indian communities. In 1949, Forbes Burnham returned from London where he had qualified as a lawyer as well as being active in anti-colonial movements there. With Cheddi Jagan, Burnham founded the People's Progressive Party. Under Jagan as its leader and Burnham as its chairman the PPP was the first nationally organised party in the colony and replaced two old sectional parties, the East Indian Association and the League of Coloured Peoples.

The policies of the party were spelled out in its weekly newspaper, *Thunder*. It called for an end to colonial rule and measures which would lead to a higher standard of living for all. In 1951 the British government agreed to changes in the colony's constitution. An assembly was to be elected by universal adult suffrage and some of the elected members were to be given portfolios in the government. In the first elections, in 1953, the PPP won a clear victory with eighteen out of twenty-four seats. Dr Jagan became Prime Minister and Forbes Burnham Education Minister. They had fought the election on a strongly socialist programme, declaring that further advances to self-rule must go alongside government control of the economic wealth of the country, then largely in foreign hands. The forcefulness of the PPP proposals and the strength of their support in the country alarmed the British government, then headed by Winston Churchill. They quickly came to believe that the PPP intended to control every position of importance in British Guiana without waiting for further steps along the road to self-government.

In the British view, one sign of this was that PPP ministers announced they would keep their positions in the trade union movement as well as serving in the government. Their suspicion increased when the PPP encouraged the Indian sugar workers to start a strike against the Sugar Producers' Association which refused to recognise their union. At the same time the PPP cabinet said it wanted two new laws. One was to bring schools managed by the Church under the control of the government. The other would end the censorship which made it illegal to bring certain political books into the country.

Opposition members in the assembly declared that the PPP intended to turn British Guiana into a communist state. In Britain and the United States there were many ready to believe the accusation. This was the time of one of the peaks of the Cold War and the United States had a constant suspicion that communism would spread to South and Central America. This fear was so strong that she was likely to believe that any strong nationalist movement was a cover for communist activity. American leaders were also alarmed that the PPP's stand against Britain would be copied by anti-Amer-

Fig. 15.4 *Supporters of Cheddi Jagan protest against British troops.*

ican movements in countries such as Guatemala. They put strong pressure on the British government to turn the PPP from power. It was a request the British did not feel able to reject, for they were by now junior partners in NATO, the military alliance of the western powers which was largely paid for by the United States.

After Dr Jagan and Forbes Burnham had been ministers for only 133 days, British troops were landed in Georgetown. On orders from Britain, the governor suspended the constitution and set up an interim government of nominated officials. The British action delayed the coming of internal self-government and independence to British Guiana for many years. But it had other serious consequences. For four years, since its foundation in 1949, the PPP had united the two major communities in British Guiana in a common cause. By destroying the PPP government the British made it difficult for the alliance of Dr Jagan and Forbes

Burnham, and of African and Indian peoples, to hold together.

The two men had different political philosophies. Dr Jagan saw his socialism more as part of an international movement while Burnham placed greater emphasis on purely Guyanese issues. In the end they might have split anyway. But the break-up of the PPP came very soon after the two were dismissed from the government. This was too early to prevent what was still a young political movement from dividing itself on racial lines. For a further two years there were two PPPs. One backed Dr Jagan and drew its strength from the Indian community who made up nearly 50 per cent of the population. The African people gave their support to Mr Burnham's branch of the party. In 1957 this party was renamed the People's National Congress or PNC. For several years after 1957 the British government used the racial basis of the Guyanese parties to turn the situation in the colony to its advantage.

Belize

The move to create trade unions involved British Honduras as well as the island territories. In 1938 the colony's first trade union, the General Workers' Union, was formed. The need for improvement in labour conditions was amply clear from the sharp criticisms in the Moyne Report about the harsh conditions in the camps provided for seasonal timber workers and the even greater sufferings of the Maya workers in the chicle industry.

At the time, the colony had only two elected members of the legislative council and the right to vote for them was limited to those with incomes of $300, or the equivalent in property. After the Second World War there was agitation in British Honduras for a greater degree of self-government. Leaders of the General Workers' Union created the People's United Party which soon captured control of Belize City Council. In 1951 the British sent a Commission of Enquiry to recommend changes in the colonial government. It reported in favour of slow development because of the undeveloped nature of the country outside Belize City (which held nearly a third of the population). The people of these rural districts were mostly Maya, Indians or Caribs and the Commission stated that 'the advances in general and political education has not been uniform among all races'.

However, there were some changes in 1953 when British Honduras was given an elected assembly of nine members. The number of people allowed to vote in the first election in 1954 was raised from 1,772 to 21,000, and most of the new voters were from the rural districts. The PUP won eight of the nine seats. The leading figure in the PUP was George Price who followed the policy of as little co-operation as possible with the colonial government. When elected members were given three ministerial posts in 1955 he refused to take one. Other PUP assembly members were willing to co-operate in this limited form of self-government and the disagreement led to a split in both the PUP and the General Workers' Union. However, in the 1957 election Price and the PUP won all nine seats. He now took a leading part in pressing for further advances along the road to self-government but aroused suspicion by having talks at the same time with the Guatemalans. He was dismissed from the executive council and once again the PUP split.

Even so, the PUP still held the loyalty of most voters. One of the two opposition parties was made up of ex-PUP members and they shared many of their old party's ideals. So it was not surprising that in 1960 all three parties came together in a United Front to press for more powers of self-government. Nor is it surprising that the PUP became the dominant partner in this alliance. Finally, in 1964 British Honduras won full internal self-government and George Price became Prime Minister of the colony, which was renamed Belize in 1973.

Assignments

1 *'Everywhere Moyne heard demands that the people of each territory should elect their own assemblies by adult suffrage . . . On the other hand Moyne heard opposition to the idea of adult suffrage, self-government and federation from many . . . who did not always wish to see the ordinary men and women have an influence in government.'*

Outline the main points that a writer in a British Caribbean territory might have made in the period 1940–45:
a) *explaining why 'the people of each territory should elect their own assemblies by adult suffrage'.*
b) *expressing 'opposition to the idea of adult suffrage, self-government and federation'.*
or
c) *Let the class debate the following:*

  'In this year 1940 the British West Indies is ready for self-government with all of its implications.'

2 *Make a chart (dividing your page in columns) to show when and how the following areas in the British Caribbean achieved self-government: Jamaica, Barbados, Trinidad and Tobago, Guyana and Belize.*

3 *Why was self-government more difficult to achieve in the Windward and Leeward Islands than in the other colonies?*

16 TOWARDS FEDERATION

Self-government and federation

By the later 1950s, all the British Caribbean territories had moved far along the road to full self-government. However, the governors held important reserve powers in every colony. No English-speaking West Indian country controlled its own foreign policy. European interests dominated their economies and Britain paid for parts of their costs of government and social welfare. Full independence had not yet been reached, nor even promised.

Between the first steps to internal self-government and independence there was the attempt, from 1958 to 1961, to make a federation of the West Indies work. It was only after the federation failed that independence or full internal self-government came to most of Britain's colonies. Many West Indian political leaders had hoped that federation would give the whole of the English-speaking Caribbean a stronger voice in world political and economic affairs. To understand why it failed we shall have to look at the background to the idea of unifying the territories and at the long negotiations which led up to 1958.

Attempts at federation before 1947

The seventeenth century

The first attempt to federate part of the British colonial empire came in 1671 when the governor of Barbados was also given charge of the Leewards. This small federation did not last long because planters on the Leewards and in Barbados were rivals for the biggest share of the trade in exporting sugar to Britain. The Leewards islands suffered from raids by Dutch sailors and some planters there complained that Barbadian planters had been pleased by this.

In 1671 the British gave in to Leewards demands that they should have a separate government. A governor-in-chief was put in charge of St Kitts, Nevis, Montserrat, Antigua, Barbuda, Anguilla and any other island which might come into the British Empire.

The nineteenth century

In the 1860s the British were looking for ways to save on the costs of Crown colony government and decided that they could cut the wages bill if islands shared the same officials. In 1869 Governor Benjamin Pine was told to organise a federation of Antigua (with Barbuda), Dominica, Montserrat, Nevis, St Kitts (with Anguilla) and the Virgin Islands. There was local opposition, St Kitts and Nevis did not wish to share their government funds with Antigua and Montserrat which were bankrupt. Governor Pine had to tell the Colonial Office that the scheme had failed because of 'local prejudice and self-interest'. All the British could do was to give the Leewards a single governor but agree that any laws or ordinances had to be approved by the councils of each island.

Governor John Pope-Hennessy was sent to Barbados in 1875 with orders to arrange a federation with the Windwards. There was a bitter opposition from the Barbados press and from the assembly of white planters and a few influential coloured men. The governor was supported by the cane workers. They hoped that federation would give them a chance to leave Barbados and work for higher wages or buy their own plots in the Windwards. They also believed the schemes for federation would help them by making it possible to emigrate freely to the Windwards.

The planters and coloured merchants set up the Barbados Defence League to fight federation. They claimed it would lead to the end of their representative system. In March 1876 estate labourers in the south rioted in support of Pope-Hennessy who was popular because he tried to force the assembly to reform prisons and hospitals. Eight people were killed. The Colonial Office then quickly removed Pope-Hennessy fearing more trouble.

The plan to federate Barbados with the Windwards was dropped. In 1886 some of the Windwards were given a similar system to that in the Leewards. There was one governor for Grenada, St Vincent, St Lucia and Tobago. His headquarters were in Grenada but each island council was responsible for its own police, law courts, social services and treasury.

The only successes in federating were the union of St Kitts and Nevis in 1882 and that of Trinidad and Tobago in 1899. Against this there was the break up of the long union of Jamaica and British Honduras (Belize) in 1886.

Why was there so much resistance to closer union or federation? The main reason was probably that islanders would not put aside economic rivalries. They would not share either profits from trade or the costs of government. In addition each island society was different from any other with its own history, laws and customs. All these made for strong local pride. They also meant that planters, merchants and other interest groups did not want to lose their influence as they would if the centre of government went to another territory.

The ex-slaves did not always share the opposition. Their main interest was in free movement so they could improve their poor conditions. But the question of free movement was one strong reason why planters opposed federation.

The twentieth century: middle class opinion

In the twentieth century, social and economic changes meant that many of the West Indian middle classes began to see advantages in federation. The old local ruling classes were shrinking in numbers and had much less influence in their territories. Many family-owned plantations and merchant businesses had been bought by multi-national companies. They often had land and other interests in several colonies and ran them as one unit. Their local managers, such as Robert Kirkwood, the

managing director of the West Indian Sugar Company in Jamaica, favoured the idea of federation for economic matters. A whole-region approach to production and marketing made more sense when radio and telegraphs brought people together. Steamships had overcome the trade winds which had once made sailing from west to east long and tedious.

Economic co-operation seemed absolutely essential in bad times when the colonies might gain a better price or larger share of the world market if they stuck together. Outside trading partners, such as Canada, often preferred to deal with one unit rather than many. In 1917, the Associated Chambers of Commerce was organised and soon came out in favour of some form of economic union. The depression of the 1930s pushed them to call for the revival of West Indian trade through the creation of regional shipping services, a customs union and clearing houses for the payment of bills.

The Colonial Office played a part in strengthening the idea of federation by creating several regional organisations in the 1920s. After 1922 the Imperial College of Tropical Agriculture, which had its headquarters in Trinidad, kept regular contact with Departments of Agriculture in the other colonies. A West Indian Court of Appeal was set up for the whole English-speaking region and, shortly afterwards, a regional meteorological service was started.

In 1926 the Colonial Office called the first of the West Indian conferences. Over the years these regional meetings studied many topics: ways of developing overseas markets, improvements to communications in the English-speaking Caribbean, promoting local industries and providing veterinary services. The meetings were rotated from one island capital to another. For a while they gave West Indians a chance to work together on regional projects. Unfortunately, the committees soon became top heavy with foreign 'experts' who had very little Caribbean experience.

Closer union

A chance to move towards federation came in the early 1930s when falling sugar prices seemed

Fig. 16.1 *The former Imperial College of Tropical Agriculture is now a section of the University of the West Indies, but it still deals with tropical agriculture.*

about to throw the Caribbean colonies once again into bankruptcy. A Royal Commission came that was headed by Lord Olivier. It recommended that a greater preference be given to West Indian sugar landed in Britain but at the same time suggested that money could be saved by uniting the governments of the Windwards and Leewards. Ever ready to cut costs, the British government sent the Closer Union Commission in 1932 to look into the possibilities.

The middle class politicians who wanted a greater share in Crown colony government saw how they might gain from the Commission. One of them was Cecil E. Rawle, president of the Dominica Taxpayers Reform Association. He immediately called leaders of the representative government associations (see page 95) of other countries to a meeting in Roseau. Rawle hoped that the meeting would agree to some kind of federation in return for a bigger share in government. The leaders from the Windwards, Leewards, Trinidad and Barbados had difficulties in deciding on how they wished closer union to work but in the end agreed on three points.

First, they would work towards a federation of the eastern Caribbean with the door 'left open' to Jamaica and British Guiana to join later. Second, they would work within the

federation to gain some form of self-government. Third, their self-government would be based on a wider franchise but still not on the right of every adult to vote. Cipriani was disgusted by this although he decided to support the proposals as an important step forward. In his parting speech he called on the 'common man' to 'agitate, educate, confederate'.

Most of the proposals from the Roseau Conference were ignored by the Closer Union Commission. They did suggest an association of the Leewards and Windwards but rejected the idea of a federation, saying it would not save on costs.

The labour movement and federation

This was the final failure of the middle classes to bring about limited political changes. In the next few years, the demands for change in the colonial system were broadened by the protests of working men and women in town and country. In the late 1930s and 1940s the leaders of the labour movement strongly supported federation. They believed that it would be an important step forward along the road to ending the Crown colony system.

In June 1938 labour leaders from all colonies

formed the first regional political organisation, the British Guiana and West Indian Labour Congress. In November that year they held a special meeting in Trinidad to consider their demands to the Moyne Commission. At the top of their list was the setting up of a federation of the West Indies. It was to be made up of self-governing states in which all adult citizens had the right to vote.

After listening to their views, the Moyne Report gave cautious support to the idea of federation. The start of the CDWO in 1940 gave strength to the idea of approaching West Indian problems on a regional basis. During the war labour politicians were gaining strength and influence in many colonies, so it was not surprising that the British government began to link the possibility of federation with their vague promises of self-government after the war. In London, it was taken for granted that most, if not all, of the colonies were too small to reach self-government on their own. At that time, it was difficult for the British to foresee the economic development that would take place as the colonies moved towards self-government in the 1950s.

In 1945, the wartime Colonial Secretary invited representatives from local governments to meet and discuss ways of bringing about political federation. Two years later the Colonial Secretary, a member of the British Labour Party, issued his White Paper promising 'guidance' along the road to self-government. For the Caribbean he suggested that this might be linked with setting up a federation. He called a conference to take place at Montego Bay to discuss the question.

Planning federation 1947–58

Montego Bay Conference

Representatives from all the territories and Colonial Office officials came to the Montego Bay Conference. Most were in favour of some form of federation but there were important differences between them. The British never made their intentions plain, but it is probable that they did not expect the colonies to become fully independent. Instead, they looked forward to self-rule on local matters for each territory, balanced by a federation over which Britain kept a good deal of control. They certainly believed it would be more efficient and cheaper to replace the governor and his staff in each colony with one governor-general and a few officials for the whole English-speaking Caribbean.

Many of the representatives of local councils and assemblies believed that regional co-operation would bring benefits in trade and cultural matters but they did not wish to link federation with self-government. In 1947 political power in most colonies was still in the hands of the older trading or plantation interests. These men had no desire to hasten the coming of self-government through elected parliaments, which would almost certainly place power in the hands of union-based parties. The main labour leader already in power, Alexander Bustamante, also had doubts about federation. He possibly feared that it was part of a British scheme to abandon responsibilities for helping the West Indies.

On the other hand, leaders of the socialist parties were still in favour of combining the question of federation and independence. The British Guiana and West Indian Labour Congress had been replaced by the Caribbean Labour Congress and this held a meeting in Kingston shortly before the Montego Bay Conference. In Kingston the CLC called for a federation with dominion status. In other words it wanted the Caribbean colonies to be united as a nation within the British Commonwealth but with the same independence that Britain granted to India in 1947.

The CLC delegates then moved to Montego Bay believing that their view would win the day. But they were faced with strong opposition from the non-labour politicians there and from Alexander Bustamante, who warned against rushing to set up a 'federation of paupers'. These cautious views had the support of Arthur Creech Jones, the British Colonial Secretary who was chairman of the conference. He suggested that committees be set up to recommend what powers the federation should have over finance, trade, immigration and customs, quite separately from the matter of self-government.

The SCAC

This was accepted by the conference. It set up a Standing Closer Association Committee to work out a form of federation which followed two main guidelines. First, the new federation would have to respect each territory's right to make its own arrangements except for matters which all agreed could be handed over to the new central government. This was almost certain to produce a federal government with very few real powers. Secondly, each territory's movement to local self-government was to be separate from the plans for a federation. This meant that the federation could contain territories which were fully self-governing alongside those still under mainly British control.

The SCAC made its report in October 1949. It suggested a federation of all the English-speaking colonies. Each was to elect representatives to a Federal House of Assembly which would be the main law-making body. There were to be fifty seats in the assembly but if they were shared out on the basis of population Jamaica would have a permanent majority, as she had over half the people of the federation. Instead it suggested that the division should be: Jamaica, sixteen; Trinidad, nine; British Guiana, six; Barbados, four; and the Leewards and Windwards two each, except for Montserrat which should have one seat. There was to be a prime minister and cabinet government, made up of elected politicians, but also a governor-general who would have reserve powers to interfere on matters such as defence and finance. Both the territories and the federal assemblies would be allowed to make laws on questions of trade, commerce, development of industries and the free movement of peoples. In the case of conflict, the federal government would have the power to overrule a territory.

British Guiana, British Honduras and the British Virgin Islands all said they would not accept this form of federation. All had interests or problems which were different from those of the rest of the English-speaking Caribbean. The Virgin Islands were linked in economic and cultural matters with their United States neighbours. British Honduras and British Guiana both saw their future in terms of relations with mainland neighbours, more than with the English-speaking islands. They had different security and customs problems due to their land frontiers. Both, too, feared the effects of immigration from the islands if free movement came about as a result of federation.

Planning the federation

Councils and assemblies in all other territories accepted the plan, but often with many doubts or reservations. Some of these were political. The SCAC had recommended only partial self-rule for the federation with wide powers left to the British governor-general. Many politicians attacked this timid scheme bitterly. Grantley Adams, who had been a member of the SCAC, said the plan would lead to nothing more than a glorified Crown colony. In Trinidad, Dr Pat Solomon said it represented no constitutional advance for the Caribbean. In Grenada, T. A. Marryshow, who had argued for federation for forty years, absolutely rejected the SCAC proposals.

Other politicians had doubts about the idea that the federal government should take 25 per cent of customs duties collected by each territory. They also disliked another SCAC scheme which was that all should join a customs union. A customs union meant that each government would have to charge the same import duties on all goods brought into its country from outside the federation. Both schemes would mean that territories would lose control over much of the income they needed for local government. The larger territories all feared that their development would be held back by the smaller, and generally poorer, colonies. Some, especially Trinidad, feared that, if the new federal state allowed free movement to all its citizens, they would be faced with unlimited immigration. The problem of the position of the federal capital produced jealousies. The SCAC had proposed Trinidad but the question was postponed for later discussion.

Fig. 16.2 *The London Conference on Federation, 1953.*

All these questions were discussed at meetings over the years between 1950 and 1958, when the federation actually came into being. As each year passed it became more difficult to reach agreement. Many of the political leaders at these conferences were the same men who had met at Montego Bay in 1947. Then they had very little power in their own countries. By the mid-1950s, they had become ministers or chief ministers with powers of government which they would not easily give up. Most territories, by then, had universal suffrage, so that politicians were bound to remember election promises and could not easily give way to the ideas of leaders from other countries.

The first of the major conferences took place in London in 1953. There, the West Indian leaders were united in demanding that some of the powers the British wanted to give the governor-general should be held instead by the prime minister of the new federation. They also agreed on arrangements for sharing the seats in the Federal House of Assembly between the territories. But, on other questions, they were not united. The site of the capital was still a

matter for argument. In London, Grenada was chosen instead of Trinidad but no one felt that this decision would be final. The most hotly disputed problem was over the free movement of peoples.

The free movement question

The question of controlling migration had lain behind the withdrawal of British Guiana and British Honduras from federation. Now, in London, Barbados and the smaller territories argued that free movement would be essential for all citizens of the English-speaking Caribbean who came under the same government. Leaders from Jamaica and Trinidad and Tobago found it difficult to disagree with this, but both countries feared that large-scale immigration from the smaller islands would lead to higher levels of unemployment and labour disruptions. For the time being the question was sidestepped when all but the Trinidad delegates agreed that it need not be settled there and then.

In 1955 a meeting was called in Trinidad

specially to deal with the problem of free movement. The best agreement that could be reached was that each territory would be allowed to follow its own immigration policies for the first five years after federation. At the end of this time, the federal assembly would decide whether to make movement of people a matter for federal laws or allow the territories to continue with their own arrangements. It was a compromise which meant that the federal government would have less power on this issue than the territorial governments. The compromise made it possible for West Indian politicians to go on planning, but they were soon involved in other issues about the division of power between the federal government and the territories.

Paying for the federation

The federal government would be powerless if it did not have some means of raising money to pay for its work. The first idea had been that each territory should pass on to the federal government 25 per cent of the money collected from local customs duties. Then in 1956 Sir Sydney Caine, the British chairman of the commission studying financial arrangements, pointed out some difficulties in this scheme. It would be unfair as some islands had few local industries and relied much more on imported goods than their larger neighbours. Therefore, their citizens paid customs duties on more everyday goods and would end up paying a larger share. Caine also said that the plan would be unreliable. If a territory had a bad trading year its imports would be lower and so would its customs duties.

Political leaders in the territories agreed with Caine's view that the scheme would be unfair. Many of them also objected to a customs union. Most governments tried to encourage local manufacturers or businesses by making the duties low on imports of raw materials or machinery. At the same time they could discourage competition from rival foreign manufactured items by high import duties on imported goods.

Some objectors to customs union also feared the coming of a free trade area. Now they agreed with Mr Manley when he argued strongly that a customs union could take away the local governments' powers to find their own duties to keep local industries. The idea was opposed by politicians who feared that more developed Caribbean states would profit at the expense of the less developed. Mr Bustamante said that free trade would allow more industrialised Trinidad to dump her manufactures cheaply in Jamaica, while smaller island leaders feared that both Trinidad and Jamaica would dump in their countries. They complained that this would be particularly unfair if their citizens were not, in return, allowed to emigrate to the larger islands for work.

The politicians were just as opposed to the scheme Sir Sydney Caine suggested instead, of paying customs duties to the federal government. This was for the federal government to raise money by excise taxes paid on purchases of spirits, rum, beer, cigarettes and petrol. Such excise duties could mean that the federal government's need for money would force up prices and the cost of living in the territories.

The question of how to pay for federal government was still undecided in 1956 when West Indian leaders met British ministers in London, for the last conference before federation began in 1958. So strong were the disagreements among the Caribbean politicians that they spent five days in a private meeting, or 'caucus', to discuss whether they favoured customs duties or excise taxes. On the fourth evening agreement was no nearer. Then Mr Bradshaw of St Kitts suggested a way out of the deadlock. Instead of giving the federal government power to collect money, each territory would make a fixed payment, or 'mandatory levy'. The next morning the others agreed to pay a levy for the first five years during which time the federal government would not have the power to raise its own funds.

Only then did the West Indians go into full conference to make the final arrangements. They persuaded Britain to cut down further on the power of the governor-general to interfere in any matters other than defence and foreign affairs. But, this did not leave the future federal government in a strong position. On the two most important questions, the free movement of people and the collection of taxes, the conferences of 1953, 1955 and 1956 had taken away the powers which the SCAC report had intended to give the federal government. For the first five years it would have only £2 million a year to spend, made up of the total of the mandatory levies. In effect, the federal government would have only three major tasks: to take over the distribution of CDWO funds, to support the West India Regiment and to develop the University of the West Indies.

Final arrangements

In London the final arrangements were made for elections to the federal assembly. There would be forty-five seats of which Jamaica would have seventeen, Trinidad and Tobago ten, Barbados five and the rest would be shared among the smaller islands.

An important decision was made that no one could be a minister or member of assembly in both the federation and a unit territory. It was hoped that this would prevent politicians finding a clash of loyalty between their work on regional and local questions. Unfortunately, it also meant that the federal parliament and government would not have the services of some of the region's most experienced leaders, who decided to stay in local politics.

Between 1956 and 1958 committees were busy with the final details. A civil service staff was recruited, a flag and coat of arms were designed and a detailed constitution written. The most difficult question was the site of the federation's capital. In the end Trinidad was chosen. Until a permanent home could be found on the island, the federal government was given a temporary headquarters in Port of Spain. It was here that Lord Hailes was sworn in as first Governor-General of the Federation of the British West Indies on 3 January 1958. His first task was to order elections, to take place on 25 March for the Parliament of the new federation.

Assignments

1 a) *What proposals for federation of British Caribbean territories were made during the nineteenth century?*
   b) *What were the main arguments of the opponents to federation during this time?*
   c) *Which groups were most in favour of federation during this period?*

2 *What do you think were the main reasons for:*
   a) *most of the British Caribbean territories and*
   b) *Britain,*
   working towards a federation between 1947 and 1958?

3 *Explain why it took British Caribbean territories so long (1947–58) to reach agreement on the terms for federation.*

17 FEDERATION AND INDEPENDENCE

Federal politics

Political parties

The elections were fought by politicians belonging to two main groups. The West Indies Federal Labour Party was well prepared. It was formed in London in 1956 by leaders of the socialist parties who agreed to fight the federal elections as one organisation. The parties which came into the WIFLP were in government in every territory except St Vincent. Because its policies were socialist, the WIFLP was given a contribution of £5000 by the British Labour Party. Norman Manley was elected president and Grantley Adams first vice-president. Other leaders who took part were Robert Bradshaw, Vere Bird and Eric Gairy. In 1957 Dr Williams' Trinidad Party, the PNM, was accepted, but only as an associate member because the PNM's policy was one of national reform rather than socialism.

The WIFLP had time to be well organised for the elections. But many of its leaders were not themselves candidates. Mr Manley argued that he could do more for the federation by staying in Jamaican politics. He left the leadership of the WIFLP in the elections to Mr Adams. Some other island politicians took the same decision. In the end, out of the chief ministers of territories, only Grantley Adams, W. H. Bramble and Robert Bradshaw decided to go into federal politics.

In each territory candidates from the opposition parties also stood for election to the federal assembly. As election day drew near they began to realise they might be stronger by coming together as a rival federal party to the WIFLP. The leading spokesman for this group was Sir Alexander Bustamante of Jamaica although, like Mr Manley, he was not himself a candidate. In the elections this alliance of opposition parties won twenty out of the forty-five seats in the federal assembly. In Jamaica they gained twelve to the WIFLP's five; in Trinidad they won six against four for the WIFLP. Immediately after the elections these twenty elected members formed an opposition party, the Democratic Labour Party.

The election results were a shock to the WIFLP leaders. As most of them had taken part in preparing for federation, they expected to win widespread support. But most of them had not tried very hard to explain why they thought federation would benefit the ordinary Jamaican or Trinidadian. As we have seen, Mr Manley and other WIFLP leaders preferred to stay in local politics which weakened the case they put forward. Perhaps this helped to convince voters to give their support to politicians who had been less favourable to federation.

Grantley Adams was placed in a difficult position. The WIFLP had just become the largest party with twenty-two seats to the DLP's twenty, so he became prime minister. But to be sure of the support of a majority of the assembly he had to rely on the votes of one or two of the three Independents who had been elected. It was a weak position for the new federal prime minister, especially as the main strength of his party lay in Barbados, the Windwards and the Leewards while the opposition had most of its support in Jamaica and Trinidad and Tobago.

The difficulties of federation

Grantley Adams' new government had to work within strict limits placed on it from two sides. On the one hand, the British kept control over foreign policies so it was impossible for the federation to build up a standing in world affairs. On the other, the territories had refused to give the federation any powers over taxation, customs or the free movement of people for the first five years. So Adams' first task was to keep the federation alive for those five years and build up the confidence of West Indians so that they could make common arrangements for independence rather than each territory winning its own.

An early example of the difficulty of agreeing whether leadership should come from the federal or local governments was the question of Chaguaramas. The Trinidad government said that this peninsula, about 2 kilometres from Port of Spain, was the best site for the permanent headquarters of the federal government. But it had been in American hands since the Second World War, when the British had leased it to the United States for ninety-nine years. In 1958, neither Britain nor the United States was willing to end the lease and hand over the site to the West Indies federal government.

Norman Manley and Eric Williams demanded the handover of Chaguaramas. Eric Williams found the documents of the 1941 negotiations which showed that the governor and his executive council had objected to the lease but had been ignored. As head of the Trinidad government, he meant to get Chaguaramas back. Manley, in support, called the refusal of the British and Americans to consider the demand 'the usual arrogance of an Imperial power'. The campaign for the return of Chaguaramas had widespread support in the West Indies,

especially in Trinidad where the peninsula included what once had been one of Port of Spain's main bathing beaches.

Grantley Adams refused to support Eric Williams' and Norman Manley's campaign. In his view the question of the site of a capital was a matter to be decided by the federal government, not the prime ministers of Jamaica and Trinidad and Tobago. He opposed Dr Williams' insistence that Trinidad be allowed an official place in any further discussions with the United States and Britain. In an attempt to avoid further bitterness, Adams accepted a proposal from the British and Americans that the negotiations be postponed for ten years. This was unpopular with West Indians who hoped that the federation would take a nationalist stand. Williams let it be known that he intended to have Chaguaramas back for the Trinidad people, with or without the consent of the federation.

Economic issues

Obstacles to partnership

In 1947 it seemed that no West Indian territory would become economically strong enough to become independent on its own. This had been the chief reason why many Caribbean leaders as well as the Colonial Office had favoured federation. But, by the time federation did come, Jamaica and Trinidad and Tobago had greatly

Fig. 17.1 *The federal government meeting the British Secretary of State for the Colonies, Reginald Maudling, who is second from the right. Sir Grantley Adams is third from the left.*

strengthened their economies. The time between 1945 and 1958 saw a great development in the Jamaican bauxite industry, while Trinidad increased her oil production and sunk her first offshore oil wells. Both islands had growing manufacturing industries. Jamaica's were mostly concerned with processing foodstuffs while Trinidad and Tobago had established factories and assembly plants for vehicles, light machinery and household goods. This meant that Trinidad had more goods suitable for export to other Caribbean islands.

Most of these changes had come about as a result of government action. Both countries (and Barbados too) had passed laws to give encouragement to industry. Many of the difficulties in planning for federation had come from the larger territories' unwillingness to hand over some of these powers. The difficulties still remained. Just as economic advance for the two largest countries had started with government action, so progress for the federation would need leadership from these larger Caribbean governments. But would Jamaica and Trinidad be prepared to hand over control of their economies? The question became a real one for Jamaica in 1959.

Jamaica's oil refinery

The Jamaican government had plans to encourage building a local oil refinery by allowing the builders to take a percentage of the local tax on petrol sales. The scheme was a reasonable way of encouraging industrial development, but it went against plans that the federation had for taxing items such as petrol once they had power to do so. It also meant that the federal government would not be given the chance to decide whether the region needed a second oil industry in addition to Trinidad's. The federal government objected and, this time, had the support of the government and press in Trinidad which had been the region's main oil refiners for years.

In October 1959 Adams visited Jamaica to reach an understanding with its government over the proposed tax rebate to the oil refiners.

He spoke up strongly for the federation but there was nothing he could really do while his government still had no power to raise taxes. Yet, while talking to the Jamaican newspapers, he hinted that the federal government might look into the possibility of collecting back the rebates once they had the power to tax. He also suggested that the federal government did not believe that an economic plan for the whole region would include the building of a second oil refinery. These comments set off a wave of anti-federation protests. To many Jamaicans it looked as if the federal government would hold up the industrialisation of their country to protect markets for Trinidad oil. The leader of the Jamaican opposition, Alexander Bustamante, brought the question into the open when he thundered:

> Rather this kind of federation be smashed to nothing than for thousands of my people to be thrown out of work through a customs union, by Trinidad dumping its manufactures here.

Paper 18

Norman Manley, the Jamaican chief minister, was a committed federalist but he could not ignore the anti-federalist feeling which was sweeping through the island. His reply came in the form of Ministry Paper 18 published in mid-1959, which set out the Jamaican government's demands for changes in the federal system. It called for seats in the federal assembly to be given to each territory on the basis of its population numbers. This would have meant that Jamaican members of the assembly would have a majority over the representatives of all the other islands combined. Paper 18 also said that there should be a permanent restriction on the taxation powers of the federal government and that a full customs union could never come about since there would always be 'a hard core of industries' which would need local government protection. Partly, of course, this showed Jamaica's concern that her plans for future development of manufactures would be handicapped by imports of Trinidadian goods.

The Economics of Nationhood

Before the federal government had time to reply to Paper 18, Trinidad and Tobago issued a call for almost the direct opposite of Jamaica's scheme. It was set out in a publication called the *Economics of Nationhood* which made it clear where Dr Williams stood on the question of the federation's future. The *Economics of Nationhood* proposed a much stronger federal government with wide powers of taxation, a customs union and a federal bank. The federal government should also, the paper said, take over responsibility for the region's borrowing from abroad, for education and for services such as the post, radio and transport.

The two proposals for changing the federation showed the widening differences which separated the two most powerful unit territories after only a year. Adams worked hard to bridge the gap between their points of view and called a conference in Port of Spain for September 1959 to open talks on revising the constitution. It was agreed to enlarge the House of Representatives to sixty seats with Jamaica's share rising to thirty and Trinidad's to sixteen. Two special committees were appointed to look into independence and dominion status.

The end of federation

Jamaica's referendum

The committees never finished their work. In Jamaica, Norman Manley was faced with the growing appeal of Bustamante's campaign against federation. He could see a clear threat to his political position and so decided to hold a referendum to allow Jamaicans to say whether they wished the island to remain in the federation. He hoped that a majority of 'yes' votes would mean an end to the strong opposition to federation in Jamaica but it was a gamble which failed.

In September 1961, the electorate chose to withdraw from the federation by a small majority. Only a little over 60 per cent of the electorate bothered to vote. Of these 54.1 per cent voted 'no' and 45.9 per cent 'yes'. Manley

Fig. 17.2 *The* Jamaican Daily Gleaner *reports the result of the referendum, with pictures of the Federation flag, Alexander Bustamante and Norman Manley.*

was bitterly disappointed but he had to accept the result. For their part, the British government showed no interest in saving the federation. Without consulting the federal government, the Colonial Secretary told Jamaican leaders, in October 1961, that Britain would accept the referendum result. The Colonial Office went ahead with the legal work to withdraw Jamaica from the federation and prepare it to become an independent member of the British Commonwealth.

Jamaica's withdrawal, and the fact that she could gain full independence before the federation, was more than Grantley Adams' government could survive. In Trinidad, Dr Williams said that Jamaica's withdrawal would make it impossible to bring about the strong and unified federation he had called for in the *Economics of Nationhood*. 'Ten minus one equals nothing' he declared and announced that Trinidad and Tobago would withdraw from the federation and seek independence. That meant the end of the federation. The British dissolved it in May 1962. In August Trinidad and Tobago and Jamaica became fully independent states, and members of the Commonwealth in their own right.

After federation

Grantley Adams tried hard to hold together a smaller federation of Barbados, the Leewards and Windwards. But he failed because of the same fears which had torn apart the first federation. The smaller units were not keen to hand over local powers to a federation which would be dominated by Barbados because of its size and population. For their part, Barbadians feared the possibility of becoming responsible for the smaller units. After three years of discussion the scheme was abandoned. In November 1966 Barbados became independent

and the remaining states worked out their own arrangements with Britain.

In 1966, Antigua along with Barbuda and Redonda, St Kitts-Nevis-Anguilla, Dominica, Grenada, St Lucia and St Vincent became associated states with Britain. Each territory received internal self-government and constitutions which guaranteed a two-chamber parliament and government by a cabinet and premier. Each associated state had its own civil service and police commission. They shared a supreme court and Britain took full responsibility for defence and foreign affairs.

Demands for independence mounted in the 1970s. Grenada was the first to break away from the associated state relationship with Britain and become an independent state in February 1974. She was followed by Dominica in November 1978 and St Lucia in February 1979. In 1978 a conference on the future independence of St Vincent took place in London. By then,

Fig. 17.3 *Antillans carry a coffin in a mock funeral as a protest against the British Commissioner in 1969.*

Antigua had also declared herself in favour of an end to association with Britain.

The situation in St Kitts-Nevis-Anguilla was complicated by the desire of the Anguillan people for separation from their partners. In 1967, almost as soon as the three-island federation became an associated state, Anguilla broke away. In 1969, the British government sent army engineers and policemen who stayed on the island until 1972. By then, the Anguilla Act of 1971 had restated Britain's claim to rule the island although it was given a great deal of internal self-government with its own chief minister. In March 1978 the government of the now smaller federation of St Kitts-Nevis negotiated with Britain for full independence. It was clear that many of the people of Nevis would prefer to stay separate from St Kitts even if that meant remaining a dependency of Britain. However, St Kitts-Nevis become a single independent state in 1983. Two years earlier, Belize had also become independent.

In 1966, Montserrat became a direct dependency of Britain as did several colonies which had not joined the federation: the British Virgin Islands, the Caymans, the Turks and Caicos Islands as well as British Honduras which was renamed Belize. Separate agreements were made for each territory.

These agreements usually granted some self-government through an elected assembly and special appointments to the governor's council. The governor kept responsibility for defence, foreign affairs, and internal security.

British Guiana becomes Guyana, 1953–66

Jagan and Burnham

British Guiana had stood outside the federation. In 1953 the British suspended her constitution in an effort to check Dr Jagan's policy of gaining full local control of economic affairs. One result had been the split between Dr Jagan's PPP and Mr Burnham's PNC which came in 1955. Another was that the country's economic development was held back. The level

of income per head in Jamaica and Trinidad surged ahead of British Guiana's, despite a rapid growth of export agriculture. Guyanese sugar production rose from 240,000 tonnes in 1943 to 340,000 tonnes in 1960 and rice output from 75,000 tonnes to 126,000. But the people of British Guiana gained little. The profits were mostly sent overseas and mechanisation in the sugar estates actually cut the labour force by more than a quarter. While Jamaica was developing her bauxite and Trinidad her oil, the mining industry in British Guiana hardly advanced.

In 1957, the British allowed elections once again for a new assembly which was to be made up of elected members and those nominated by the governor. Some of the elected members were to be allowed to serve on the governor's executive council. In these elections, Dr Jagan's PPP won a clear victory, taking nine of the fourteen elected seats against three won by the PNC and one each for two parties which had support among the middle classes, the United Democratic Party, led by John Carter, and Lionel Luckoo's National Labour Front.

In the election both Dr Jagan and Mr Burnham spoke out against making the issues racial but in fact most of the votes were cast on community lines. After the result, the PNC began to argue that the electoral system would give the East Indian community a permanent majority. The reason was that African voters were concentrated in the urban areas which had a minority of the seats in the assembly. A proportion of African voters were estate workers and voted in country constituencies, but they were always outnumbered by East Indians.

In 1960 the British called a constitutional conference in London to work out details for the internal self-government which had been delayed since the landing of British troops in 1953. At the conference, Mr Burnham argued for proportional representation – which would give seats in the assembly to each party according to the number of votes it received in the country as a whole. The British refused to agree and in 1961 elections were held for thirty-five members each from a single constituency.

The elections were to choose the government

which would lead British Guiana as an internally self-ruling nation. It would have the power to take public control of industry and education and fear of these changes led to the rise of a party representing middle class business interests. This was the United Force, led by Peter D'Aguiar, one of the colony's wealthiest men. D'Aguiar found it easy to use his warnings that the country would go 'communist' to win financial support from overseas, from bodies such as the United States anti-communist crusade, some church organisations, and the international MRA or Moral Re-armament campaign. The United Force made it even more certain that Dr Jagan's PPP would win the election because it split the possible support for the PNC in the towns. In fact, although it had only 42.6 per cent of the votes, Dr Jagan's PPP gained 20 seats against the PNC's 11 seats with 41 per cent of the votes.

Jagan in power

Once again in power as premier, Dr Jagan set about a programme of laws to change the way the country's economy was managed. As we have seen, there was a good case for measures to prevent the expatriation of profits and to redistribute wealth within the country more equally. The British refused to give loans without strings to the new government, despite the fact that a large government debt had been built up in the years since 1953. So the Jagan government's budget of January 1962 said it would control the movement of money in and out of the country, increase taxes of wage-earners and tax capital gains (the increase in the value of businesses or shares in them). At about the same time the government, once again, proposed to take public control of church schools so that a full nationwide system of primary education could be developed. All these were quite mild measures, of the sort that other Caribbean colonies had brought about after self-government. But in British Guiana there was a difference. The urban workers would have to pay more than people in the countryside. The sense of unfairness was made even more severe because many sections of government workers,

such as teachers and civil servants, were in dispute with the government over pay claims.

Mr Burnham opposed the budget and his opposition had a strong racial content. The teachers and civil servants unions were largely African, as were most tax payers in the towns. As well as their grievances against the budget, Africans shared a widespread fear that the Indian population was making more social progress than they were in the towns. In 1965 an international group of lawyers described ways in which Indians had begun to throw off the social and educational disadvantages of their origins as indentured labourers. By then there were more male Indian primary school teachers than African or mixed race, and Georgetown's public health department employees were more than half Indian. There were other examples of Indians entering work and professions which had once been almost entirely African.

The country now had a government which seemed to favour the Indians and an opposition which did not hesitate to appeal openly to the Africans. From early 1962 Guyanese politics had a racial basis even if the root problems were similar to those in other states, such as the clash between town and country interests. The racial basis was clear when African workers in Georgetown went on strike against the budget. The strike was supported by Mr Burnham and, in a rather more underhand way, by D'Aguiar and the United Force. Many businessmen, for instance, closed their businesses and paid their employees to go on strike against the budget.

Dr Jagan ordered the use of tear-gas on demonstrators in the streets of Georgetown. Widespread, racially based riots broke out. Much of the town centre was damaged. With the situation out of hand, Dr Jagan called in British troops, which the governor already had standing by.

Dr Jagan's government was forced to withdraw the budget. The only people who really benefited from the riots were those, in Britain and America, who wished to believe that Jagan was determined to become a communist dictator and that the country would never accept his government.

This belief was strengthened by the protests

Fig. 17.4 *A PNC demonstration at the time of the riots in Georgetown, 1962.*

which followed Jagan's Labour Relations Bill, put forward in early 1963. The bill proposed that workers in industries and on estates should hold a poll to decide which unions should represent them in negotiations with employers. There were good reasons for the bill. Many union leaders of the time were not primarily concerned with the best interests of their members. Some were even members of the United Force Party. CIA funds were channelled to Georgetown through at least one American union which had close relations with a Guyanese union. In the sugar estates, the MCPA had taken funds from the Sugar Producers' Association. At the same time the Sugar Producers would not recognise the GAWU which had far more workers.

There was also a strong racial aspect to these issues. The MCPA was almost entirely African while the GAWU was largely an Indian workers'

organisation. As there were more Indian estate workers, the vote would have gone in favour of making their union the one to negotiate with the employers.

The PNC and the UF, for different reasons, opposed the bill and gave their backing to a general strike. In an effort to beat the strike Dr Jagan declared a state of emergency, but this could not prevent it being successful and the bill being withdrawn.

A new constitution

With the memory of these events still strong, the leaders of all three parties went to London in October 1963 for discussions on arrangements for full independence. The Colonial Secretary asked all three to sign a letter giving him full powers to make decisions on all the questions discussed. Dr Jagan did so, followed shortly by

Mr D'Aguiar, while Mr Burnham only signed under the threat that Britain would postpone the conference unless he agreed.

The Colonial Secretary then decided that independence would be discussed only after further elections. They would be held in 1964 on the proportional representation system. The whole country would be counted as one constituency and seats in the assembly allocated in proportion to the votes given to each party. The decision had some justice, for the previous electoral system had been weighted against the interest of the PNC and the African community. But, again, it had the unhappy consequence of seeming to threaten the interests of the other community – the Indian people.

The GAWU called a strike in protest. In many parts of the country there were outbreaks of violence with people from the two racial groups being forced to barricade themselves against attack and house burnings. It was yet another episode in two years of inter-racial violence which divided the colony into warring camps and cost scores of lives.

The imperialists, however, acted. Encouraged by the United States the British government altered the Guyanese constitution to give the governor power to declare an emergency and call in British troops. They stayed while elections were held on 7 December 1964. The PPP gained 45 per cent of the vote, the PNC 40.8 per cent and the UF 12.5 per cent. Under the new system, this would give the PNC and UF together a majority of seats in the assembly and the right to form a coalition government. Mr Burnham became Premier and D'Aguiar, Finance Minister.

The new Burnham government was now in a position to seek full independence which the British agreed to in 1966. With independence came the new spelling of an old name: Guyana. With independence, too, came a decline in the position of the UF. D'Aguiar was opposed to many of Burnham's policies, such as the steps he took to cut the number of expatriates in senior posts in Guyana. He also objected to the PNC's proposals to make Guyana a republic. The break came in 1967 when the UF broke away from the PNC and offered its support to the PPP. However, this did not affect the strength of the PNC. In the 1968 elections, in which overseas Guyanese for the first time had the right to vote, the PNC won an overall majority with 55.81 per cent of the votes to the PPP's 36.8 per cent while the UF's support had slipped away to 7.42 per cent.

Assignments

1 *What problems did Grantley Adams face as the federal prime minister in 1958?*

2 *Dr Eric Williams: 'Ten minus one equals nothing'.*
   a) *What did Dr Williams mean by this statement?*
   b) *Explain Jamaica's withdrawal from the federation in 1961.*
   c) *Why did the other territories not federate without Jamaica and Trinidad?*

3 *What were the most important reasons for Guyana and Belize not being a part of the 1958 federation?*

4 *Why do you think that full independence followed so quickly for some islands after the failure of federation?*

18 CHALLENGES TO COLONIALISM: THE FRENCH, DUTCH AND SPANISH CARIBBEAN

The French-speaking territories

Links with France

The history of the French-speaking colonies has always closely matched developments in France. We have seen how the Haitians took their first steps to independence at the time of the French Revolution. Emancipation in the other French-speaking territories then came with the second revolution in 1848.

Emancipation was not the only change in 1848. The new Republican government in France also ordered that the West Indian colonies should each elect three representatives to sit in the French assembly in Paris. The right to vote was based on property, but the limits were set low enough to give a large number of colonial people the vote. In 1848 the voters chose Victor Schoelcher, the hero of the emancipation movement and one other white man from Martinique. All the other representatives were coloured West Indians.

In 1852 the Republican government collapsed and was replaced by the Second French Empire under Napoleon III and Caribbeans lost their right to a voice in France's government. They regained it when the Second Empire collapsed and was replaced by the Third Republic in 1871. From then on elections were held regularly and the right to vote was given to all adult males. Caribbean representatives, nearly all coloured, again sat in the assembly in Paris.

Assimilation

No other European country would have accepted the idea that coloured people should have a say in law-making in the middle of the nineteenth century. The fact that the French accepted their presence shows how their thinking about colonialism and race was different from the British view. The French believed that their culture was far superior to that of any colonised people. But they also believed that it was possible for people of any race to learn the customs, language and manners of the French. Then they would become 'assimilated' into French civilisation and would be French whatever the colour of their skin.

Assimilation meant that the French government believed that the way forward for their colonies was to develop closer links with the government in France. This was the opposite of the British Colonial Office's policy of trying to cut the costs of owning West Indian territories. Politicians in the French Caribbean usually accepted assimilation and wanted more say in French affairs while English-speaking political leaders were trying to win more power in their own countries.

The effects of war

The French colonies' share in the political life of the French Empire headed off discontent with colonial rule in the 1930s. In 1940 most of France was occupied by the Germans but the French Caribbean territories remained loyal to those who fought on. In 1943 they agreed to follow the leadership of the 'free French' forces who were fighting to drive out both the Germans and the French puppets who ruled part of France for them.

The leader of the free French forces was Charles de Gaulle. He knew that nationalism was growing in north Africa where armed groups were organising to fight against French rule in the post-war period. The same was happening

Fig. 18.1 *General de Gaulle in Brazzaville 1944.*

in the French colonies in Indo-China.

De Gaulle decided to head off trouble in other parts of the empire, especially in west Africa and the West Indies. He met with the nationalist leaders of the colonies south of the Sahara at Brazzaville in 1944. The meeting decided that the colonies would be allowed to vote on their own future between four choices. They could continue as before the war; they could become self-governing and join in a French Union, they could become independent or they could be politically amalgamated with France. The African colonies, except one, voted for self-government. In the 1950s, however, they all changed their mind and decided for independence.

Departments of France

Martinique, Guadeloupe and French Guyana all voted for political amalgamation with France,

as did the Indian Ocean island of Réunion. In 1946 the colonies became four new French *départements* with the same rights and privileges as the ninety départements in France itself. The colonial governors and their staffs were replaced by departmental administrations. At the head was a prefect who was appointed, like the 90 prefects in France, by the central government in Paris. The prefect was responsible for carrying out directives from the central government and controlled local public services such as sanitation, road and bridge maintenance, health care and education. In the Caribbean departments the prefects were given special powers such as the control of the armed forces and the right to declare martial law.

The people of each overseas department elected deputies to sit in the French National Assembly and Senate. Locally there were elected general councils. At first they were only advisory bodies to explain local needs to the prefects and were forbidden to express political

Fig. 18.2 *A demonstration for autonomy in Martinique. The crowd is waiting for the President of France to pass by.*

opinions. This was changed in all overseas departments following a riot in Martinique in 1959. The riot arose out of a dispute between a white and black man. The Martinique council protested at the brutality of French troops in putting down the riot. It went on to complain about the racial arrogance of some white Frenchmen, as well as widespread unemployment, low wages and high taxes.

The Martinique council was joined in its protests by the other Caribbean councils and the French government decided to give them greater powers than the general councils in the departments in France. The 1960 decentralisation decrees laid down that French laws intended to apply to the overseas departments should first be sent to their councils for consideration. At the same time, the councils were given the right to put their own proposals for laws to the Minister of State in France who would present them to the central government. Overseas councils were also given wider control over the spending of government investment funds.

Political parties

The creation of overseas departments in 1946 quickly led to the formation of political parties to fight for seats in the general councils and the assembly in Paris. The most important dividing issue was over the question of departmentalisation. The supporters of overseas departmentalisation were mostly found among the more conservative political groups, especially those representing the owners of businesses and agricultural estates. White and coloured people were more likely to be departmentalists than the black population. Most of these groups made alliances with conservative political parties in France.

Other political movements in the Caribbean wanted the overseas departments to have more self-government or autonomy. Most of the Caribbean autonomist groupings linked themselves to French socialist parties. They were partial autonomists because they supported departmentalisation but wanted the overseas territories to have more local power. They argued that the councils should have special law-making powers because of their distance from France and their different social and economic conditions.

The French Communist Party went a stage further. It described departmentalisation as being another form of colonialism and called for full autonomy. Since 1958 both Martinique and Guadeloupe have supported strong local communist parties. In the 1970 election they received over 45 per cent of the popular vote. Even many who did not back the party's call for complete local autonomy often supported its call for agrarian reform, nationalisation of the big sugar and banana properties and programmes of industrialisation.

Caribbean identity

Support of local autonomy often had other reasons than political or economic demands. Many French-speaking West Indians felt that complete assimilation with France would destroy the best and the unique aspects of their own culture. One of the first black writers from the French colonies to emphasise the culture of his homeland was Aimé Césaire of Martinique. Since 1939 his poetry and prose writings emphasised the beauties and depths of the island's cultural heritage. Like many black English-speaking writers and leaders in the West Indies, his work stressed the strength and richness of the African heritage and the common roots of the Caribbean peoples in slavery.

Césaire rejected the idea that western European culture is in any way superior to that which developed from the Caribbean experience. His views led him to take an active part in the political life of his country, first as an elected deputy to the National Assembly in France and then as founder and leader of the Parti Progressiste de la Martinique. The central political belief of Césaire and his party was that the central government in France can never understand the needs and desires of West Indians.

Another writer from Martinique, Franz Fanon, became one of the world's best known spokesmen for black nationalism. An early admirer of Aimé Césaire, he spoke out against departmentalisation in Martinique and, still more forcefully, against all forms of colonisation. He objected strongly to the educational system in the Caribbean that taught French values and tried to instil French nationalism in students. Such an education, he declared, could only lead the black student to frustration and disillusion. In one of his first books, *Black Skin, White Masks*, he argued that it was impossible for a black man with his own history and culture to become 'like' a Frenchman.

After spending several years in France, Fanon moved on to Algeria when it was still under French rule. He worked there as a psychiatrist and became aware how devastating European colonialism could be to the lives and spirit of subjugated people. He witnessed first-hand how the colonised were robbed of their wealth, human dignity and responsibility for their own actions. In *The Wretched of the Earth* he showed how political élitism and racism survived long after the colonial power had been driven out. Ex-colonial societies and their leaders could not rid themselves of subservience to the economic and cultural forces of the colonial past. His conclusions were blunt. Subjected people must stand up to both the colonial rulers and those national leaders who had not freed themselves from European culture. For this, the use of violence would be inevitable and necessary. Before his death in 1961, Fanon's message had been acted upon by many of the world's oppressed peoples. His ideas influenced the rise of militant black power groups in America, who argued that the peaceful campaigning methods of the older improvement associations were playing into the hands of the white majority.

Social and economic consequences

Despite the many criticisms, departmentalisation has brought some benefits. As departments of France, the overseas territories share in funds from the central French treasury for the improvement of roads, health services and schools. School enrolments increased steadily from 82,000 to over 190,000 students in 1965.

Many critics, however, complained that the studies were too much concerned with French literature, history and general culture. Central government funds were also used to start massive housing programmes for middle and lower income families. An important development was the buying of unused or abandoned land for redistribution to landless families. Between 1962 and 1965 over 4,000 hectares of land was bought in this way in Martinique and distributed among 1,282 families. In Guadeloupe 5,000 hectares were subdivided into farms for 1,193 families.

In 1957 France was one of the six countries which founded the European Economic Community. As departments of France the Caribbean territories were inside the Community. This meant that their agricultural products could find their way into countries such as Italy and Britain at the same low or nil rates of duty as if they had come from metropolitan France. The reverse is also true. Manufactured goods from any of the member countries could pass to the Caribbean territories at the same rate of duty as they would be charged to enter France.

The EEC has greatly increased its farm production so that milk and cheese are shipped to the French-speaking Caribbean – although the price is very high because of subsidies paid to European farmers to guarantee them a high standard of living. The EEC spends large sums on grants for the development of the poorest parts of the Community and the Caribbean departments of France have had a share in this money. It has been used to develop the tourist trade, build better shipping ports and pay for studies on future economic growth.

Despite the advantages, departmentalisation has not freed the French West Indies from the economic problems faced by most other Caribbean countries. The central place given to export agriculture has led to seasonal unemployment and low wages. On the other hand, the French Caribbean people are entitled, as French citizens, to social security payments in times of unemployment and sickness and these have protected them from the harshest effects of poverty.

French Guyana is the least developed of the

Caribbean departments. The country seemed to have great possibilities because of its large forests and a great deal of uncultivated land. It was thought to have mineral wealth, including bauxite. But up to 1970 little had been done to exploit these possibilities and the main earnings came from the export of small quantities of sugar, pineapples and bananas. French Guyana is thinly populated so the central government has tried to use it as a solution to the unemployment in Martinique and Guadeloupe. In the 1950s many young Antilleans went to seek work in France. In 1961 a scheme was started to redirect the flow of emigrants to French Guyana. All male French citizens have to do a period of military service, so many from Guadeloupe and Martinique were sent to do their service in French Guiana. Recruits for this plan of 'adapted military services' worked on forestry projects, agriculture, mining exploration and road building.

The Dutch-speaking territories

The tripartite kingdom

In the Dutch Caribbean the old colonial system had remained almost intact until 1939. The colonial assemblies, or statens, continued to be dominated by the old Dutch classes of planters and merchants. The colonies' governments were presided over by a governor appointed in Holland.

By 1939 the power and influence of the statens was coming under attack from the new middle classes, mostly made up of oil refinery workers. Among them grew up a number of political parties campaigning for home rule. However, their campaigns were never as bitter and fierce as those of 'Buzz' Butler's oil field workers in Trinidad. The immediate demands of the Dutch Caribbean parties were met in 1949 when the colonies were granted universal suffrage and internal self-government.

In 1954 the Dutch colonies were made partners in a tripartite kingdom in a scheme laid down in the Charter of the Kingdom of the Netherlands. Under the Charter, the three equal members of the one kingdom were declared to be the Dutch Antilles, Surinam and the Netherlands. Each of the kingdoms was to keep its full internal self-government while defence and foreign affairs were to be a joint responsibility. The Dutch, who had lost their colonies in the East Indies, were keen to develop

Fig. 18.3 *The Dutch architectural influence in Willemstad is still obvious in this photograph taken in the 1970s.*

something along the lines of the British Commonwealth as a means of holding the rest of their past empire together. At the same time, by linking all six Antilles colonies into one kingdom they were putting into practice a scheme for Caribbean federation – again at a time when the British West Indians were drawing up plans for their own federation.

To many Dutch Caribbean politicians the idea of a tripartite kingdom was preferable to complete independence, for this might have meant the withdrawal of Dutch aid and preferential trading with the West Indies. At the same time, many nationalists believed that close political ties with the Netherlands were preventing the growth of a sense of national identity based on Caribbean roots. They also had good grounds for pointing out that the Netherland's greater wealth and population meant that she was always dominant in the kingdom's foreign policy decisions.

These views were strengthened when economic difficulties arose in the 1960s. Some stemmed from mechanisation programmes in the oil fields, which cut the number of workers in the industry by a quarter. The island governments tried to make up for the lost jobs with schemes to encourage light industry and tourism. They had some success but they never produced enough work for all the young people looking for jobs.

Economic difficulties resulted in labour unrest and calls for a new political order. The most serious disturbances began in Curaçao in 1969. They began as a demonstration for higher wages by 5,000 workers in Willemstad. Four people were killed, 150 injured and 50 buildings damaged or destroyed. Almost $40 million worth of property was damaged. Royal Dutch paratroops were flown in from Holland to restore order and supervise elections for a new government. The government that was elected in September 1969 contained members who were willing to raise again the question of independence for the Dutch Antilles.

Surinam

After the riots, the Dutch Parliament at The Hague, in Holland, debated the question of giving full independence to the two American parts of the tripartite kingdom. Although nationalist feeling remained strong throughout the 1970s, no action was taken towards independence for the Dutch Antilles. This was not the case with Surinam.

Bauxite and timber meant that in 1974 the people of Surinam enjoyed the highest per capita income in Latin America and a favourable balance of payments totalling over $15 million. Nationalist leaders in Surinam were confident that independence was possible and desirable. Under the leadership of Henk A. E. Arron, independence from the tripartite kingdom was negotiated and agreed on in November 1975.

The Spanish-speaking territories to 1898

Liberators on the mainland

Between 1814 and 1821, the creole people of the Spanish Empire in Central and South America won their independence from Spanish rule. The revolutionary movement began with the *juntas*. These were committees of creoles who had managed the affairs of their colonies between 1808 and 1814 when Spain herself was ruled by the French emperor, Napoleon. In 1814, Napoleon was defeated and King Ferdinand placed back on the Spanish throne.

The colonial juntas demanded that they keep their new freedom in government, self-defence and trade. Ferdinand refused to even discuss these demands and was immediately faced with creole revolts. The juntas called upon their militia commanders to lead their men against the Spanish armies. These commanders became the Liberators who created the nations of Central and South America almost as they appear on the modern map.

The first Liberator to take the field was San Martin. He led an army which drove the Spaniards from the viceroyalty of La Plata. It was soon divided into the three independent states of Argentina, Paraguay and Uruguay. San Martin then crossed the Andes and helped Bernardo O'Higgins, an Irish-Spaniard who

Fig. 18.4 *Simon Bolivar, the Liberator.*

Map 14 *Independent Latin America after the battle of Ayacucho.*

beat the Spanish armies at the Battle of Maipu in April 1818. The new state of Chile was now free from Spanish rule. San Martin then moved into modern Peru but retired to make way for another great Liberator, Simon Bolivar.

Bolivar had defeated Spanish forces in New Granada, out of which were created the modern states of Venezuela, Colombia and Ecuador. He now completed the overthrow of the viceroyalty of Peru. One of Bolivar's generals, Sucre, had the honour of driving the last Spanish garrison from South America at the battle of Ayacucho in upper Peru on 9 December 1824. The states of Peru and Bolivia were carved out of this area.

In New Spain a widespread revolt against Spanish rule was led by two priests, Manuel Hidalgo and José Maria. This prepared the way for Augustin de Iturbide to lead the independence movements which resulted in freedom for Mexico and the small Central American states.

Loyalty on the islands

The three Spanish island colonies of Santo Domingo, Puerto Rico and Cuba did not follow the mainland people into independence. The Spanish made a bid to keep their loyalty by making government land more freely available to settlers and allowing in plantation supplies free of import duties. Most important of all, the Spanish government continued to encourage the import of slaves, despite a treaty which it signed with Britain promising to end the trade.

These measures gave most creoles in Puerto Rico and Cuba strong reasons for wishing to remain under Spanish rule. Above all, there was the fear of revolt by the black people of the islands. In Cuba in 1817 the 224,000 slaves and 115,000 free coloureds outnumbered the 291,000 whites. Of those whites, many were refugees from Santo Domingo who had suffered severely when Haiti had ruled their colony. Fear of revolt was increased by their stories and grew even stronger when Haiti again overran Santo Domingo in 1822.

Fear of slave revolt and the example of Santo Domingo meant that most creoles in Puerto Rico and Cuba stood aside from the small revolutionary groups which wanted to fight for independence from Spain. Most of the rebels were teachers, lawyers and writers and they got little support from the other groups in society who feared to lose their property, their slaves or their profitable businesses. In 1823, the Spanish uncovered a plot by the young Cuban poet, Heradia. He and his supporters were exiled from the island. Conspirators in Puerto Rico were dealt with in the same way.

After this, there was little objection when Spain placed both islands under military rule, headed by captain-generals who had great personal powers backed up by large numbers of troops from Spain. The rule of these 'little Caesars', as they were called in Puerto Rico, lasted for fifty years. The end of their rule came at the same time as emancipation for the slaves.

The Liberals

In the 1830s opposition to Spanish rule grew up among Cubans who took the name of Liberals. Many of them were young students, journalists and lawyers. Often the Liberals were divided between those who wanted full independence from Spain and those who preferred Cubans to have a share in their own government but stay inside the Spanish Empire. But they were united in their opposition to the captain-generals and many of them were forced to live outside the island.

Committees of Cuban Liberals were found in the capitals of all the independent Latin American states around the Caribbean, although the most important group of exiles was always in New York. From these places of safety they wrote pamphlets, issued proclamations and sometimes plotted uprisings. Between 1849 and 1851 the Venezuelan revolutionary, Narciso Lopez, led three raids of Cuban exiles, carrying American arms, on the Cuban coast. He was finally captured and shot with about fifty followers.

The Liberal movement had little chance of success while it had no support among those Cubans who depended for their wealth on slavery. After the great slave revolt at Matanzas many began to believe that it would be better to do without slaves than risk Cuba becoming a black republic and began to use indentured labourers. Then Spain finally put an end to the slave trade in 1866 and announced that slavery itself was to be ended. The large planters resisted emancipation, but the small estate owners on the east of the island were now ready to accept it.

The Ten Years War, 1868–78

The question of emancipation now became bound up with the demand of the Cuban Liberals for self-government. The execution of Narciso Lopez in 1852 had not stopped the activities of the Cuban exiles in New York and other mainland cities. Support for them spread among the small planters who were grieved by heavy taxes and a feeling that the island's affairs were in the hands of the Spanish officials and their wealthy supporters in the west. A movement for independence grew up, led by Carlos Manuel de Céspedes, a lawyer and eastern land-owner. Arms were smuggled in from America. In 1868 de Céspedes emancipated his own slaves and then opened a revolutionary war for Cuban independence with the declaration of Yara – or *grito de Yara* – which called for freedom from Spain, a republican government and the abolition of slavery. He ended with the cry:

> Gentlemen . . . the power of Spain is decrepit and worm-eaten. . . . If it still appears strong and great it is because for over three centuries we have regarded it from our knees. Let us rise!

The war which followed lasted for ten years. Most of the fighting took place on the eastern end of the island and the rebels had little chance of success, especially after the Spanish soldier, Martinez Campos, was sent to fight them in 1876. But their struggle did help to bring forward the time of emancipation. In 1878, Campos signed the Treaty of Zanjon with the revolutionaries. They agreed to end the war in return for an amnesty for their rebellion. The Spanish promised to abolish all slavery and allow creoles a share in the government of Cuba.

American influence

The years after the Ten Years War were harsh times for most Cubans. The Spanish government broke its promise of amnesty and confiscated the estates of rebels. The fighting had ruined the coffee plantations and they never recovered. The sugar planters were forced to pay heavy taxes for the costs of the war. Then came an even more bitter blow, the Spanish government began to give bounties to beet growers in Spain itself. Cuban planters found they could no longer export to Spain.

The Cubans' difficulties became a time of great opportunity for the United States. American companies moved in to buy up factories and plantations. Sugar production boomed but the wealth went to America. The United States put heavy duties on refined sugar which meant it was imported raw in to the USA and refined by workers there. The same thing happened to tobacco. By the 1890s the most important fact of life in Cuba was the strength of the American control over its economy.

War for independence

In 1895 a new war for independence from Spain broke out. Unlike the earlier revolts it had widespread support. *Colonos*, small farmers, and their labourers all suffered from the low prices for cane. Wealthier Cubans complained of high taxes and were determined to take control of the island's affairs from the Spanish. Since Spain had stopped importing Cuban sugar there was no longer any profit in remaining the 'ever-faithful island'. Many believed that American duties against Cuban sugar would be dropped if Cuba was no longer a colony of a European power.

As in earlier wars, an important part was played by Cubans in exile. José Marti, the son of a policeman, had fled to the United States after being in prison for his part in the Ten Years War.

His writings were widely known throughout the Americas. They described the Cuban revolutionary movement as a struggle for freedom, justice and democracy against a European tyranny. Once again it was on the eastern end of the island that most support could be gathered for a revolution. It was here that Marti declared war on the Spanish government of Cuba in 1895.

A few weeks later Marti was killed but the war went on. As we shall see in Chapter 19, the Cuban rebellion was the main cause of war between Spain and the USA in 1898. The Americans soon won and Cuba gained her freedom from Spain, but only at the cost of falling even more directly under American control.

Independence in Puerto Rico

In Puerto Rico, the chief political division lay between the wealthiest classes, who often owned businesses trading with Spain, and the smaller farmers, shop-keepers and professional people. The wealthy groups were the Conservatives, loyal to Spain and friendly to the peninsular officials in the island. The less wealthy, especially from the educated classes, often became Liberals who sought freedom from Spanish rule. Groups of them plotted revolution from places of exile in Latin America or New York.

In 1865, one of the conspiracies broke out into revolution, led by a Venezuelan, M. Rojas, and an exile from New York, Matiás Bregman. The revolutionaries began in Cuban style with the declaration – or *grito* – of Lares which called for independence and slave emancipation. But the Puerto Rican rebels were quickly crushed by the Spanish military forces.

The defeat of the 1865 revolution did not stop the growth of the Liberal movement. Their numbers were so large that the movement split between those who called themselves autonomists and other who were sometimes known as unconditionalists. The unconditionalists were stronger among the exiles and they sought complete freedom from Spain. In 1895, when Marti's revolution broke out in Cuba, Puerto Ricans in New York joined the Cuban Revolutionary Party and formed a section known as the Borinquen Chapter, using the Amerindian name for Puerto Rico. The Chapter prepared to fight the Spanish in Puerto Rico.

The autonomists, on the other hand, did not want total independence. Instead, they were ready to bargain with Spain for self-government within the Spanish Empire. Many feared that a fully independent Puerto Rico would be swiftly brought under United States control. The autonomists were the stronger Liberal group on the island itself. Their leader, Manōz Rivera, got a promise from the Liberal Party in Spain that it would grant self-government to Puerto Rico once it had power in Spain. This happened in 1897 and the promise was kept. A new Puerto Rican constitution was agreed by the Spanish Parliament, or Cortes, in February 1898. Elections were held in the island in March and the Liberal Autonomist Union Party formed the new Puerto Rican government in July.

For the first time since the Spanish settled on the island, the creole population was free from Spanish government restrictions. Yet the freedom lasted only a few days because the island found itself caught up in the war which broke out in 1898 between the United States and Spain. The roots of the war lay in American support for the rebels in Cuba but the fighting quickly spread to all Spain's overseas colonies.

From the time of the 1898 war, the history of Cuba and Puerto Rico was no longer bound up with the Spanish Empire. Instead their politics became involved with the development of American imperialism.

Santo Domingo until 1844

Before the revolution in Haiti, there had been 120,000 Spanish in Santo Domingo. By the time the first Haitian occupation had ended, one-third of them had already fled to other lands, mostly to Cuba, Puerto Rico and Venezuela. During the second Haitian occupation from 1822 to 1844, most of the remaining whites followed.

For all but one of the years of occupation the ruler of Haiti and Santo Domingo was Jean Boyer. His outstanding achievement was to emancipate the slaves in Santo Domingo far earlier than they were freed in Cuba and Puerto

Rico. For the rest his rule was mostly remembered for attempts to destroy the country's Spanish culture. The universities were closed and the Roman Catholic Church forbidden to have contacts with Europe. Haitians replaced Santo Domingans in public positions and Haitian laws, often based on French traditions, replaced the old Spanish laws.

These policies broke almost entirely the dominant position that the white creoles once had in Santo Domingo. The estates of white landowners who fled were divided into farms too small to produce for export. However, Boyer's rule created grievances among Santo Domingo's mulatto population. They expected to take over the positions left by the whites but this was impossible while their country was ruled by Haitian soldiers and officials. Many suffered imprisonment or saw their property looted by the occupying forces.

The mulattos' sense of grievance gradually turned into a movement for independence. They gave their support to Juan Pablo Duarte who led a successful revolt against the occupiers in 1844. After the expulsion of the Haitians, Duarte declared that Santo Domingo would become a new independent Dominican Republic.

The Dominican Republic

The first problem for the new Dominican Republic was how to prevent a third occupation from Haiti. The Liberals, led by Duarte, believed that the country should defend itself. But their Conservative opponents favoured protection from some outside power. One of these, Pedro Santana, arranged in 1861 for the country to become once again a colony of Spain. Santana was appointed captain-general of the new colony. Spanish troops were sent to garrison the colony and a number of white immigrants settled there, some reclaiming lands and property lost by their families during the Haitian occupation.

The rule of Santana and the Spanish quickly became unpopular. Spain found herself having to spend money on putting down revolts and sending new troops to replace those who had died from yellow fever. The island was bringing her no profit and her re-occupation of a New World colony had led to complaints from the United States. In 1865, therefore, the Spanish were glad to withdraw and leave behind a second Dominican Republic. Now it was the turn of another Conservative leader, Buenaventura Baez, to seek protection from another power, the United States. He persuaded President Grant, in 1870, to agree to annex the Dominican Republic to the United States. In the end this was prevented because the United States Senate refused to accept the arrangement made by the President.

After the failure of his scheme, Baez was forced to leave the Republic. For the remainder of the 1870s it fell into a state of lawlessness with three groups struggling for power. There was so little difference between them that they were best described by their colours: blue, red and green. This state of confusion and disorder was almost bound to lead to dictatorship and in 1881 this came in the person of Ulises Heureaux.

Ulises Heureaux

Heureaux ruled until 1899. It was a harsh dictatorship which allowed no opposition. Heureaux built up a large, efficient army to put down any disorders and any rebellion against his rule. The work of the army was supported by police spies and a vast civil service made up of officials who owed their jobs to the favour of the dictator. At the same time there were many improvements in education, in transport and roads. Perhaps the most important result of Heureaux's dictatorship was to awaken the interest of other nations in the possibilities of investing in the Dominican Republic. Americans and Europeans, especially French and German businessmen, saw that Heureaux's attempts to modernise the country would create a need for machinery, postal and telephone equipment and help with developing public services such as water and power supplies. Because the country was orderly it seemed to be a sound place in which to invest. Other overseas businessmen and companies were interested in buying land to start producing export crops.

Unfortunately for the future of the Dominican Republic, Heureaux spent far more on his schemes for modernisation than the country could afford, especially as he also spent heavily on his women and other pleasures and on the army and police. In 1899 he was assassinated. His death left the Dominican Republic with two problems. There was no regular system of government and there were enormous debts owed to overseas companies.

Assignments

1 *In what ways were twentieth-century political developments in the French Caribbean different from political developments in the British Caribbean?*

2 a) *What alternative to metropolitan rule developed in the Dutch Caribbean in the twentieth century?*
   b) *How did this differ from the path taken in the English and French Caribbean territories?*

3 *Describe the movements towards independence in Cuba and Puerto Rico up to 1891. What similarities and differences were there?*

4 *Explain why some people in the Dominican Republic wished to return to colonial government.*

19 THE UNITED STATES IN THE CARIBBEAN BEFORE 1900

The USA to 1865

Rivalry with Britain

The United States became an independent nation after the thirteen American colonies had defeated British forces in the War of Independence from 1775 to 1783. For many years after independence, the American people occupied only the eastern part of their huge territory. In the southern states small numbers of white Americans controlled the lives of the slaves who worked their tobacco and cotton plantations. In the northern states, there was a much larger population of European peoples who were active traders, ship-builders and manufacturers. They hoped that freedom from British rule would make it possible to replace Britain as the main trading and shipping power in the American hemisphere.

Up to the early nineteenth century, however, British ships and traders still sold twice as many goods to Latin America as the Americans did. British ships sailed across the Atlantic with manufactured goods, especially textiles and iron products. They sold these in the Caribbean islands or mainland and then sailed north to pick up cotton and other produce for shipping back to Europe.

Between 1812 and 1814 Britain and the United States fought a war over this trade. It began when the British claimed the right to stop and search American ships which might be supplying goods to their enemy, the French Emperor Napoleon. After the war there were further quarrels when the British government tried to prevent American goods carried in American ships being sold to her Caribbean colonies. In reply, the United States closed American ports to British ships sailing from Canada or the West Indies. The British then gave way and allowed American goods into their Caribbean islands, provided they paid extra duties of 10 per cent. The 10 per cent duties caused a second round of arguments. They were settled in 1830 when the two countries finally allowed each other's ships to move freely. By then, the United States had made her attitude to European activities in the western hemisphere quite plain.

The Monroe Doctrine

The United States and Britain were both pleased at the revolt of Spain's colonies in South and Central America. The new countries set up by the Liberators were no longer bound to obey trading regulations made in Spain and they bought increasing amounts of goods from British and American traders. So Britain and the USA were both alarmed when the King of Spain called on the rulers of other European countries to supply him with ships and troops to win back his colonies.

In 1823 the British Foreign Secretary, George Canning, asked the Americans to join in a warning that the United States and Britain would resist the scheme to reconquer Spain's colonies. The American President, Monroe, however, went further and issued an independent warning which also applied to Britain. It was delivered in his annual message to Congress in December 1823. The part of the speech which became known as the Monroe Doctrine said:

> The American continents by the free and independent conditions which they have assumed and maintained are henceforth not to be considered subjects for future colonisation by European powers.

He went on to say that any European attempt to interfere in 'any portions of this hemisphere' would be seen as 'the manifestation of an unfriendly disposition to the United States'. In other words, the Americans were making it clear that they were the major power in the American hemisphere – not any other European country, including Britain.

Central America

Twenty years after the Monroe Doctrine the United States was involved in a quarrel with Britain over Central America. The beginnings of the quarrel lay in the steady American expansion into Mexican land. In 1848, after much pressure and warfare, Mexico was forced to sell Texas, New Mexico and California to the USA. In the same year, gold was discovered in California. The next year, tens of thousands of prospectors were trekking across America to take part in the great Californian gold rush. These prospectors became known as the 'forty-niners'.

At that time no railways crossed the continent. The only means of carrying goods by land was by horse or waggon. If the west coast was to be opened up a new transport system was needed. Many Americans favoured the idea of a canal linking the Pacific and Atlantic across Central America. Cornelius Vanderbilt was already making a good business by ferrying prospectors across Nicaragua on an inter-connecting system of steamboats and railways. An improvement on the scheme would be to build a canal along the San Juan river valley.

The Clayton-Bulwer Treaty

The British did not welcome the American plans, partly because it might mean that the United States could move her fleets quickly from the Atlantic into the Pacific and on to the Far East

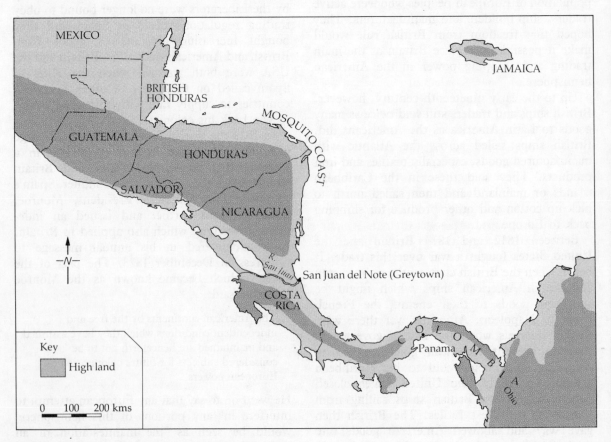

Map 15 *Central America at the time of the Clayton-Bulwer Treaty.*

where Britain was the most powerful European nation. But another reason was that there were settlements of British, mostly logwood-cutters, in Honduras, the Bay Islands and on the Mosquito Coast. To stop the canal scheme the British seized San Juan del Note (which they re-named Greytown) at the mouth of the San Juan river. The Americans demanded that the British withdraw but they held firm until 1850. Then a treaty was worked out by the American Secretary of State, John M. Clayton, and a British minister, Henry Lytton Bulwer. The treaty declared that if a canal was built across Central America it would not be used for military purposes and would be under the joint control of the Americans and British. It was also agreed that neither side would occupy or attempt to rule Nicaragua, Costa Rica, or the Mosquito Coast.

The treaty meant that Britain would have to evacuate the Bay Islands and Mosquito Coast. For some time the British government tried to argue that they ought to be allowed to keep a protectorate over these areas for the good of the inhabitants. Eventually, they decided to withdraw and signed agreements with Nicaragua and the Republic of Honduras handing over the Bay Islands and Mosquito Coast.

The treaty said nothing about Belize, which was then known as British Honduras. So, Britain kept this one territory in Central America. In 1862, British Honduras was made into a Crown colony with a lieutenant-governor who worked under the orders of the governor of Jamaica.

The real lesson of the Clayton-Bulwer Treaty and the British withdrawal was that the United States had a stronger position in Central America than the world's greatest naval power of the time.

Cuba

America's determination to be the strongest power in the western hemisphere led her to take a particular interest in Cuba. It began in 1819 when she bought Florida from Spain. After that the southern tip of the United States was only 149 kilometres from Cuba. Some political leaders talked of taking over the island so that it could become an advance base for the mainland. The move was strongly supported by Southern slave owners who were eager to add another 'slave' state to the United States to balance the growing number of Northern 'free' states where slavery was prohibited.

Other Americans argued that Cuba was a natural place for a United States naval base to protect a central American canal if it were built. Others, such as members of the 'Young America' movement, supported plots against Spanish colonial rule. They gave arms and money to Narcisco Lopez in his three attempts to invade Cuba. American eagerness for taking over Cuba led President Pierce to try to buy the island from Spain. In 1854, he ordered the American minister in Spain, Pierre Soulé, to offer $130 million. Soulé was a Southerner who keenly wanted Cuba to become American. Before making the offer to the Spanish government, he met with two other American ambassadors at a hotel in Holland. Together, they wrote a despatch to the government in Washington, saying that if Spain refused to sell, the United States should take Cuba by force. News of the despatch leaked out. Spain protested but so did politicians from the Northern states who described the despatch as a 'slave-holders' plot'. In face of their opposition Pierce backed down, much to the disappointment of some Cuban 'annexionists' – slave-owners who wanted the scheme to go forward.

The question of the United States replacing Spain in Cuba was put aside in the 1850s. But it was not forgotten. After the American Civil War, it was the turn of Northern businessmen to take up the idea again. As we shall see, they got most of what they wanted in 1898.

Slavery in the United States

In 1808, the year after Britain abolished the slave trade, the United States government made it illegal to import any more slaves. However, it refused to join forces with Britain in naval action to prevent slaves being brought to the Americas. The United States made the work of anti-slaving patrols difficult by refusing to agree that ships carrying her flag should be stopped and searched for slave cargoes. So slaving vessels from other nations often sailed under the American flag. Merchants from the Southern states of the

United States itself were also active in the trade, some of them using boats capable of carrying between 600 and 800 slaves. Most of the slaves carried across the Atlantic after 1808 were taken to Brazil or Cuba and few landed directly in the United States. A number were imported from Cuba, but the yearly totals were much smaller in the nineteenth than the eighteenth century.

As the import of slaves declined, it was replaced by the new evil of an internal slave trade. Corn and tobacco farmers in Maryland, Virginia and Kentucky had more slaves than they needed. From these states, coffles of heavily guarded slaves were moved south, on foot or by boat, to the cotton fields of the Deep South in Mississippi, Alabama and Georgia.

The planters of the South were convinced that their way of life needed slavery. Increasingly the people of the Northern states thought differently. There was no shortage of European immigrants seeking work on the farms or in the cities. By 1804, all the Northern states had abolished slavery. Then they tried to stop it being

Fig. 19.1 *A slave 'coffle' passing through an American town.*

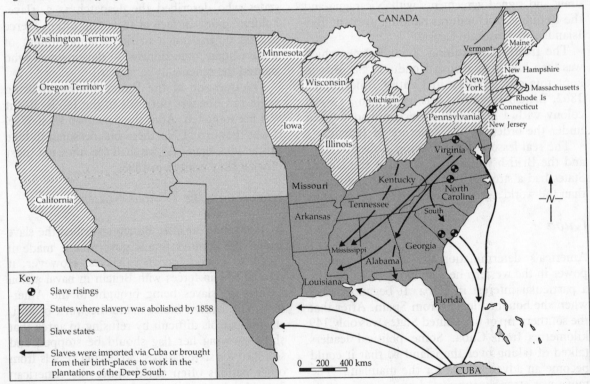

Map 16 *Slavery in the United States.*

Key

⊕ Slave risings

▨ States where slavery was abolished by 1858

▨ Slave states

➝ Slaves were imported via Cuba or brought from their birth-places to work in the plantations of the Deep South.

0 200 400 kms

allowed in the new states created by the movement of American people into the west.

Until the 1850s, only a few Northerners campaigned to make slavery illegal throughout the United States. Then pressure for emancipation grew rapidly. Some Northerners believed it would bring economic benefits. At that time, the United States kept her customs duties low to encourage the import of manufactured goods. These low tariffs served the interests of slave-owners who wanted cheap plantation supplies. They were against higher duties in case they led to Europeans replying with higher tariffs on cotton and tobacco. Northern industrialists, however, wanted high tariffs on manufactured goods to keep out foreign rivals to their own products. To change the tariff policy meant weakening the influence of the plantation interest. One sure way of doing this was to end slavery.

Emancipation and Civil War

Other Northerners attacked slavery itself, pointing out that it was contrary to the American ideals of freedom and democracy. Both the humanitarian emancipationists and the industrialists pressed for laws abolishing slavery in all states. Alarmed by the threat to their way of life, eleven Southern slave states broke away from the United States and formed a separate Confederacy. President Abraham Lincoln declared he would fight to keep all states in the one Union. The Civil War which followed lasted from 1861 to 1865. During the fighting, in September 1862, Lincoln declared that all four million slaves would be freed on 1 January 1863.

The USA after the Civil War

Economic development

The Civil War ended in 1865. Most slaves became poor sharecroppers and Southern whites were still determined to deny them education, the right to vote or the chance to take employment outside agriculture and domestic work. In the country as a whole, however, a great industrial boom began during the war and continued well into the

Fig. 19.2 *Broadway, New York, in about 1900.*

twentieth century. In forty years from 1865 the population of the United States grew from 31 million to 76 million. In the same period the length of railway lines had grown from 48,270 kilometres to 321,800 kilometres carrying a thousand million tonnes of goods each year. America had discovered great wealth in oil, coal and metals of every kind. By 1900 her output of steel was greater than that of Germany and Britain together.

For the first fifteen or so years after the war, most of this great boom in American business took place within the United States itself. The rapidly growing population could make use of most of the new goods produced. New inventions such as the typewriter, the telephone and the electric light, were installed in America in the 1860s and 1870s before they moved into the international market. There was little need to export iron and other metals when American railway builders bought so many million tonnes each year. During these years, businessmen, politicians and newspapers writers were generally opposed to American expansion into neighbouring countries. But by the 1880s opinion was changing. Behind the change was a new wave of activity by American businessmen and manufacturers.

American business in the Caribbean

In Chapter 10 we saw how Baker and Keith discovered the profits to be made by importing bananas and other foods from the Caribbean and Central America. Other Americans were making fortunes from railways, mines and public works in Central America, often with the help of West Indian immigrant labour. But the biggest interest in expanding American business came from industrialists and bankers. They made huge profits in the United States and looked for new places where they could invest their surplus funds.

They found many opportunities in the Spanish-speaking Caribbean. During the 1880s, American bankers took over the foreign debt of the Dominican Republic. Within a few years they actually controlled the country's customs service. At the same time, millions of dollars were invested in the Cuban sugar industry. By the 1890s, American trade with the island was valued at $100 million each year. Americans had gained the most important share of the trade of Puerto Rico, Haiti, the Dominican Republic, San Salvador, Honduras and Guatemala. All together, the markets in the circum-Caribbean and the Caribbean itself made up over 40 per cent of all the American overseas investment.

American imperialism

This change in American opinion came at the time of a new surge of imperialism by European powers. France, Britain and Germany were active in areas which had not before been colonised. Between 1880 and 1900 they carved up the whole of the interior of Africa between them. In roughly the same period, China was forced to allow Europeans to control her ports and rivers, railway building and her customs service. Islands and coastal strips throughout the world were seized to provide coaling stations for the new steamships which linked the world-wide trading networks.

American leaders began to feel that this race to colonise the remaining free parts of the world would create a threat to American interests. Military and naval experts, such as Captain Alfred Mahan, thought that these interests should be protected by the United States becoming imperialistic herself. Mahan studied the way Britain defended her empire and overseas trade. He believed that America, too, needed a chain of overseas bases and a strong navy, backed up especially by a large force of marines who could be carried to wherever there was a threat to her interests.

So, from the late 1880s, America herself became an imperialist nation. Some of the first moves were made into the Pacific where she gained several island possessions. But most Americans thought that Latin America and the Caribbean were more important. They believed, as James Blaine stated in 1884, that 'It is the special province of this country to improve and expand its trade with the nations of America.' In 1888 Blaine, who was now Secretary of State, called a Pan-American Conference which met in Washington the following year. Blaine

Fig. 19.3 *A German cartoon of 1894, which had the title 'Only a small step and Uncle Sam will be in Cuba'.*

hoped that the USA and each of the Latin American states would sign a treaty to help each other in trade and defence. He failed because the Latin American countries would not agree to long-term arrangements binding them closely to the United States.

In the end, the only lasting result was an organisation, later called the Pan-American Union, for encouraging trade and cultural exchanges between the American nations. From Blaine's point of view the conference was a disappointment, but it was a way of announcing to the world that the United States was ready to take up the leadership of the Americas which she had claimed in the Monroe Doctrine. It was a step on the road to a full military imperialism which came about when the United States was drawn into a colonial war with Spain in 1898. The main cause of this was the state of affairs in Cuba.

The USA and the Spanish colonies

Background to the Cuban rebellion

As we saw in Chapter 18, José Marti and his supporters began rebellion against Spanish rule in 1895. By then few Cubans could see any value in remaining under Spanish rule. Now the slaves were emancipated, Spanish soldiers were no longer needed to deal with threats of revolt. Spain was the least important of Cuba's overseas customers and bought only 6 per cent of all the exports from the island. Yet all classes in Cuba suffered from the taxes demanded by the Spanish government.

The most important group of foreigners in Cuba were the American businessmen who had invested money in sugar, tobacco, railways and harbour works. The biggest part of Cuba's exports went to the USA, yet the gain was more America's than Cuba's. The United States placed high tariffs on cured tobacco and refined sugar so that American, and not Cuban, workers would have the jobs in curing and refining. In 1894 the USA also placed a high tariff on raw sugar. Cubans came to believe that America would lower these tariffs if their island was no longer a Spanish colony.

Many Americans were in sympathy with the Cuban Liberals and their struggle against Spain. Some were businessmen with interests in Cuba but others were ordinary people who had read the stirring articles on the Cuban liberation movement which José Marti wrote in their newspapers.

173

The Cuban struggle

José Marti was killed only a few weeks after the rebellion began, but his followers went on with all-out war. The struggle was a cruel one. Spain sent 200,000 troops but they found themselves faced by rebels from all classes and in every part of the island. The fighting was so widespread that the island's economy was almost completely ruined. In three years sugar production fell from 1,500,000 tonnes to 200,000 tonnes. Both sides tried to force the peasants and smallholders to join them. The rebels' leaders deliberately destroyed crops and buildings to make the island worthless to Spain. The Spanish commander-in-chief drove peasants into concentration camps to stop them being recruited by force into the rebel armies. This move brought most American opinion firmly on to the side of the revolutionaries, who were shown in the American press as fighters for freedom and democracy against an Old World monarchy.

The Maine

The United States government began to see that intervention in the war would be popular.

Fig. 19.4 *The wreck of the* Maine *in Havana harbour.*

Americans who owned land or businesses which were being ruined in the fighting called on their government to send aid and bring about a quick rebel victory. Army and navy commanders pointed out that American defences would be stronger if Cuba was under United States influence. President McKinley hesitated and took time to think the question over. Meanwhile, he sent the warship *Maine* to Havana to protect American lives and property. On 15 February 1898 the *Maine* exploded in Havana harbour with the loss of 266 American lives. It had been blown up by an underwater bomb. Americans immediately blamed the Spanish. In fact the bomb was probably placed by Cuban patriots who saw the disaster as a way of bringing the United States into the war on their side.

The Teller Amendment

Public opinion in the United States demanded war against Spain, although there were still some American politicians who feared that it would be used as an excuse for adding Cuba to the United States. Their fears were dealt with in an amendment to the Act of Congress which declared war on Spain. The amendment was put forward by Senator H. M. Teller and said that, once Cuba was free and peaceful, the United States would 'leave the government and control of the island to its people'. The amendment was passed. America was at war with Spain and prepared to fight her not just in Cuba but in the rest of the Caribbean and the Pacific.

The Spanish-American War, 1898

The first fighting in the war took place in the Philippines, half way around the world from Cuba. An American naval squadron, led by Commodore George Dewey, seized the Spanish naval base at Manila. Immediately 11,000 American troops were sent to occupy the islands which Spain surrendered to the United States on 13 August 1898. Hardly an American life was lost. Shortly afterwards the Pacific island of Guam was also occupied.

In the Caribbean, American victories were just as complete. A small army landed in Cuba and entered Santiago a few weeks later. Another force marched through Puerto Rico as if it were on a holiday parade. The poorly organised Spanish simply gave up in the Caribbean. They agreed that Cuba should be left to the patriot forces and Puerto Rico was to be occupied by the Americans until a peace conference decided its future.

Paris peace conference

The peace conference opened in Paris on 1 October. The American delegates said that they would abide by the Teller Amendment but that they would keep their army in Cuba until a suitable civilian government was set up. The Philippines, Puerto Rico and Guam were to become American territories but not states of the United States. Spain was to be paid $20 million for the loss of these territories. The treaty was signed in December 1898. It came as a disappointment, especially to the Filipino patriots who had fought with the Americans against the Spanish. They had not expected to exchange Spanish rule for American. When news of the treaty reached Manila the patriots turned on the Americans; 70,000 American troops took three years to restore their control over the islands.

American colonialism

Now it had won the Spanish colonies, the American government had to work out a colonial policy. It had to please two sets of opinion, the expansionists and the isolationists.

American expansionists wanted to see outposts of the American way of life around the world. They looked on the new possessions as a chance for missionaries, teachers and charitable organisations to take a better way of life to less fortunate people. Many businessmen thought it would be safer to invest money in factories, plantations and public works in countries which were under American rule backed by American troops. Military leaders wanted naval and marine bases in the seas to the east and west of the United States.

There were not so many isolationists but they put their point of view forcefully. American liberals made the point that ruling colonies was against the spirit of their own political system. They reminded Americans that their own Declaration of Independence began by stating that all men are created equal. Labour leaders feared that immigrants from the new colonies would take jobs away from Americans. Some Southern politicians objected to the thought that there might be more black and coloured people in the country.

The ideas of expansionists and isolationists were brought together in the way that the American government managed the affairs of Cuba and Puerto Rico. Neither was turned into a full colony like those owned by Britain or France, and yet the United States kept control of their affairs. This pleased both expansionists and isolationists. The United States gained the greatest share of the wealth created by the people of these islands without allowing immigration into America. This satisfied both businessmen and labour leaders.

Cuba

Following the defeat of Spain, Cuba was placed under American military governors. They worked hard to give the Cubans what they thought of as the blessings of American civilisation. The first complete census of Cuban population was taken. New schools were built and the University of Havana re-opened. Roads, railways and docks were built. New cattle and breeding stock were imported to replace the herds slaughtered in the fighting. A health-care programme under Dr Walter Reed and Carlos Finlay eliminated malaria and yellow fever. Political prisoners of the Spanish were released and the Cuban Patriot Army was disbanded and given resettlement money, totalling $3 million, paid for by the United States.

Most of the improvements were welcomed by the Cubans. Yet some looked further ahead. They pointed out that the railways and docks tended to aid American-owned sugar properties more than the Cuban enterprises. The road-building programmes gave work to American engineers and used American equipment. Even the textbooks in the schools were Spanish translations of American publications. They were written, printed and bound in the United States for sale in Cuba. Many Cubans complained of the length of the American military occupation. Led by Tomas Estrada Palma, they called on Americans to honour the promises made in the Teller Amendment.

The Platt Amendment

In 1902 the Americans prepared to hand over the island to its own people. A constitution was drawn up for the new government and Tomas Palma was elected free Cuba's first president. But before they left, the Americans insisted that the constitution included the Platt Amendment. This gave the United States the right to interfere in Cuban affairs whenever Congress felt that important economic, military or human interests were threatened:

> Cuba consents that the United States may exercise the right to interfere for the preservation of Cuban independence and the maintenance of a government adequate for the protection of life, property and individual liberty.

The Platt Amendment also laid down that the Cuban government could not sign foreign treaties or accept foreign loans without approval from the United States. This obviously pleased American businessmen and her military leaders who were allowed to keep naval bases in Cuba, such as the one built at Guantanamo Bay.

Puerto Rico

The United States had not been able to make Cuba into a colony because of the Teller Amendment which promised to hand the island over to its own people. The Teller Amendment had not applied to Puerto Rico, but the United States government did not wish to go too strongly against the opinion of American anti-expansionists. So, after a short period of rule by a military governor, Congress passed the Foraker Act in 1900. This gave the island a civilian government and a law-making body of elected Puerto Ricans. But final power rested in the hands of the United States through the Senate which was made up of an American governor and five 'official' members appointed by the American government. Judges in the Puerto Rican supreme court were also appointed by the United States. American labour leaders and racist politicians were satisfied by another section of the Foraker Act which stated that Puerto Ricans were not American citizens and could not travel freely to the United States.

Americans quickly became active in Puerto Rico, carrying out programmes such as those in Cuba. Malaria, yellow fever and other diseases were controlled. Work started on large-scale harbour repairs, road-building schemes and irrigation projects.

Assignments

1 a) *Draw a map of the United States which shows the mainland territory she acquired which enabled her to expand her boundaries in the nineteenth century.*
   b) *How did these extensions of mainland territory increase her interest in the Caribbean and Central America?*
   c) *On your map indicate the areas of the Caribbean and Central America which most interested the USA. Can you summarise what the map shows about the reasons for United States activity outside her own frontiers?*

2 *Using the cartoon on page 173 answer the following questions taken from the CXC Examination, June 1986.*
   a) *What was the cartoonist trying to show?*
   b) *How would each of the following react to the situation which the illustration suggests?*
      (i) Spaniards; (ii) Cuban nationalists; (iii) United States business interests.
   c) *Identify the ways in which the United States was involved with Cuba during the nineteenth century.*
   d) *Give four reasons for this involvement in Cuba during the nineteenth century.*

20 THE UNITED STATES IN THE CARIBBEAN AFTER 1900

The USA and the Caribbean basin to 1918

A new balance of power

The powerful European nations had not objected to the way that the United States had gained control over Cuba and Puerto Rico. The islands had belonged to Spain who had been far too weak to resist, either as a trading nation or a military power. But the American government was just as interested in the independent states of Latin and Central America. England, Germany and France had important interests in most of these arising from the large sums of money they had invested in banks, plantations and railways. On the other hand they were too distant to maintain large forces in the area, so the United States was able to replace them as the major power in the Caribbean basin.

President Theodore Roosevelt

The moves to bring about a new balance of power began with President Theodore Roose-

Fig. 20.1 'Teddy' Roosevelt when he was colonel of the 'Rough Riders'.

velt. He had been lieutenant-colonel of the Rough Riders, an American cavalry troop which fought in Cuba in the Spanish-American War. From then his political rise was swift. He first became governor of New York State and then, in 1900, vice-president of the United States. In 1901 the president, McKinley, was assassinated and Theodore Roosevelt took his place. He was re-elected for the term from 1904 to 1908 and in his seven years as president laid down new lines for American foreign policy towards the Caribbean basin.

Roosevelt's first interference in the affairs of Latin America came in 1902. Venezuela's president had failed to make the payments his government owed to bankers in Britain, France and Germany. In an attempt to force payment the British and German governments sent several gun-boats which blockaded Venezuela's ports and destroyed some of their harbour defences. President Roosevelt was alarmed at the possibility of these European powers occupying Venezuela. Roosevelt quoted the Monroe Doctrine to make it clear that the United States would not permit a European state to use military power in the western hemisphere. He threatened that the United States would send troops to the area unless Venezuela and the European powers worked out a settlement. This they did quickly. Britain, at least, was quite ready to see the United States and not herself face the costs of becoming involved in Latin American affairs.

The Panama Canal

After the war with Spain, the United States needed a means of speedy communication between her colonies and trading interests in the Pacific and Atlantic. The best way would be by a canal which linked the two oceans. The need for a canal was made clear in the Spanish-American war when it took the USS *Oregon* more than two months to sail from California around Cape Horn to join the action in Cuba. The war was almost over before the ship arrived.

The canal scheme was too important to the United States for her to be willing to allow Britain a share. However, both powers were bound by the Clayton–Bulwer Treaty under which they had agreed not to occupy any part of Central America. But Britain was now willing to agree to the United States breaking the treaty if she promised that the future canal would be 'free and open to the vessels of commerce and war of all nations'.

Fig. 20.2 *Panama City at the beginning of this century. The American consulate is the first building to the right.*

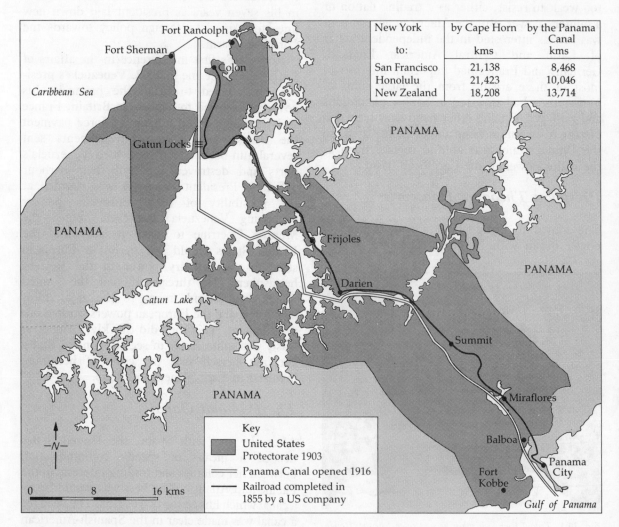

New York to:	by Cape Horn kms	by the Panama Canal kms
San Francisco	21,138	8,468
Honolulu	21,423	10,046
New Zealand	18,208	13,714

Key

United States Protectorate 1903

Panama Canal opened 1916

Railroad completed in 1855 by a US company

Map 17 *The Panama Canal Zone in 1914.*

The next step for the Americans was to select a route for the canal. They favoured Nicaragua at first, both because Americans already had road and waterway interests in the area and because the route could take in Lake Nicaragua. But American interest soon swung to a new route across the Isthmus of Panama which was part of a province in the Republic of Colombia. The Panama route was more rugged, covered with jungle and drenched by tropical rains. But it was only 80 kilometres across the Isthmus and a French company, headed by Ferdinand de Lesseps, had already carefully surveyed the route and begun excavating. The company was now bankrupt but its main shareholder, Philippe Buneau-Varilla, was willing to sell the used machinery at a very low price. In 1903 President Roosevelt's government bought it for $40 million.

Roosevelt had more difficulty dealing with the Colombians. At first, the Colombian representative in Washington signed a treaty with the United States. The United States agreed to pay $10 million and an annual rent of $250,000 for a ninety-year lease on a 10-kilometre wide corridor. The Colombian senate rejected the treaty claiming that it threatened their rights in Panama. They were also insulted that the United States had paid the French company $40 million for rusty machinery, and offered them only $10 million for the right of way. They demanded $25 million plus $10 million worth of shares in the French company that was being sold to America.

This alarmed Buneau-Varilla who feared that Roosevelt would break his agreement to buy the French company. In November 1903 he organised a few Panamanians to declare independence from Colombia. The disorders that followed gave Roosevelt the chance to send a cruiser to 'keep order'. In fact the cruiser was used to stop the landing of a Colombian force which arrived to arrest Buneau-Varilla and put down the tiny revolt. Buneau-Varilla then signed a Treaty with John Hay, the American Secretary of State. The treaty stated that Panama was an independent state and said that the United States had the right to build the canal and own a zone of land on each side.

The zone was increased to 17 kilometres from the 10 offered to Colombia. Instead of ninety-years it was leased to the Americans 'in perpetuity'. Inside this zone the treaty said that America could act as the 'sovereign of the territory' and Panama had no rights there. In addition the United States had the right to keep police and shipping officials in the port cities of Panama and Colon. Nine years after the treaty, the United States agreed to pay an annual rent of £250,000. Shortly afterwards, in 1914, the first vessels passed through the canal. All work was finished in 1920 and the canal was open to regular shipping.

Roosevelt's Corollary

Roosevelt was unashamed of the way that his government had played a leading part in overthrowing Colombia's rule in Panama. He later said, 'I took Panama. It was the only way the canal could be constructed.' But he also knew that the United States' neighbours were becoming troubled at the sort of behaviour they had seen in Cuba, Puerto Rico, Venezuela and Panama. It was time for his government to state its general lines of policy towards such countries. The statement came in a speech by Roosevelt to Congress in 1904.

He began by declaring that his government would continue the policy of the Monroe Doctrine and not allow European nations to attempt to bring about boundary changes in the American continent. But then came the famous Corollary to the Monroe Doctrine. Often, Roosevelt said, Latin Americans managed their affairs so badly that they gave European powers a genuine reason for interfering. To avoid this difficulty in future, the United States would have to see that her neighbours behaved. He later told Latin American and Caribbean representatives in Washington that they need not fear intervention if they knew how to act with 'decency'. But if they showed 'brutal wrongdoing' or weakness 'which results in a general loosening of the ties of a civilised society', they must expect intervention by a 'civilised nation' and America, therefore, would not hesitate to step in.

Dollar diplomacy and war

It would have been difficult for Roosevelt to be more insulting to America's neighbours, but his language made his intentions clear. The other states in the Americas had to accept that the United States had taken over leadership in the region. In any case it had become increasingly difficult to shake off United States' pressure because of the rapid spread of American trading and business interests.

This expansion of American activity was given strong support by the government of Howard Taft who became president in 1908. Subsidies were given to shipping, public works and mining and construction companies which wished to invest in the Caribbean or Latin America. American-owned plantations were helped by placing high customs duties on sugar, bananas, coffee and other crops which did not come from areas where Americans had investments in agriculture.

Taft spoke of this policy as 'dollar diplomacy'. By helping the economic development of poorer neighbours, the United States could gain influence and cut down the interference of European powers without having to use force. Dollar diplomacy, he believed, was a better way of carrying out America's foreign policy than the threatening attitude of Roosevelt's Corollary.

However, Latin American and Caribbean states still fell in debt to European bankers and many still suffered from political upheavals and disorders. So direct interference by the American government continued. Then, in 1914, war broke out in Europe. The United States entered the war in 1917 but, before that, she was concerned that European powers would seize positions in the Americas as naval bases or for supplies of raw materials and food. To prevent this, and to check any threat to her own defences, the United States herself sent troops to several neighbouring countries to ensure that their governments remained friendly.

Haiti

It was difficult for Haiti to stand up to dollar diplomacy. The majority of its people farmed for their own subsistence although some grew coffee for export. These people of the interior lived a life almost completely separate from that of the French-speaking population of the towns. Among these, political leaders struggled for power, not because they had programmes to develop their country but because running the government gave a chance to make personal fortunes from a share in the customs duties or from taking bribes to allow foreigners the right to build railways and public services or open banks.

With such weak and corrupt government it was not difficult for a group of American bankers to gain control, between 1900 and 1915, of Haiti's National Bank, railways, public utilities and customs houses. In some cases the Americans were acting as local managers of businesses set up by German and French investors. The activities of the American bankers made the political situation in Haiti more unstable. Between 1908 and 1915 seven different men seized the presidency of Haiti and at least three were murdered to make way for a rival.

When the First World War broke out in 1914, Germany was eager to gain an American supply base to help her in her fight against Britain and her allies. She saw the chance offered by the disturbances and threatened to seize Haiti for nonpayment of debts to German lenders. To the Americans this was a clear case where the Roosevelt Corollary should be acted on, but in this time of war they also had the support of France and Britain who were fighting together against Germany. They supported the American occupation of Haiti in July 1915.

American marines seized Port-au-Prince where Admiral Caperton set up an office to manage Haiti's affairs. One of his first moves was to find a puppet president through whom he could rule the country. He chose Sudre Dartiguenave and forced him to agree to a ten-year 'occupation' treaty. In the treaty Dartiguenave agreed to appoint Americans to run the customs service, the treasury, and police force. Other Americans were to be in charge of public works, health programmes and new agricultural training schools.

The Dominican Republic

Ulises Heureaux was dictator of the Dominican Republic from 1881 to 1899 when he was assassinated. His firm rule had dealt brutally with revolts but the country was ruined. It had to pay for the dictator's private army, his spy network, his mistresses and his debts to European bankers and to the San Domingo Improvement Company of the United States. Heureaux had given this company the right to collect customs duties as a means of reclaiming the money it had loaned.

In 1903 the Dominican Republic's government took over the funds of the Improvement Company without paying compensation to its American shareholders. President Roosevelt objected along the lines of his Corollary. In 1905 he forced the Republic to allow him to appoint an agent to collect customs duties for the purpose of paying compensation to the company and debts to European bankers.

During the years since Heureaux's assassination, the Republic had had a succession of dictator presidents, each lasting for only a short while. Then, in 1906 Ramón Cáceres became president and gave the country five years of firm government and a chance to put its finances into order. However, in 1911, he too was assassinated and civil war broke out. The short-lived presidents who followed him allowed the Republic to fall further into debt, especially to Europeans. In 1916, the United States government acted to prevent a German effort to make claims on the island. Marines were landed to put an end to the civil wars and to install American military government. The country remained under American control for eight years.

Nicaragua

The story of intervention in Nicaragua also begins with the country's failure to pay its debts to Europe. Most of the debts had come about under the misrule of President José Santos Selaya. In 1909 he was forced to flee the country after a revolt which had been encouraged by American officials in Washington. Now the

Fig. 20.3 *A small sign of United States' activity in Managua, Nicaragua, in the 1930s.*

country was without a government, England and France threatened to invade unless interest was paid on loans. The Americans who had been active in the background were not surprised to be invited by some powerful Nicaraguan families to send an administrator to restore the country's finances and bring about stable government. They sent a civil servant, Thomas C. Dawson. He forced the Nicaraguans to accept a puppet president and then set to work in the standard American way. An American was in charge of customs and others had the task of sharing out the collected money between the Europeans and Nicaraguans. Day-to-day funds were provided by New York banks; in return they were given a share in the

Nicaraguan State bank and the national railways.

In 1912 Nicaraguan patriots organised an armed revolt against the puppet president. American troops were immediately landed and the puppet president was kept in power while the Americans carried out their improvement schemes and trained an armed police force.

Danish Virgin Islands

A slightly different example of the new American foreign policy was seen in the little Danish colonies of St Thomas, St John and St Croix. The American navy saw their value as a first line of defence against an attack from the Atlantic on the Panama Canal. It became even more anxious for the United States to own them when she entered the First World War against Germany in 1917. Eventually Denmark agreed to sell the islands for $25 million. The islands became known as the American Virgin Islands and they were administered by the United States navy until 1931.

Cuba

Haiti, the Dominican Republic, Nicaragua and the Virgin Islands were all examples of the new foreign policy based on dollar diplomacy and the Roosevelt Corollary. The Americans set out to dominate their neighbours and to keep European powers out of the area. Another example was the events in Cuba which are described in Chapter 21. It shows how American business spent so much money in the island after 1902 that it became the best example of dollar diplomacy. But there was also political interference along the lines of the Roosevelt Corollary. American troops were landed in 1906 and 1917 to ensure that Cuba had a government to the United States' liking. Between 1921 and 1923, the American, General Crowder, was the real power in the island.

US policy after 1918

From the early 1920s, the United States government began to see disadvantages in so much direct interference in Latin American and Caribbean affairs. After the war, there was no risk of a European power sending forces to the continent. France and Britain owed the United States huge sums from wartime loans and dared not displease her. Germany was ruined and not allowed to rebuild her navy. At an international conference in Washington in 1922, it was agreed that the American and British fleets of battleships should be the same size but that no other power should have such a large naval forces. American politicians were also aware that their activities had made them unpopular with the people in many Caribbean and Latin American states, especially where American marines or officials were obviously in control.

In 1922 a new president, Warren Harding, took office and, shortly afterwards, his Secretary of State, Charles Evans Hughes, announced that the United States had a 'deep interest in the prosperity, the independence and the unimpaired sovereignty of the countries of Latin America.' This recognition of the rights of Latin American states to independence and non-interference was taken a step further under the next president, Calvin Coolidge. In 1928 his government said that it no longer accepted the Roosevelt Corollary to the Monroe Doctrine. Under the Corollary the United States had claimed the 'right' to interfere in the affairs of American neighbours if she thought they had behaved wrongly. Calvin Coolidge restated the aims of the original Monroe Doctrine under which the United States said she would prevent American nations being occupied or attacked by a foreign power.

It was the next president, Herbert Hoover, who first spoke the words 'good neighbour' to describe the new American policy. But the phrase is always connected with the man who followed him, Franklin D. Roosevelt, who used it in his first address to the nation, saying, 'I would dedicate this nation to the policy of the good neighbour – the neighbour who resolutely respects himself, and because he does so, respects the rights of others.'

The marines go home

The new declarations of policy went alongside United States withdrawals. Unfortunately, the events which followed made it clear just how unsuccessful the occupying forces and officials had been in helping the development of democratic government. In several countries the police forces, which had been trained and armed by the Americans, became the backers of dictatorships.

In 1922 President Harding sent Sumner Wells to the Dominican Republic to arrange for the withdrawal of American forces after the free election of a civilian president. In 1924 Horatio Vasquez was elected and the American marines returned home, leaving a financial adviser behind to administer the country's customs service. Before they left, the Americans had also trained a well-armed local police force. When Vasquez tried to retain power by a corrupt election in 1930 he was driven out by the police force led by Rafael Leonidas Trujillo. Trujillo then used the police to build up his own personal dictatorship which lasted until 1961.

In 1925 the United States took the first steps in withdrawing from Nicaragua. The marines were recalled but returned in 1927 when civil war broke out again. In 1928 elections were held under American supervision and José Maria Moncada was elected president. He ruled with the support of the marines until 1933. During this time the United States trained a national police force to replace the army as the organisation for keeping law and order inside the country. Within a few years the leader of the police, General Samoza, had overthrown the elected president and taken his place. His family held on to power in Nicaragua from 1937 until 1979.

The United States withdrawal from Haiti followed a similar pattern. In 1930 the Americans began preparations for a presidential election. At the same time they began to train a local police force, the Guarde d'Haiti. The United States marines were then called home in 1934, although an American commission remained to protect American financial interests. This stayed until 1941. It was in 1946 that the Haitian president was overthrown by the American-trained police. After this the constabulary made and unmade several presidents until 1957, when François Duvalier created his

Fig. 20.4 *President Duvalier, protected by bodyguards.*

personal dictatorship.

In 1936, Roosevelt's government announced that it no longer claimed the right to interfere in the affairs of Panama or to keep police in Panama City and Colón. At the same time, he insisted that the United States should be allowed to undertake joint action with Panama if any other nation threatened the Canal's safety. The United States Senate was not satisfied with this and would not sign a new treaty until 1939, when Panama agreed that America could act to defend the canal before consulting Panama.

The good neighbour policy actually strengthened American economic interests in Latin America and the Caribbean. By the 1930s, American businesses played a central part in the economic life of many Latin American and Caribbean nations. In 1938 American stockholders controlled 32 per cent of Chile's copper production. The United Fruit Company had a monopoly of Central America's banana industry, owning plantations, wharves and trading companies. The sugar industries in Cuba and the Dominican Republic were controlled by

Fig. 20.5 *President Franklin D. Roosevelt.*

large American-owned refineries. Many of the utility companies in the region were owned or controlled by either the American Foreign Power Company or International Telephone and Telegraph.

The Second World War

The outbreak of war in 1939 had three important consequences for relations between the United States and her near neighbours. First, it boosted production of goods bought by America and either used there or passed on to Britain. Sugar in Cuba and oil from the Dutch islands were two obvious examples.

The second consequence was the involvement of some Latin Americans in the fighting. While men from the West Indies were in the British armies, Brazilian troops were fighting alongside American forces in Italy and Mexican pilots were flying missions against the Japanese in the Far East.

Perhaps most important of all, the war saw a deepening of the American presence in the Caribbean. Bases on Cuba, Puerto Rico and the Virgin Islands were increased in size and many more troops were stationed there. Britain granted long-term leases of land in her Caribbean colonies for the United States to build naval and military bases. At the same time, she agreed to the Americans having a powerful influence in planning the future economic and social development of the Caribbean. In 1942, the two powers jointly set up the Anglo-American Commission which was later named the Caribbean Commission. In the First World War, American activity had been confined to the Spanish-speaking territories in the Caribbean. By the middle of the Second World War it was clear that Britain could not survive without the military and economic aid of the United States and had to agree to her involvement in the affairs of the English-speaking Caribbean.

Assignments

1 *What evidence is there that the United States had taken over leadership in the Caribbean and Latin America after 1900?*

2 a) *Explain and give examples of the 'dollar diplomacy' policy of the United States, as seen in the Caribbean after 1900.*
   b) *What was the 'good neighbour' policy? In which ways could it be seen at work in the Caribbean?*

3 *What do you imagine would have been the response of the people of Panama, Haiti and the Dominican Republic to the presence and involvement of the United States in their countries?*

21 Cuba: Cubans and Americans 1902–62

From the Platt Amendment to 1933

American business in Cuba

The Platt Amendment of 1902 made it possible for American interests to become increasingly powerful in Cuba without the island becoming a colony or a state of the United States. This was seen most obviously in the sugar industry. American finance paid for huge new centrals, mostly on the land once owned by small land-owners in the east. Between 1908 and 1918 the island's sugar production rose from 1,500,000 tonnes a year to 4,000,000 tonnes. Until 1918 many of the new factories were owned by Cubans, who had borrowed the money from Americans to build them.

In the next two years, most of the factories and much of the plantation land was bought outright by American businesses attracted by the new high prices for sugar. One consequence of this new sugar boom in Cuba was a steady stream of seasonal migrant workers from Jamaica and Haiti. But there was also a movement into Cuba of American businessmen, clerks, engineers and other employees of the new American-dominated industries, banks or public works undertakings. These years also saw the beginnings of a tourist industry, backed up by a widespread gambling business which was to turn Havana into a playground for Americans who had nothing to offer Cuba except the dollars they spent.

American marines in Cuba

Events after 1902 showed that the Americans would not hesitate to intervene in Cuban

Fig. 21.1 *Crowds gather in Havana in 1913 to see the inauguration of President Menocal.*

political affairs if her interests were threatened. The first case concerned the new president, Estrada Palma. He had accepted office under the constitution drawn up by the Americans and his opponents criticised him for being a puppet of the United States. After Palma won the 1906 election, the Liberal leaders, José Gomez and Alfredo Zayas, accused him of cheating and called for his overthrow. Disorder spread across the island. Palma did not wait for the United States to act under the Platt Amendment. He himself asked for American troops to be landed to restore order. Once this had been done, President Roosevelt sent a personal friend, Charles Magoon, to manage the day-to-day business of the Cuban government.

In 1909 Magoon supervised a new election which brought Miguel Gomez to power. Gomez acted as president with American support until he was replaced by Mario Garcia Menocal. In 1917, after the United States had declared war on Germany, a revolt broke out against Menocal. Menocal's government was corrupt and extremely unpopular, but the American government believed that it had to protect its sugar supplies and its defences on the eve of war. So President Wilson sent marines; their presence, and the threat of further intervention, was enough to check the revolt.

Crisis in the 1920s

The wartime sugar boom was followed by a slump in world sugar prices which began in 1920. The slump had a harsh effect in Cuba where sugar was the leading business and the biggest provider of jobs. Many estates went bankrupt and there was a new wave of selling to American private businessmen and banks. The government of Cuba was also heavily in debt.

The economic troubles led to political chaos. It came to a head in the elections of 1921 which were won by Alfredo Zayas, a close supporter of Menocal. Opposition groups immediately said the election had been rigged. The country was about to break into anarchy and the United States sent an unofficial adviser, General Crowder, to help restore order. Crowder got his

way by using the fact that Cuba needed large American loans to avoid bankruptcy. He arranged for Zayas to stay as president, but insisted that he ran the country along guidelines that Crowder laid down.

Many Cubans objected to Crowder's position in the government and the Americans called him home in 1923. In 1925 new elections brought another pro-American, Gerado Machado, to power as president. He built up a personal dictatorship based on heavy bribes and the thuggery of his force of private gunmen, the 'Porristes'. Machado's rule began a new stage of American business involvement. Even more sugar factories, estates and public works passed into American hands. These were also years when hundreds of thousands of pleasure-seeking Americans turned to Cuba. The boom for hotels, nightclubs and casinos was helped by the fact that alcohol could not be sold in the USA in the years of prohibition from 1919 to 1933.

The end of the Platt Amendment

The Americans had not objected when Gerado Machado changed the Cuban constitution to allow himself to stay in office for ever. But they changed their policy in 1933. By then Machado's rule was so cruel and corrupt that there was widespread unrest on the island. President Roosevelt felt that this might damage American interests and ordered the American ambassador to demand that Machado resign so new elections could be held.

Before that could happen, Machado was forced out of office by an army revolt. Carlos Manuel de Cespedes was chosen as provisional president until elections took place. But his rule lasted only a few days before his government was overthrown by another army revolt led by Sergeant Fulgencia Batista.

America did not interfere in these changes. She sent warships but they only stood by in case American interests were threatened. To Roosevelt the overthrow of Cespedes showed that America would never gain from interfering in Cuban affairs in the way that the Platt Amendment said she could. In May 1934 he signed a new treaty with the Cubans. It cancelled the Platt Amendment so that the United States government had no position in Cuban politics. Officially, all she had left was the naval base which had been built at Guantanamo during the time when the Platt Amendment was in force.

The Batista years, 1933–59

Fulgencia Batista

Batista had begun his working life as a barber and, sometimes, a cane-cutter. He then joined the army where he learned to read and write. He became stenographer and personal secretary to several high-ranking officers. At first hand, he discovered how corrupt and inefficient the military had become under Machado. His humble background, his quick wit and his knowledge of the High Command's outrageous behaviour made Batista popular among the rank and file soldiers. It was their backing which gave Sergeant Batista the chance to begin a political career on 4 September 1933. He calmly drew his revolver, walked into the chief of staff's office, dismissed him and promoted himself the new chief of staff with the rank of colonel. From his new command, he fired 500 of his former officers, replacing them with common soldiers loyal to him.

Batista's first dictatorship

With the army firmly under his control, Batista had no difficulty in driving out Cespedes. He did not need to take the risk of becoming president himself. It was easier and wiser to be a behind-the-scenes dictator, ruling through puppet presidents who could be sacked as soon as they became unpopular. In seven years he made, and unmade, seven presidents. Throughout this time, the real power lay with Batista and the army and armed police forces which together numbered more than 30,000 men. Batista made sure that the new officers never forgot that they owed their position to him. The enlisted men's loyalty was taken care of by pay rises, fine new barracks and playing fields, good food and adequate pensions.

Fig. 21.2 *Armed police and troops in the streets just before Batista seized power in Havana, 1933.*

Because he ruled through the might of the army and not votes, Batista was quite willing to let the elected congress, the newspapers and student groups criticise his government officials. Labour unions were encouraged and their leaders given seats in the cabinets of Cuba's puppet presidents. Batista even had the support of communist groups.

The 1940 constitution

By 1939 Batista felt it was safe to experiment with a democratic form of government for Cuba. Elections were held for a Constituent Assembly to write a constitution. The 1940 constitution gave both men and women the right to vote in elections and form political parties. Presidential elections were to be held every four years. As well as giving these basic political rights, the constitution laid down that it was a duty of government to tackle unemployment, to provide at least eight years' primary education, to introduce schemes of social insurance and to regulate the working hours of employees.

With the constitution accepted, Batista laid down his office as chief of staff in the army and stood in the first presidential election. The election was carried out fairly, although Batista was able to spend far more money and draw more attention to himself than the other main candidate, Dr Ramon Grau San Martin. Not surprisingly, Batista won by a three to two majority. Among his supporters were men and women from most social groups, both businessmen and workers from town and country, and from many political groups including the communists.

While he was president, Cuba benefited from the great economic boom which followed the upsurge of American industry and trade during the Second World War. The United States agreed to buy all the sugar Cuba could produce at low rates of import duty. American companies opened the first nickel and magnesium mines in the island. Cuba enjoyed a time of relative prosperity while Batista and American and Cuban businessmen grew rich together.

The breakdown of democracy, 1944–52

Unlike most Latin American dictators, Batista retired quietly from office in 1944 and allowed a free election for a new president to take place. He himself did not stay in Cuba but preferred to live on his estate in Florida. There he was well away from any investigations which the new government might make into his years as ruler of Cuba.

The 1944 election was won by Dr Grau San Martin. San Martin included both communists and conservatives in his cabinet and promised to move ahead with social and economic programmes. He soon found that it was not easy to follow eleven years of Batista's rule. The army and police continued to behave as if they were independent of the elected government. San Martin found it impossible to stop the corruption which Batista had permitted to keep

the top civil servants loyal. Most of the money put aside for social improvement programmes still found its way into their pockets.

The coalition gradually broke up as first the communists and then the labour leaders withdrew. Popular support for San Martin himself crumbled when it became known he was building himself a country estate complete with private zoo and stables. One of his cabinet ministers drove a truck to the treasury, loaded millions of dollars into suitcases, went to the airport and flew to Miami where immigration authorities accepted him as a political refugee!

In 1948 Carlos Prio Socarras was elected on the promise that he would end dishonesty in government. It soon became clear that he was no more honest than San Martin. No one was very surprised when it was known that he was building himself a $3 million house out of his $25,000 salary. In March 1952 Batista returned from Florida. Fearing a complete breakdown of the government, most business interests and the army backed him in a bid to overthrow Socarras' elected government. Socarras did not fight but left quietly for exile. The United States was relieved at the change of government and was quick to recognise Batista as president.

Batista's second dictatorship

Batista had described his first dictatorship as 'mild, suave and sweet'. The second was no such thing. Cuba had changed and he could no longer rule quietly behind the scenes. During the chaotic democratic years since 1940, patriotic movements had grown up, especially at the University of Havana. Many put forward socialist or communist programmes and all were anti-American. Throughout his second dictatorship Batista was faced with outbreaks of student riots, and anti-American campaigns directed at the American-owned businesses.

A survey in 1956 showed that Americans owned over 90 per cent of telephone and electricity services, 50 per cent of public transport and railways and 40 per cent of raw sugar production. United States banks held a quarter of all Cuban bank deposits. The only case where American ownership was falling was in sugar.

Fig. 21.3 *Night life in Havana in the 1950s.*

The Cuban-owned share of the industry had risen from 22 per cent in 1939 to 60 per cent in 1950. But the American influence had grown rapidly in Havana where most of the American-owned banks and utility companies had their head offices and American staffs. It was also a centre for American tourism which had led to the building of new hotels, casinos, nightclubs and race tracks. The contrast between the free-spending Americans and the grinding poverty of most Cubans led to open anti-American feeling.

Batista had taken power at the same time as a sharp fall in the international sugar market. In a single year, between 1952 and 1953, average incomes fell by 18 per cent. The land-less sugar workers and the small farmers who sold cane to the centrals were hit hardest. The sugar barons who owned about three-quarters of the land lived an American style of life in Havana and never came to see the hardships of their labourers. The effects of declining prices for sugar soon led to unemployment in the cities. Batista tried to put some back to work on short-term public works programmes such as building a tunnel under Havana Bay. The works programmes drained the national treasury but did little to ease unemployment. Workers began to support leftist trade union leaders. The Bank Workers' Union and the electricity workers began anti-government strikes. In 1955 they were joined by sugar workers who struck in the three eastern provinces. In 1957 a general strike paralysed cities all over the island.

As discontent and opposition grew, Batista's dictatorship became more totalitarian. He gave up any pretence of welcoming criticism and allowing freedom of speech. His rule became more gangsterlike. The military and police used to round up possible opponents; courts-martial and pre-dawn firing squads became common. Much of Cuba's national treasury was used to buy support. It is probably true that Batista himself grew rich from protection money paid by American crime syndicates such as the Mafia which controlled much of Havana's gambling and prostitution. The brutality and wholesale corruption lost Batista the support of the more honest businessmen and landowners who had welcomed his return in 1952.

Castro and the 1959 revolution

The rise of Castro

In 1956 Batista's opponents found a new leader, Fidel Castro. He was a well-educated lawyer and a member of a wealthy landowning family in Santiago. As a student he had travelled widely throughout South America. There he came to believe that the poor could be helped only by giving them back the wealth they earned for landlords and industrialists. The corrupt dictatorships and their wealthy supporters could only be overthrown, he believed, by armed rebellion.

In 1953 Fidel, his brother, Raul, and 165 young followers began a revolution to free their homeland from Batista's corrupt dictatorship. In their 26 July Manifesto, the revolutionaries condemned Batista, the colonial mentality of wealthy Cubans and the economic control of the island by foreign interests. Immediately after-wards they launched an attack on the Mancado army barracks in Santiago. It failed miserably. Half of the young revolutionaries died in the first round of machine-gun fire. The survivors, including the Castro brothers, fled. Batista retaliated quickly and brutally. Those suspected of sympathising were rounded up, tortured for information and condemned by court-martial to death.

Fig. 21.4 *The Moncada barracks with the bullet marks from the fighting in 1953.*

To stop the massacre Fidel and Raul surrendered on 1 August. They were sentenced to fifteen years in prison. Eleven months later Batista pardoned them. He hoped the pardon would win some support for his regime while making it look as if he had nothing to fear from such young rebels. He was badly mistaken. Fidel Castro immediately fled to Mexico where he began gathering new recruits for his next attempt.

The Sierra Maestra

On 2 December 1956, Castro landed on the south-east coast of Cuba with a band of 82 men. They were met by Batista's troops armed with the latest automatic weapons. Only Fidel, Raul and ten others escaped by making their way into the jungle-covered mountains of the Sierra Maestra, west of Santiago. When news of their survival reached the outside world, medicine, arms and supplies were smuggled to them by sympathisers in Mexico, the United States and Venezuela. New Cuban recruits made their way to the Sierra Maestra. Batista helped the rebels when he closed the University of Havana because of its opposition to his dictatorship. Many ex-students and young educated Cubans made their way to join Castro in the Sierra Maestra.

From their mountain stronghold the revolutionaries made expeditions into nearby plantations and villages. Here they were given food and gradually built up support among the peasants who saw the rebels as new folk heroes fighting the absentee landlords and Batista's dictatorship. New rebel camps appeared throughout the island. Raul set up another stronghold in the Sierra del Cristal in the Oriente Province. In March 1957, twenty-one young revolutionaries shot their way into the national palace and almost killed Batista. He stopped appearing before crowds and continued to divert money from the national treasury to his bank accounts in foreign countries.

Growing support

In 1958 there was growing support among middle class Cubans, especially in Havana, for a change in the system of government. They could accept many of Castro's political ideas. He declared that he would replace the dictatorship with a government elected along the lines laid down in the 1940 constitution. He wished to see an end to the American domination of Cuban economic affairs and would rid the island of the worst features of the tourist industry which had allowed reckless spending by Americans on gambling, prostitution and other pleasures while Cubans lived in wretched slums.

University teachers who had seen their university closed by Batista, as well as lawyers and journalists who had to work in courts and on newspapers controlled by the dictator, hoped for his overthrow. So did officials and technical staff who often worked in inferior positions in American-dominated businesses or public services and saw the corruption that went on. Even Cubans who owned land and businesses believed they would only prosper under a freer and more honest government. The Church added its voice. In 1958, the island's bishops published a letter calling for 'a government of national unity which can restore our country to a peaceful political life'.

The USA changes policy

In March 1958 pressure from Cuban businessmen and landowners persuaded the United States government to hasten the end of the dictatorship by stopping the sale of arms to Batista. The United States government heard from many Americans in Cuba that they wanted an end to the dictatorship. Businesses were suffering from the disorder, corruption and labour unrest. Some businessmen openly preferred Castro's revolutionaries. One described them as 'just nice kids'. The American ambassador reported on them as 'friendly, courteous, capable of preserving order among the populace and displaying no anti-American sentiment.' Unfortunately, Britain did not also stop the sale of arms and the conflict dragged on throughout the summer and into the fall.

Batista departs

In November 1958, Batista made one last effort to save his dictatorship. He tried to step into the background by having a new president elected.

Map 18 *Cuba in the 1950s.*

But nobody took the election seriously. In December, top ranking army officers began to defect away into exile and safety. On 1 January 1959, Batista and his family were driven to the airport and left the island for the last time.

The new government

The new government was made up of the revolutionary bands which had forced the downfall of Batista. Fidel Castro was premier. His brother, Raul, was chief of the armed forces and Ernesto (Ché) Guevara, an Argentinian doctor, was economic adviser. Yet the revolution had also depended on the goodwill of middle class Cuban liberals who supported the return to a democratic system of government. They too had places in the cabinet and one of them, Manuel Lleo Urrutia, became the first president under the new system.

The new government quickly showed that it meant to be thorough in its changes. A first step was to make sure that its policies would be carried out. Most of the senior government officials were dismissed. In their place new ministries were set up, staffed by men loyal to Castro and the revolutionary party. He demanded, and got, complete honesty, a state of affairs unknown in earlier Cuban civil services. The police, army, air force and navy were purged. Top ranking Batista aides and officers who had not fled were put on trial. By official count, 483 were executed after having been found guilty of serious crimes against the Cuban people.

Fig. 21.5 *Women soldiers parade outside the American embassy in Havana.*

Cuba between the USA and the USSR

Agrarian reforms

The Cuban revolutionaries believed that the greatest cause of their countrymen's hardship was that most of the best land was owned by a small number of extremely wealthy corporations and families, both Cuban and foreign. In June 1959 the first Agrarian Reform Law outlined plans for the expropriation, or taking land away, from the owners of the cattle, sugar and tobacco estates. The expropriations were to be carried out by a new National Institute of Agrarian Reform (INRA). Owners were to be allowed to keep a small percentage of the lands. The rest would be taken by the state and paid for in government bonds. These would give the ex-owners a yearly $4\frac{1}{2}$ per cent dividend, starting in four years' time. Machinery and cattle were expropriated without compensation. The expropriated estates were to be divided among

Fig. 21.6 *Cuban soldiers planting trees.*

landless families at the rate of 27 hectares per family. The expropriations continued throughout 1959 and 1960. By the end of that year most of the land belonging to United States firms, including 100,000 hectares of United Fruit estates, was in Cuban hands.

Industry

The revolutionaries were determined to bring the island's major industrial and commercial enterprises into government hands. In November 1959 the government appointed 'interveners' to oversee American-owned companies such as the Cuban Telephone Company and the Compania Cubana de Electricidad. The interveners ordered them to improve and extend their services and cut their charges. But government control of public enterprises was only a first step. At the centre of Castro's schemes for a new Cuba were plans for a massive development of government-managed industry. He believed the island could only pay for social reforms and

start new housing and road works if the government owned mines, metal works, engineering factories and supplies of fuel and building materials. Unless the Cubans created their own wealth, according to government plans, and kept it in the country, they would never be free of the need to borrow from abroad.

In the early stages outside help would still be needed but the revolutionaries would not take American money. As Ché Guevara said in March 1960, 'Our hardest fight is against the North American monopolies . . . private foreign capital comes here only for profit and does nothing for the people of Cuba.' Instead, Castro turned to the communist states of the world, the USSR and her allies. In all of them industry was state-owned and run by state planning organisations.

Under Batista, Cuba had been an American-dominated state. In the cold war which followed the Second World War, the USA and the USSR were extremely hostile to each other. Batista had followed the United States policy towards

Fig. 21.7 *'Ché' Guevara at a building site near Havana.*

communist countries by not trading with them and not having diplomatic relations with them. Castro immediately changed this policy. By early 1960 there was a Soviet ambassador in Havana and in February the first trade agreement was signed between Cuba and the Soviet Union.

The Soviet Union agreed to buy 5 million tonnes of sugar over a five-year period, and granted Cuba a loan of $100 million at an interest rate of only 2.5 per cent. The loan was to be used to buy goods from the USSR which would help Castro to launch his industrialisation plans. They were to include petroleum, iron, steel, aluminium products, chemicals and fertilisers as well as complete factories with their machinery and with Soviet technicians who would set them up and train Cubans to run them. In April another trade pact was signed with Poland who agreed to buy sugar in return for similar help to Cuba's industrialisation. In July a deal was worked out with the People's Republic of China to exchange sugar for rice.

Economic war with the USA

The plans for industrialisation and the dealings with communist countries soon brought the Cuban revolutionary government into open disagreement with the United States. In 1960 Cuba cancelled leases held by American companies to mine iron ore, sulphur, cobalt and nickel in the island. A little later, three American oil refineries in Cuba refused to refine petroleum which was imported from the USSR. In reply, they were expropriated by the Cuban government. Then all American-owned sugar-mills were expropriated. The United States government complained that the suggested compensation was too little and would not be paid immediately.

When Castro refused to reply to their complaints, Congress cancelled the purchase of Cuban sugar at preferential rates for 1960 and 1961. This could have ruined Cuba but in July 1960, the USSR came to her aid by agreeing to buy nearly all the Cuban sugar crop. From then on Cuba and the United States carried on an economic war. The American government warned its citizens not to visit Cuba and thus stopped the island's income from tourism. It also placed an embargo on all trade with Cuba except in food and drugs. For his part, Castro refused to give in to these economic pressures. He pressed ahead with expropriations but now without any suggestion that compensation would ever be paid. By November 1960, over $1 billion worth of American-owned enterprises had been seized as well as many which were mostly owned by Cubans.

US support for Castro's enemies

The United States then began to look for political ways of destroying Castro's government. Towards the end of 1960, just one year after the revolution, it seemed that his enemies would have support from many Cubans. Castro's plans for rapid industrialisation had lost him much support from the middle classes. Cuban businesses as well as American had been expropriated by the state. It was clear that new industries paid for by communist aid would be managed by supporters of Castro. Jobs would not go to Cubans who did not wholeheartedly support him. There were growing fears among some liberals that Cuban communists were playing too great a part behind the scenes in the affairs of the government. Most of the liberals in the cabinet had been dismissed or forced to resign as had the liberal president, Manuel Urrutia.

One important sign of the growing middle class discontent was the number of Cubans who went into exile into the United States. There, many campaigned for American support in overthrowing Castro's government which they said was communist controlled and dominated by the USA's enemy, the Soviet Union.

The Central Intelligence Agency of the United States (CIA) and staff of the American embassy in Havana began to support opponents of Castro's government. Castro counter-attacked in a four-hour-long speech at the United Nations. He attacked the United States and its economic imperialism in so many Latin American countries. In January 1961 he took action against the political plotting in the American embassy and ordered that its huge staff should be cut down to eleven. There was uproar in the United States Congress and President Eisenhower gave way to demands that all the staff should be withdrawn. Diplomatic relations between the United States and Cuba were broken off.

Almost immediately afterwards, John F. Kennedy took office as American president. Like Eisenhower, he was under pressure to take action to destroy the new revolutionary government before it became a communist armed base only 149 kilometres from the United States mainland. But Kennedy would not agree to an outright military invasion. It was sure to be condemned by the Latin American republics. Both Eisenhower and Kennedy were also well aware that an invasion of Cuba might lead to something everyone feared – nuclear war. In May 1960, the USSR's premier, Nikita Khrushchev, had promised that 'rockets will fly' to protect Cuba and her revolution.

The Bay of Pigs

Since they dare not act openly, both Eisenhower and Kennedy continued to plot secretly. The CIA recruited, armed and trained Cubans who had fled from Castro's rule, at secret camps in Florida and Guatemala. Over 2,000 men were made ready to land at the Bay of Pigs in Cuba on 17 April 1961. The CIA command had let itself believe that the invaders would win support from the majority of Cubans. This did not happen. The Cubans remained loyal to Castro and the revolution.

The invasion was also poorly planned. The invaders should have been landed at several places which would have given some a chance to escape into the interior as Castro had done in 1956. The attacking force was given absolutely no American back-up force because the United States government feared that this would reveal its part in the affair. As it was, the invasion came as no surprise to Castro. The secret plans were simply not secret. In their haste for volunteers, the CIA had recruited several of Castro's own spies! They kept him informed of the exact time, date and place of

the invasion. As a result when the men waded ashore they were met with the best troops, guns and tanks Castro could muster. Within 72 hours, 1,179 survivors were rounded up and hustled off to Cuban prisons. There they remained until July 1975 when they were ransomed back to the United States for $53 million worth of drugs and food.

The Bay of Pigs fiasco was a blow to the prestige of the United States government at home and abroad. In the United States, critics condemned the blunders of the CIA and demanded that its future schemes should be brought under some sort of control by Congress. In the wider world Castro received much support and sympathy as a victim of American aggression. In Latin America, the United States' popularity fell further. She was now forced to turn to an open appeal to the Organisation of American States to join in her anti-Cuban campaign, but her success was only limited.

At the January 1962 meeting of the OAS the United States put forward a proposal to expel Cuba from the OAS. A very slight majority of the ministers present accepted the proposal and Cuba was expelled. At least six ministers, from Brazil, Argentina, Chile, Mexico, Ecuador and Bolivia, refused their support. They spoke for over 139 million Latin Americans, half the continent's total population. It was hardly the unanimous support the United States had looked for.

The missile crisis

On 29 August 1962, high-altitude flights over Cuba by American spy planes showed what might be surface-to-air nuclear missiles being installed in the western provinces by Soviet technicians. Premier Khrushchev assured President Kennedy that his intelligence reports were wrong. But on 14 October, photographs were delivered to the White House which proved that Khrushchev had lied. They clearly showed launching pads and missiles in western Cuba. Why Khrushchev had gone ahead with plans which were bound to endanger the safety of the whole world is not clear. Perhaps the blunders

Fig. 21.8 *Fidel Castro (right) in Moscow with Leonid Brezhnev (centre), President of the USSR.*

of the Bay of Pigs and the unpopularity of the United States in Latin America had led him to think there was no risk. If so, he was wrong.

Kennedy spent some time discussing his course of action with advisers. He then acted decisively. He informed the OAS of the danger from the missiles to both the United States and the Latin republics. He demanded and got OAS support for a plan to stop and search all Soviet ships heading for Cuba. He then contacted Khrushchev and demanded the removal of the missiles. Without waiting for a reply, he ordered 145,000 American troops to stand by in Florida and Nicaragua. Faced with the possibility of clashes which could lead to all-out war, Khrushchev backed down. On 29 October he ordered ships heading for Cuba to turn back and work to start on dismantling missiles on the island.

Cuba and communism

By 1962, it was clear that Castro had decided that Cuba should be governed along the lines of a communist state. A single party for all supporters of the revolution was created – the Party of the Socialist Revolution. In October 1965 this was re-organised to become the Communist Party of Cuba (PCC). Those who could not give whole-hearted or full-time support to the revolutionary movement were excluded from the PCC, which began with a select membership of only 55,000. Other supporters were enrolled into mass political organisations such as the Federation of Women.

The ruling organisation of the PCC was its hundred-member Central Committee, elected by members of the party's local branches. In practice most decisions were taken by two smaller groups, the party's secretariat and its leading policy-making body, the politburo (or political buro). As First Secretary of the party, Fidel Castro was in control of the secretariat and therefore of the appointment of party officials throughout the island. Members of the politburo also held most of the important posts in the government. Castro was both the leading figure in the politburo and the head of Cuba's government. He was also commander-in-chief of the armed forces.

Thus by 1962, Castro had abandoned his first policy of returning Cuba to a system of democratic government along the lines of the 1940 constitution. Now there was no question of allowing criticism in the press or on the radio or letting other parties grow up in opposition to the PCC. Two forces had driven Castro along this road to communism. One was the attempts by the United States to destroy his revolutionary movement which had forced him to turn to the USSR for aid and protection. The other was the development of his plans for state-controlled industrialisation. These had been opposed by middle class Cuban liberals who had gradually gone into opposition to his government. For guidance on planning and for help in starting up industries, Castro had again turned to the USSR. Signs of Soviet influence were seen in the Cuban Central Planning Board (JUCEPLAN) set up in 1960 along the lines of state planning organisations in communist states. In 1961 Castro announced Cuba's first Five Year Plan. Such plans were used by all communist states which followed the Russian model.

Assignments

1   a)   *What was the purpose and what were the main results of the Platt Amendment of 1902?*
    b)   *To what extent did the United States leave the government and control of Cuba to Cubans after 1898?*
    c)   *How would you describe the means by which Cuba was governed up to 1933?*

2   *What problems did Batista face in his two periods as president of Cuba and how did he respond to these problems?*

3   a)   *Explain how Fidel Castro set about tackling the problems of his country up to 1962.*
    b)   *How did the United States react to Castro's policies?*

22 THE UNITED STATES AND PUERTO RICO

Politics and economics to 1939

A United States protectorate

Since 1898 Puerto Rico has been a special case in the story of United States activities in the American hemisphere. After the Spanish were driven out by American forces, the island was made into a protectorate of the United States. The Foraker Act laid down the way in which the United States would control the government of Puerto Rico without granting full American citizenship to its people. The Puerto Ricans complained bitterly about the unfairness of this and about the increasing power of American businesses in their island.

In an effort to quieten the opposition, the United States Congress passed a new law in 1917, the Jones Act, which made new arrangements for Puerto Rico. Under the Jones Act, Puerto Ricans were granted full American citizenship. However, since Puerto Rico was not made a state of the United States, it was impossible for her people to use rights, such as voting in United States federal elections, unless they moved to the mainland.

The USA also placed limitations on the new system of government in the island. Puerto Ricans could elect thirty-nine members to the lower chamber of the legislature and nineteen to the senate. But real power was held by the governor's executive council. The United States continued to appoint the governor along with the commissioner of education and the attorney-general. The governor was able to veto budget items even if they were agreed by the elected chambers. As a further safeguard for United States' control, the United States Congress and the president could disallow laws passed by the local Puerto Rican legislature.

Political parties

With the new system of government in Puerto Rico, new political parties grew up. The Republican Party kept close ties with the Republican Party in the United States and was generally seen as representing the interests of big business in the island. The Liberal Party's strongest support lay among educated Puerto Ricans. Both Republicans and Liberals were opposed by the outspoken Nationalist Party led by Pedro Albizu Campos. He called the United States an 'interloper' and demanded outright independence for his country. Campos was extremely popular among the poorest Puerto Ricans but by 1932 he was able to win only 2 per cent of the vote in elections.

By this time popular support was turning to the Socialist Party which was allied with the

Fig. 22.1 *Demonstrators demand the release of Pedro Albizu Campos from prison.*

American Federation of Labour. The Socialist Party called for social and economic reform and for the island to become a full state of the United States. In 1914 the Socialist Party had won only 4,000 votes. In 1928 it captured eight seats in the senate and eight in the lower chamber. In 1932 it was strong enough to be invited to form a coalition government with the Republican Party.

The growing support for the socialists and their call for full statehood was a sign of the Puerto Ricans' growing opposition to the policies of the American governors who ran the island. Few spoke Spanish and none showed understanding of the island's problems. Most Puerto Ricans looked on them simply as representatives of American business, government or military interests.

American business in Puerto Rico

By 1930 American investors owned 60 per cent of public utilities and banking, 80 per cent of tobacco manufacturing plants, 60 per cent of the sugar industry and all of the overseas shipping. Smaller American businesses were also attracted to the island to make use of cheap labour. Puerto Ricans rolled tobacco into cigars for only pennies a day; women sewed gloves which had been pre-cut in the United States for a few cents per pair; as many as 40,000 young

girls worked as embroiderers for six cents an hour. With good reason Puerto Rico became known as the sweatshop of the United States.

It was in agriculture that American control led to the greatest distress. After 1898, Puerto Rican sugar was allowed into the United States at favourable tariff rates. Money from the American mainland was soon being heavily invested in the island's sugar industry. The law which forbade corporations to own more than 243 hectares was ignored; by 1917 there were 477 holdings greater than this. All were owned by four American organisations which had built up enormous holdings on the fertile coastal plains. The industry was served by modern roads, mills, railways and seaports. By 1940 the big four corporations owned land worth $60 million and factories and equipment worth as much again. The largest corporation, the Eastern Puerto Rico Sugar Company, owned 22,400 hectares of which less than half was planted in crops.

Small Puerto Rican farmers could not compete with these American companies. Many sold their land after falling into debt. Those who managed to avoid losing their land found that the American-owned central factories paid extremely low prices for small farmers' cane. Another result of the decline in small farming was a drop in the amount of food crops grown for the local market. Farmers who

Fig. 22.2 *Large sugar fields, owned by the Eastern Puerto Rico Sugar Company, around the town of Maunabo.*

continued to grow provisions had to compete with a flood of cheap food from large and highly mechanised farms in mainland United States. Before 1898, Puerto Rican farmers had grown all the island's rice, which was the main food of the poor. In 1934, 6½ million dollars worth was imported from South Carolina and California.

All these changes destroyed the small plantation owners and independent peasants who had been the main agriculturalists in nineteenth century Puerto Rico. Under American rule, the Puerto Rican rural population was forced to depend on work at the centrals or the plantations that fed them with cane. With this came the two evils of low wages and seasonal unemployment. By 1930 seasonal unemployment in the out-of-crop season had risen to 30 per cent of the total labour force.

Coffee planters were hard-hit by the American occupation. Before 1898 coffee had been the island's main export crop and was grown on over 40 per cent of the island's farmed land. The coffee growers were not offered a protected market when the United States took the island from Spain. The smaller producers soon found that they could not compete with the large plantations in Brazil and Central America. The coffee industry was well into decline before a severe hurricane in 1928 destroyed many trees. From 1929 thousands of coffee pickers joined the ranks of the unemployed.

A few small farmers switched to tobacco growing. Demand increased as the Americans opened cigar-rolling factories because of the island's cheap labour. In 1898 only 243 Puerto Rican hectares were planted in tobacco; by 1929 there were 12,141. As in Cuba, tobacco remained a poor farmer's cash crop.

Thus Puerto Ricans had little to be happy with after thirty years of American rule. Politically, the government had only a limited freedom and the island was no longer self-sufficient in food. The major industries, utilities and agricultural enterprises were owned by absentees. Unemployment had risen to over 30 per cent of the labour force. Most of those who had jobs were employed in unhealthy and low-paid work. The average income per capita was less than $120 a year. The majority lived in villages, or towns like El Fanguito (little mud) built on a swamp outside the capital, San Juan. Social services were deplorable: there was little sanitation and far too few schools and medical services. The illiteracy rate was about 70 per cent. In 1930 it was estimated that at least

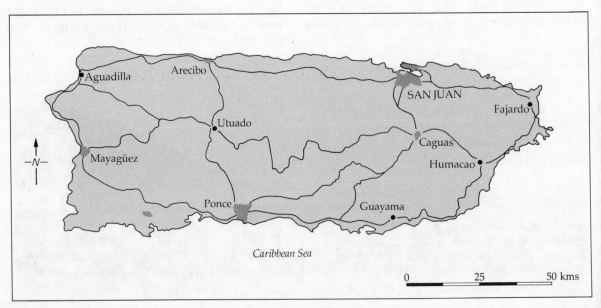

Map 19 *A map showing the main towns and roads in Puerto Rico.*

30,000 people suffered from tuberculosis, 200,000 from malaria and 600,000 from hookworm. Life expectancy was about forty-five years, almost twenty years less than in the mainland United States.

Puerto Rico and the depression

The great depression of the 1930s hit Puerto Rico hard. As America went into economic slump her people stopped buying, and imports from Puerto Rico were cut savagely. Cigar and cigarette factories were forced to close. Thousands of sugar workers lost their jobs in 1934 when the industry had to cut its production by half, as ordered by an act of the United States Congress. The landowners received compensation; the workers were given nothing. The needlework industry dwindled away as exports valued at $20 million in 1937 fell to less than $5 million in 1940.

Franklin Roosevelt was elected United States President in 1932 during the depression. In his first term of office he began his promised 'New Deal' programme to get Americans back to work. Billions of dollars of government money were spent on forestry schemes, dams, roads and social insurance schemes. The programme was extended to the overseas protectorates of the United States. In Puerto Rico it became known as the 'Little New Deal'.

The first step was to set up an Emergency Relief Administration in Puerto Rico to provide immediate help for the most distressed workers. Like the ERA in the United States, the Puerto Rican Emergency Relief Administration offered work on public works programmes. As much as one-third of Puerto Rico's workforce earned some wages from ERA schemes. Then responsibility for social and economic programmes was taken away from the Department of War and given to the Department of the Interior. This department helped set up the Puerto Rican Reconstruction Finance Corporation and the Puerto Rican Reconstruction Administration. By 1938 these two bodies had spent over $57 million on relief schemes.

The Little New Deal saw Puerto Rico through the worst depression years but did little to correct the deep-rooted problems of the island. Too much money had been spent purely on relief and too little on starting schemes which would provide long-term employment With good reason Governor Beverley criticised the whole programme and charged that too much of the relief money had ended in the pockets of local politicians as well as doctors, lawyers and officials hired to run the schemes. Both American administrators and local politicians were discredited by the charges. This helped to win support for a new political movement begun by Puerto Ricans who believed that the time had come to solve their own economic problems.

'Operation Bootstrap'

Munoz Marin

The hardships of the depression gave rise to labour politics in the English-speaking territories. They had a similar effect in Puerto Rico where support grew for the Popular Democratic Party led by Munoz Marin. In the 1940 election campaign, Munoz Marin put forward plans for land reform, better public housing, more equal social insurance and a new state socialism by which the government would spend public funds to make work for the unemployed. The Popular Democratic Party won the election and Munoz Marin became president of the senate and leader of the Puerto Rican government. Some American Congressmen objected to this new Puerto Rican socialism but President Roosevelt ignored them. He appointed a new governor, Rexford Guy Tugwell, who was sympathetic to Munoz's plans. Together Tugwell and Munoz Marin set about remaking Puerto Rico. Their programme was later nicknamed 'Operation Bootstrap', a title which made it clear that Puerto Ricans would have to pull their country together by their own efforts.

Sugar

One of the first steps of the new government was to enforce the 243 hectares law. As money became available, land was expropriated from the large holders. The foreign-owned sugar corporations lost most by the expropriations. On the other hand, Puerto Rican owners were usually able to avoid expropriation by dividing their land among family members in 243-hectare lots. As a result, the expropriations did not provide land for small farmers as Munoz Marin had hoped. Today half of all farm land is still in the hands of 3 per cent of the landowners.

The government did manage to provide some new land by swamp draining. Munoz Marin also tried to bring part of the sugar industry under government control. Plantations were kept in production through a profit-sharing scheme with the workers. In 1960 there were 63 of these farms making up about a tenth of the cane fields in Puerto Rico. Under Munoz Marin the government acquired two sugar factories but he never proposed outright government control of the whole industry which probably would not have been permitted by the United States. Instead, most processing was left to privately owned centrals. In this cautious way, Munoz Marin prevented the sugar industry from being ruined as it might have been if American capital were withdrawn after a full programme of public ownership.

Alternative crops

Munoz Marin paid attention to the need to make Puerto Rico less of a one-crop island. New crops, such as pineapples, were sown on government lands. Seeds and suckers were then sold to private landholders. Experimental farms for beef and dairy cattle, pigs and chickens were also set up. The success of these government schemes was clear by 1958. Beef, dairy products and vegetables made up about half of the earnings of Puerto Rican farmers. The rest was shared between the export crops of tobacco, fruit, coffee and sugar.

The agricultural labourers were not forgotten in Munoz Marin's schemes. He recognised the longing of the landless for even a small holding. On government lands, labourers were granted quarter-hectare plots on a lifetime lease. Areas not needed for sugar were often divided into family-sized farms and sold to the poorest farmers on a long-term payment basis. Small farmers were helped with money and expert advice to set up rural co-operative stores, credit unions, schools and playing fields.

Top priority was given to rural electrification and housing projects. The 400-dollar house scheme helped to replace thousands of thatched shacks with solid hurricane-proof homes. Materials and trained supervisors were provided at cost price by the government and the future owners gave their own labour free. They paid $15 down and the rest on interest-free instalments each month. By 1948, 90,000 farmer-tenants lived in their own houses.

Industry

Munoz Marin and Tugwell believed that agriculture was not the main key to providing an adequate living standard for Puerto Rico's growing population. By 1950, the island had two million people, double the number in 1898. New industries were clearly needed to provide jobs. In 1942, the Puerto Rican Development Company was organised along with the Central Planning Board and a government-funded Development Bank. Attempts were made to build factories which could use the island's natural resources. Local limestone was processed in a cement plant and silica was used by a bottle factory. Fruit processing plants canned the new pineapple crops while leather goods were made out of hides from the new cattle herds. A pottery factory made use of the island's abundant clay deposits. The Planning Board also provided many new jobs in public works programmes to develop water supplies, sewerage and road and transport systems.

A place for private enterprise

Many of the government schemes were not economic successes. By 1947 the only factory to make a small profit for the government treasury was the cement plant. The others were kept open by public subsidies. Opposition party members complained that the cost was too great and that the two thousand jobs in government factories made little difference to the overall rate of unemployment. So, all the factories except

Fig. 22.3 *A dam and hydro-electric power station in Puerto Rico, in 1946.*

the cement plant were sold and Munoz Marin began a new policy of providing government aid to private enterprise.

This approach was later copied across much of the English-speaking Caribbean, as you can see in Chapter 14. Companies willing to open factories on Puerto Rico were exempted from paying taxes on their profits for ten years. Those who built in areas of very high unemployment could have tax exemption for twenty-five years. Government assistance was given in finding sites and building the factories. In some cases they were built by the government and leased to the manufacturer. The Economic Development Administration opened schools to train workers and provided information about markets. When it was needed the Development Bank provided loans. By 1967 it had lent over $167 million to new industries and enterprises.

Almost a third of the new factories made clothes. Next in importance came food processing, electrical goods assembly, footwear manufacture, metal production, machine

assembly and chemical production. By 1955 manufacturing and processing earned more for the island than agriculture. In 1940 one out of four Puerto Ricans earned a living from agriculture. By 1973 the figure was only one out of fourteen. In 1958 there were 500 new factories; in 1972 there were 1,700. Between 1947 and 1972 these plants provided approximately 100,000 new jobs. The earliest factories were mostly for light industries or screwdriver assemblies but the later ones gave work in heavy industries such as oil, petro-chemicals and die-stamping. Income per capita rose steadily from $279 in 1950 to $1,129 in 1968.

The wealth created by the new economic schemes was used to invest in public works and social welfare programmes. Electrical power plants built under 'Operation Bootstrap' increased electrical output from 130 million kilowatt hours in 1940 to 6,200 million kwh in 1968. By 1948, 200,000 children were being enticed into new schools by a free lunch programme. Illiteracy fell steadily to less than 15 per cent in

1970. During the same period, life expectancy increased from forty-six to seventy years.

Criticisms of 'Bootstrap'

Despite its remarkable achievements, 'Operation Bootstrap' had many opponents. They pointed out that unemployment was still high, partly because of the increasing population and partly because of mechanisation, especially on the farms. Many Puerto Ricans still had to leave for the mainland United States in search of jobs and better living standards. Between 1945 and 1973, 750,000 took up permanent residence there, and often had to accept the poorest jobs and housing.

Many Puerto Ricans became *Independentistas*, who wished to see their island more, or completely, independent of the United States. They criticised the 'Americano' industrial invasion and the disruptions it caused to traditional Puerto Rican society. They pointed out that the new assembly industries which had exemptions from tax were able to make quick profits at the expense of Puerto Rican labourers. The Fair Labour Act which supervised the wages and benefits of workers in the United States had not been applied to Puerto Rico. In 1973 two out of every three workers on the island lived below the poverty line set by the United States government for its own mainland people. Small farmers still suffered from the fact that 'Operation Bootstrap' did not solve the problem of imports of cheap American food.

The Commonwealth
A Puerto Rican president

While he was working on 'Operation Bootstrap', Munoz Marin also set out to reduce the powers of the United States president and Congress over his government. Again he found a friend and an ally in Governor Tugwell, who agreed that the power to appoint important officials should be given to a Puerto Rican governor elected by the islanders. When Tugwell resigned in 1946 he persuaded President Truman to appoint a Puerto Rican, Jésus

Pinero, as interim governor for two years. The next year the United States Congress amended the Jones Act so that future governors of Puerto Rico should be elected, not appointed by the American president. In 1948, Munoz Marin became the first elected governor with the power to appoint his own cabinet.

A year later, Munoz Marin began to prepare his case for making Puerto Rico a Commonwealth, no longer under the direct control of the United States but 'freely associated' with her. He wanted the island to be completely self-governing in internal affairs while the mainland was responsible for defence and foreign affairs. The United States Congress gradually gave in to his demands. In 1949 they gave permission for 92 Puerto Ricans to be elected to a convention which was to write a new constitution. The work was finished later in the year. Congress agreed to what the convention had suggested and the people of Puerto Rico voted for it in an island-wide plebiscite, or referendum.

The Commonwealth

In July 1952 Puerto Rico became a Free State or Commonwealth associated with the United States. The power of the United States president to appoint officials was removed. The United States Congress could no longer over-rule laws passed in Puerto Rico. However, the United States remained responsible for defence and foreign affairs. On the other hand some United States laws, such as those of minimum wages, had to be accepted by Puerto Rico. The island also remained firmly inside the American customs area and the American dollar was still its currency. Puerto Ricans were still recognised as United States citizens but still could not vote in presidential elections. There was to be a Puerto Rican representative in the American Congress but he too could not vote.

The constitution of 1952 gave Puerto Rico some powers of self-government which went further than those held by many English-speaking Caribbean islands before independence. On the other hand in some ways they were tied more closely to the United States than the British colonies had been. For instance, the

American Congress insisted that the 1952 constitution included the phrase 'the island of Puerto Rico and the adjacent islands *belonging* to the United States'. Many Puerto Ricans naturally protested that they did not belong to the USA. On the other hand many welcomed the advantages of being linked to the United States and having the right of free entry there. In 1967 a referendum showed that 60 per cent of Puerto Ricans were satisfied with Commonwealth status.

Assignments

1   *In what ways was Puerto Rico i) different from and ii) similar to, other Spanish-speaking territories in the Caribbean between 1900 and 1939?*

2   *How did 'Operation Bootstrap' attempt to improve living and working conditions in Puerto Rico?*

3   *Account for the growth of the 'Independentistas' movement in Puerto Rico.*

4   *Can you find any similarities between 'Operation Bootstrap' and schemes for development in the English-speaking Caribbean?*

23 THE UNITED STATES AND THE ENGLISH-SPEAKING CARIBBEAN

Before 1939

In the years before the Second World War, United States activity in the Caribbean and Central America was directed mostly at the Spanish-speaking territories. As we have seen in Chapter 21 she had taken the place of Spain as the dominant economic and political power in Cuba and Puerto Rico. In countries such as Panama, Nicaragua or the Dominican Republic her interests were mostly concerned with defence or maintaining stability so that no European power was tempted to enter the western hemisphere.

The English- and French-speaking territories were then still colonies directly run by European powers and the USA made little attempt to become involved in their politics. There was no need to interfere from a defence point of view, at least until the labour disturbances of 1938, which the Americans saw as a threat to stability in the Caribbean.

Trade and investment

The years between the First and Second World Wars actually saw a fall in United States trade and investment in the English-speaking Caribbean. In 1913 the five largest British colonies had sent 31 per cent of their exports to the USA and took 35 per cent of their imports from her. By 1933 the trade was much smaller. Only 13 per cent of imports came from the USA and 7 per cent of exports went there. In the last year before the Second World War, the export figure was still only 8 per cent. There were two reasons for this. On the one hand, tariffs on imports to the USA made the price of Caribbean goods very high. On the other hand, Britain and Canada began to give preferential treatment to West Indian sugar and food products.

American companies such as United Fruit kept the plantations they had started in the nineteenth century. Some of their plantation holdings were even increased but there was no large-scale expansion of American-owned businesses to compare with those in Cuba and Puerto Rico. One British writer noted in 1936:

> it is commonly whispered by those who distrust the monopolistic ways of the United Fruit Company that it stays in Jamaica at a loss, only that it may keep a hold on a dangerous rival, while looking to its cheaper holdings in the Central American Republics for its real profits.

Negative effects on the Caribbean economy

The real impact of United States business on the Caribbean in these years was of a more negative kind. The growth of American-financed centrals and huge sugar, fruit and coffee plantations made it hard for British colonies to compete with their rivals in the Spanish- and Portuguese-speaking territories. In the same way, the growth of an American tourist industry in Cuba meant that few Americans took their holidays in the British West Indies.

Another example of a negative effect came in 1924 when the United States closed her doors to immigration from the West Indies. That cut off the movement of several thousand workers from the English-speaking Caribbean who had entered the USA each year in search of work. Along with the decline of trade with the United States, this check to labour migration was a major reason for the poverty which led to the unrest of the 1930s.

The Second World War
Bases

The Second World War began in September 1939 when Hitler invaded Poland, and Britain and

France declared war on Germany. The United States did not join in the fighting until December 1941, but from the start she was concerned about the defence of the western hemisphere. This was particularly important because Holland and France, who both owned colonies in the West Indies, were overrun by Germany in 1940. The Americans immediately made it clear that German attempts to take French and Dutch colonies would be opposed. They also prepared to deal with threats from German submarines to shipping in the Caribbean and the western Atlantic.

The first concern of the United States was to safeguard freedom of movement for her navy and airforce. To do this, she needed to add to the bases she already held in Panama, Cuba, Haiti, Puerto Rico and the Virgin Islands. In September 1940, President Roosevelt came to an agreement with the British government. They were desperately short of warships to track down German submarines, so Roosevelt gave them fifty destroyers which were out of date in design but could still strengthen Britain's navy. In return the British agreed that the USA could set up naval bases in Trinidad, Guyana, St Lucia, Antigua, Jamaica and Bermuda. The position of the bases helped to protect the sea routes to the French and Dutch colonies and to the USA herself. Their importance was shown by the fact that German submarines were still able to cause heavy damage. In 1942 they sank five oil tankers in one raid near Aruba and sank more than 300 ships carrying trade from one part of the Caribbean to another.

The most valuable result of the bases was the employment they gave to the English-speaking Caribbean. The first to benefit were the local people of the territories where bases or new airstrips were built. Others migrated for work. For example many people from the eastern Caribbean found work at the base at Chaguaramas near Port of Spain which gave employment to 30,000 West Indians. Some islands benefited directly from the works. For instance, the USA built

Fig. 23.1 *Antigua international airport in the 1980s. Many planes will be carrying tourists to and from the island.*

military airfields on Antigua and St Lucia. After the war, she handed over the one at Antigua which became the first airfield in the eastern Caribbean able to take large aircraft. The one in St Lucia was handed over in 1960 and it too became an international airport.

The base at Chaguaramas was popular with the local people because of the varied work it offered but some Trinidadians questioned why it should be so large or why it should take up Port of Spain's best bathing beaches. Others resented the fact that the base became American territory where United States law and currency were used. Racial tension followed the behaviour of some white American troops towards Trinidadians and the people in other territories where bases were built. Bases often drew workers away from other occupations. Trinidad's sugar industry, for instance, suffered a labour shortage as workers moved for higher American wages.

American influence

The war made the United States reconsider the value of the English-speaking territories in the Caribbean. As Americans joined the armed forces, she needed men to replace them on the farms and in the factories. More than 100,000 British West Indians went to work in the United States during the war years. The war gave the natural resources of the Caribbean a new importance, too. Jamaica's bauxite had lain untouched in the ground since it was first found in the 1860s. By 1942 there was a shortage of aluminium which was an important light metal used in making aircraft. American companies began to plan to mine it in the island, although no works were open until after the war. American investment also helped the great expansion of Trinidad's oil fields and refineries during wartime.

The Caribbean Commission

In 1942 the United States joined with Britain to set up the Anglo-American Caribbean Commission. The main purpose of the Commission was to increase American influence in the area. In 1944 its headquarters were set up in Trinidad, where it had a chance to monitor opinion among West Indians. It made arrangements for the movements of workers to the naval bases or jobs in the USA. It also developed a few welfare projects similar to those run by the CWDO. But its chief concern was to increase West Indian support for the United States and to prevent any outbreaks of sympathy for Germany. As in other parts of the world where American influence increased, an important way of doing this was by radio. The Commission beamed its own programme, the *West Indian Radio Newspaper*. In 1946 the Commission became the Caribbean Commission and was joined by the governments of France and Holland, now free from German rule. It was one sign that the United States intended to keep a more active interest in the Caribbean in the post-war years.

From war to independence

American investment

After 1945 the growth of United States influence in the English-speaking Caribbean matched the decline in the power and wealth of Britain.

Fig. 23.2 *Part of the oil refinery at Point à Pierre, Trinidad, in 1949.*

The first clear sign of this was American investment in local industries. The most important examples were bauxite in Jamaica and oil in Trinidad. Jamaican bauxite was heavily dominated by American or American-Canadian companies from the start. The same was true of the smaller bauxite industry in Guyana. In Trinidad, American companies gradually bought up the smaller local companies until the bulk of the industry was United States owned.

American companies took advantage of the steps taken by West Indian governments to boost the industrial side of their economy. The local governments of the 1950s and early 1960s were eager to attract foreign capital to launch industries which would bring work to the people of their territories and help them break away from dependence on exporting foodstuffs. As we saw in Chapter 14 the policy had a great deal of success especially in Jamaica, Trinidad and Barbados.

More than three-quarters of the money used to set up new manufacturing and tourist industries was foreign and the greatest part of this came from the United States. It is not surprising that general trade began to flow in this direction too. By the year of independence 39 per cent of all Jamaica's trade and about 33 per cent of all Trinidad's was with the United States.

A serious problem was that the new American investment often led to a flow of money out of the country. For every $100 invested in Jamaica in the mid-1960s more than $200 went back to the USA as profits. Other territories suffered in the same way. This was one of the reasons that independent West Indian governments began to take steps in the 1970s to take a bigger share in the profits of foreign owned companies.

The cold war and the Caribbean

The Soviet Union had been a wartime ally of the United States and Britain. Almost as soon as Hitler was defeated, the United States and the USSR became hostile to each other. Each feared the other's intentions to expand in Europe and the Far East. Each believed that the other would try to undermine their control of the states which lay closest to them.

In the Americas, the United States kept a watchful and suspicious eye on all her neighbours for signs of unrest which would lead to a growth of communist influence. In 1953 this watchfulness and suspicion led her to put pressure on Britain to act in British Guiana. Elections had brought the PPP, led by Dr Cheddi Jagan, to power (see pages 136 to 137). The new government intended to take control of foreign businesses in the country as a step along the road to full independence.

The United States feared that the Guyanese example would spread to other countries. She put pressure on the British government to suspend the constitution of British Guiana and remove Dr Jagan from his post as prime minister. Britain sent warships and troops after Jagan had been in power for only 133 days. After the collapse of the PPP government, US interests continued to work in Guyana. American funds were used to influence trade unions, to back the opposition United Force Party and to change opinion through the 'Christian Anti-communist Crusade' and Moral Re-armament.

Guyana was the only example before independence of direct American interference in a British colony. On the other hand the United States interfered in the politics of Latin American countries when her interests appeared threatened. One case was in Guatemala in 1954. There the CIA actually armed the enemies of the government after it took state control of United Fruit company lands. The American aid helped the rebel leader to overthrow the government in July 1954.

The greatest of all cold war issues centred on Cuba where Fidel Castro had come to power in 1959. Within months he had begun to expropriate American-owned mines, lands and businesses. The USA first cut off diplomatic relations and trade which forced the Cubans to turn to the USSR to buy her sugar and supply her with arms. In 1961, the American government backed the Bay of Pigs invasion which failed completely. The main result of this invasion was to unite Cubans behind Castro's policy of drawing closer to the USSR and turning Cuba into a communist state.

Fig. 23.3 *The Caribbean Development Bank in St Michael, Barbados.*

Aid and the independent governments

The USA's break with Cuba came as the British West Indian territories were drawing close to independence. By then the United States had already replaced Britain as the major trading partner for most products. The Cuban disaster led the USA to consider ways of strengthening her position in the English-speaking Caribbean even further. One early sign was the agreement in 1961 to give up most of the land at Chaguaramas in Trinidad and to aid some road building and housing projects on the island.

As well as trade and investment by American companies, the 1960s saw a series of United States aid schemes which aimed to ensure that the new Caribbean states were not tempted into following

the Cuban path of economic and political development. The activities of American agencies such as the Agency of International Development, and the Caribbean Development Bank, the Peace Corps and the USCIA (The United States International Communications Agency) belong mostly to the story of the independent Caribbean after 1962. So does another important result of the American break with Cuba. The island was closed to American tourists who turned to the beaches, nightclubs and hotels of the English-speaking Caribbean. Together, these changes created an even stronger economic link with the USA so that by 1974 over 45 per cent of all English-speaking Caribbean exports went there, as did large sums of profit made on the American investment and repayments of aid loans and grants.

Assignments

1   a) *How would you define the USA's interest in the British Caribbean before 1939?*
     b) *What new interest did the USA show in the British Caribbean in 1940?*
     c) *List the advantages and disadvantages for the English-speaking Caribbean of United States' involvement from 1940.*

2   a) *What were the economic effects of US involvement in the Caribbean between 1939 and 1962?*
     b) *What cultural influence did the USA have in the British Caribbean between 1900 and 1962?*

GUIDELINES FOR THE CXC EXAMINATION

Form of the examinations

The examinations each consist of a multiple-choice paper, an open response paper and a course work component, worth respectively 14, 56 and 30 per cent of the total marks.

Paper 1   1 hour 15 minutes. This paper is common to the Basic and General Proficiency examinations. There are sixty multiple-choice questions on the Overview. Five items will be set on each of the ten listed topics: the remaining ten items will not be identified with a specific theme, but will be concerned with general trends and overall chronology.

Paper 2   Separate papers will be set for Basic Proficiency (1 hour 40 minutes) and General Proficiency (2 hours 10 minutes). Each paper will be set on the thirteen themes detailed in the syllabus. Two questions will be set on each theme. Each question will take the form of an essay or stimulus material to which the candidate is invited to respond. The stimulus material may include extracts from documents, pictures, cartoons, maps, statistical tables and graphs and the response called for may be a single sentence, a short paragraph or an essay. Candidates must answer one question from each of the four sections of the syllabus. (Where CXC has accepted an alternative theme from a school, the candidates from that school must answer one of the two questions set on that theme as their response to the section in which it is located.)

Paper 3   (Over three terms.) Nine pieces of work set and marked in the school, three per term, for three terms, with the option of substituting a project for the course work of one term. (The pieces submitted should be the exercises which a teacher would normally give and should be treated as an examination in itself.) Teachers should begin recording in the Course Work Record Book by the beginning of Term 3.

There is also the option of using a project instead of three pieces of course work. Projects usually cover *an entire theme* of the syllabus. Further details are outlined on page 19 of the CXC syllabus.

The project as course work

A project may be substituted for all or part of the course work assignments for ONE TERM ONLY. A project may therefore be allocated all the marks for the term's work. However, if the teacher feels that the project does not merit a total weight of 60 marks, one additional course work assignment may be set in the term to bring the total assignment weight up to 60 marks.

The written report of a project will normally call for 25–30 sides of letter-sized paper (8.5″ × 11″). Such a report must have the following features:
1 a specific title;
2 a list of contents which shows the material in the report arranged in chapters or sections;
3 a bibliography and a list of all other sources used, e.g. museums, personal interviews, visits to historical locations;
4 illustrations and diagrams wherever appropriate;
5 an interpretation and evaluation of the information gathered;
6 a clear indication of the work for which each student was responsible, in the case of group projects.

In addition, there should normally be:
1 a clearly and briefly stated aim;
2 a brief statement by the candidate of what was achieved in relation to the stated aim, and some indication of any difficulties encountered.

FURTHER READING

General

P. Ashdown, *Caribbean History in Maps*, Longman, 1979
F. R. Augier *et al*, *The Making of the West Indies*, Longman, 1960
A. Garcia, *A History of the West Indies*, Harrap, 1965
S. C. Gordon, *Caribbean Generations*, Longman, 1983
D. G. Waddell, *The West Indies and the Guianas*, Prentice-Hall, 1967

Easier Books

R. N. Murray, *Nelson's West Indian History*, Nelson, 1971
A. Norman, P. Patterson and J. Carnegie, *The People Who Came*, Books 1 and 2, Longman, 1987, 1989
P. Sherlock, *West Indian Nations*, Jamaica Publishing House, 1973

For Teachers

Gordon K. Lewis, *The Growth of the Modern West Indies*, M. R. Press, 1968
J. Parry and P. Sherlock, *Short History of the West Indies*, Macmillan, 1971
E. Williams, *From Columbus to Castro*, Deutsch, 1970

The English-speaking Caribbean

George L. Beckford, (ed), *Caribbean Economy, Dependence and Backwardness*, ISER, Jamaica, 1975
George L. Beckford, *Persistent Poverty*, Oxford University Press, 1972
N. Bolland, *Belize, A New Nation in Central America*, West View Press, 1987
B. Brereton, *A History of Modern Trinidad*, Heinemann, 1981
A. Lewis, *Labour in the West Indies*, New Beacon Books, 1977
V. A. Lewis, (ed), *Size, Self-determination and International Relations*, ISER, Jamaica, 1975
J. Mordecai, *The West Indies: The Federal Negotiations*, Allen and Unwin, 1968
B. Semmel, *The Governor Eyre Controversy*, McGibbon and Kee, 1962
William Sewell, *The Ordeal of Free Labour in the British West Indies*, Frank Cass, London, 1968
Hugh Springer, *Reflections on the Failure of the First West Indies Federation*, Harvard University Press, 1962

Pan-Africanism and Black Power

W. E. DuBois, *Souls of Black Folk*, Blue Heron Press, 1953
I. Lynch, R. Hollis (eds), *Edward Wilmot Blyden: Black Spokesman*, Cass, 1971
T. G. Vincent, *Black Power and the Garvey Movement*, Ramparts Press, San Francisco, 1971
E. Williams, *The Negro in the Caribbean*, Negro Universities Press, 1942

Nineteenth-century Immigration

J. G. La Guerre, *Calcutta to Caroni*, Longman, 1974

K. O. Laurence, *Immigration into the West Indies in the Nineteenth Century*, Caribbean University Press, 1971

H. Tinker, *A New System of Slavery*, Oxford University Press, 1974

The Caribbean Region

R. D. Cresswaller, *The Caribbean Community. Changing Societies and U.S. Policy*, Praeger, 1972

H. P. Davis, *Black Democracy. The Story of Haiti*, Biblo and Tannen, 1967

J. E. Fagg, *Cuba, Haiti and the Dominican Republic*, Prentice-Hall, 1965

P. S. Foner, *A History of Cuba and its Relations with the United States*, International Publishers, 1962

H. Herring, *A History of Latin America*, Alfred Knopf, 1968

R. A. J. Van Lier, *Frontier Society, A Social Analysis of the History of Surinam*, Nijhoff, The Hague, 1971

J. B. Martin, *U.S. Policy in the Caribbean*, Westview Press, 1978

K. Wagenheim, *Puerto Rico, A Profile*, Praeger, 1975

F. Ward, *Inside Cuba Today*, Crown Publishers, 1978

H. J. Wiarda, *The Dominican Republic*, Praeger, 1969

INDEX

Note: Page references in *italics* indicate illustrations; references in **bold** type indicate maps.